# INDIAN
# Cricket
## CONTROVERSIES

# INDIAN CRICKET CONTROVERSIES

**K. R. WADHWANEY**

**ISBN- 81-288-0113-9**

*Publishers :* Ajanta Books International
1-UB, Jawahar Nagar, Bunglow Road, Delhi-110007 (India)

**Distributors : Diamond Pocket Books**
X-30, Okhla Industrial Area, Phase-II, New Delhi-110020
*Phone :* 011-8611861, 6386289, 6386341
*Fax :* 011-8611866, 6386124

*E-mail :* mverma@nde.vsnl.net.in
*Website :* www.diamondpocketbooks.com

*Printers :* **Adarsh Printers,** Delhi-110032

Indian Cricket Controversies                    Rs. 195/-

# Dedication

The book is dedicated to cricket whiners who, if they happen to read it, should be men enough to restrain themselves from throwing stones at others.

As many as 117 controversies have been listed in the book which has been written after in-depth research from among piles of clippings, meticulously stocked and stored.

The book is not a fiction; nor it is a figment of imagination of any one.

There is no malice against any one. The controversies have merely been put together. They portray how flimsy, frivolous and fussy have been our stars since India's entry into international cricket in 1932.

# Acknowledgement

All photos have been graciously provided by Pradeep Mandhani, one of the finest photo-journalists in cricketing world.

# A Foreword

There is a story which runs something like this. A football fanatic played as the custodian for his club side. Nothing wrong with that. But the trouble was that every night he would dream and fancy playing football. Sensing that something was droll, he went to consult a psychiatrist. In the process of questioning, the patient was asked 'Don't you ever dream of anything else? Not even of girls?'. 'How funny', was the response, 'I dream of buxom bunnies and let slip a goal'.

Like the soccer goalkeeper of the story, Kishin Wadhwaney, is entranced with cricket, he swallows cricket, eats cricket, munches cricket and of course dreams cricket. In his love for the game of the willow he seemingly yields to none at least I know of, and I have known him now for more than half a century, when I joined Lucknow as a probationer. I had then the good fortune of knowing him intimately as I had also been bitten by the cricket bug. Fortunately again, Uttar Pradesh then had a Postmaster General, Mr PKS Chari, who would go any length to give a fillip to sporting activities and it was his ardent aspiration that Posts & Telegraphs should win the Lucknow District Cricket Championships. We did not let him down and won it 2 years running.

But Mr Chari did something unprecedented, brushing aside all impediments, cited in the office files, he ordered a concrete pitch for our net practice, arguably one of the very firsts in this country, a step which Don Bradman had, at a point of time, advocated for India. Our happiness was unalloyed but Kishin Wadhwaney was over the moon.

With an athletic figure, lithe and balanced physique, Kishin Wadhwaney was energy personified. His indomitable coverage, specially when chips were down, boosted our morale. He was an all rounder and as a bowler he could manage to get a lot of pace off the wicket. As a new ball bowler he would bowl outswingers of more than medium speed, switching on to off-breaks as the ball wore down, which turned noticeably, and rising menacingly made the task of any batsman none too palatable. We used to marvel at his stamina. As a batsman he was audacious, innovative, hard hitting, his reflexes being sharp. Needless to say that his shots were loaded with power and his batting colourful. Kishin clearly enjoyed playing cricket. And in fielding he exhibited hawk-like alacrity.

One could not imagine, at least not I, that in later days Kishin Wadhwaney would wield his pen as effectively as he wielded his cricket bat on the play field. It is a tribute to his passion and fascination for cricket. And over the years he has matured, like vintage wine, into a seasoned and celebrated writer of books of a game which 'flannelled fools' played at a point of time and which, as of now, is a commercial leviathan.

Kishin Wadhwaney knows his mind and while writing speaks it loud and clear. His thirst for information on cricket is seemingly insatiable and he would go high and low to seek it. Record of performances of cricketers, famous and not-so-famous, are on his finger tips and that is how he knows the hawks from the hernshaws among Indian cricketers.

He is blessed with prodigious industry and enviable memory and his capacity to rummage through mountains of material to seek the facts and his capacity to separate the wheat from the chaff, could be the envy of many sports writers.

What is no less praiseworthy is that although most unfortunately—and strange are the ways of destiny—he is not as mobile as he was expected to be yet he has refused to pity himself and become a couch potato. May be, somewhat oddly though, he reminds me of James Stewart in the Alfred Hitchcock film 'Rear Window' where the sleuth in Stewart, confined to a wheel-chair, manages to pin down a criminal.

Kishin Wadhwaney writes with candour and singleness of purpose. Wielding a facile pen, writing lucid prose and making pungent remarks when occasions so demand, he may seem opinionated occasionally but in the process he never twists or distorts facts. His opinions are his own but based invariably on the material he has amassed. He has written about controversies but has never allowed himself to slide down into its quagmire, even if in his view reputation of some of the famous names stand smirched. It is possible that the book may trigger off more debates and controversies than it seeks to settle. It must however be acknowledged that Kishin Wadhwaney has chosen a knotty subject and in the process, is perhaps walking on thin ice. It is possible that the book has been written because of the anguish the writer had felt in his heart on the state of health of Indian cricket. Certain abrasive happenings in the Indian cricket scenario has disturbed him, and his dreams about Indian cricket have gone sour and acerbic. What Kishin Wadhwaney has ventured to disclose reminds me of what the US President Franklin Rossevelt once said, 'At the bottom of every case of criticism and obstruction we have found some selfish interest, some private axe to grind.'

But what indeed ails Indian cricket? Why is it that India's continuous fluctuating performances cause so much ceaseless palpitations in hearts, timid or otherwise? This seems to be an open question. But I suppose it no longer remains an open question when one questions the physical toughness of an Indian sportsman. Physical toughness is a sine qua non and an Indian sportsman is a poor example of it. Say, in soccer, India is not even in the first 120. In tennis, talent may be there but it never matches the stamina. The same is the story in badminton, in hockey and other major games.

In cricket, interestingly, a recent study shows that some of the West Indian cricketers of Indian origin have hit the headlines only as batsmen and spin bowlers but never as pace bowlers. It is the bowlers of West Indian origin who specialise in four-pronged attacks of relentless nature and blinding speed or as once Ian Botham put it 'hunting in fours'. In India, Mohammad Nissar was perhaps an aberration.

Dilating on this theme Kishin Wadhwaney in a preface to one of his books had commented on the food habits of the Indian sportsmen. I would tend to agree, though I know it would ruffle many a feather. I am inclined to think that as long as the goal of an Hindu, and an overwhelming number of Indians are Hindus, is to attain salvation or 'Moksha' for his own self and as long his food habits remain unchanged through centuries, any dream of outshining others in international arena will remain a distant one.

Now, as for the author Kishin Wadhwaney he is a rough diamond and as for the book, in one word, it is 'inputdownable!

*N.C. Talukdar*
S-80, Greater Kailash, Part-II
New Delhi 110048

Note : N.C. Talukdar was one of the renowned UP Ranji Trophy all-rounders in 1950s. A member of the UP Governor's XI against Commonwealth XI at Lucknow in 1951, he was invited to attend Test trials. He led Agra University to Rohinton Baria Trophy final in 1948.

# Preface

Cricketing 'babe' India indeed has been in relation to England and Australia. But, since its entry into the arena of international cricket in 1932, it has encountered far greater quantum of controversies than all ICC (International Cricket Council) members put together.

If the growth of country's cricket, governed by British Raj, princes and zamindars, was turbulent, its adolescent years were tentative. Then, amidst unprecedented bloodbath, the body was severed into two with Pakistan taking a birth as a new baby out of the Indian womb.

The present has been equally uncertain; it has in fact been topsy turvy. It is now besieged by sordid happenings of betting, bribery and match-fixing. The match fixing may indeed have taken worldwide ramifications, but it is born out of the sub-continent, particularly out of India. This is a fact. If in this unholy scandal, India is the father, Pakistan mother and all other nations have fallen prey to the greed of money, more money and black money.

Unlike in most other sports-minded countries, where cricket is, by and large, governed, managed and administered by cricket players, of cricket players and for cricket players, here cricket has been firmly in the clutches of politicians and bureaucrats. From British Raj and princes, we have merely travelled into the lap of politicians and bureaucrats who consider cricket as a launching pad to their progression.

Quality, it is said, emerges from quantity. Here, quantity from school to Test level has been enormous. The following by masses even more enormous. There are academies and clinics in every part of the country. There is no dearth of money. In fact, the number of cricket players and following by masses, even by illiterate ones, is much more than all other cricket playing countries put together. Yet we merely stand between sun-shine and dreary nights.

Regardless of triumphs and failures, which are part and parcel of any competitive discipline, Indian cricket has, sadly, been built wrong way. It has encountered far more downs than ups. No general or captain, no matter how shrewd or tactician or understanding , can keep a 'losing army together'.

This is a fact. India, in 70 years of its baptism, has faced more defeats than triumphs. What is most shocking is that India wears a tag that Indians are tigers at home and lambs for slaughter abroad. What is sadder than this is that India has surrendered more quantum of matches than any other country.

The task of piecing together country's controversies and happenings has not been difficult as they have existed in one form or the other. The intrigues and manoeuvrings have continued unabated. Only the main actors have changed from princes to politicians/bureaucrats. The subject (players) is the same though some of them may not be as docile and meek as was the case in days prior to partition.

The Indian history shows that players have been pawns in the hands of the manoeuverers. It is not that the manoeuverers are smarter than players. But players, egoistic as they are, are unwilling to unite. There are as many divisions among Test stars as there are languages spoken in the dressing room. Take the case of North Zone. Three top stars are on different wave-length. Each is ready to stab the other. A junior super star, for example, accepted a higher position and emoluments than a senior player who had played a key role in junior player's career during his formative years. This was in Steel Authority of India where good-for-nothing officials rode over men of merits. For more than six years, the minister's son-in-law fired many shots from his rustic gun. The senior star, who is more committed to cricket than any other individual, wanted to quit the department. But he was advised against by a sports loving Margaret Alva, who was once a popular minister.

There was no quarrel with any one if the junior star was getting higher position on his merit and achievements. But he was inducted to spite the senior star who, in disgust, might have gone out of the SAIL.

There is indeed little future for Indian cricket until players bury their personal differences and rise as a unit. They cannot get into the board straightaway, but they have to enter in state bodies after breaking the monopoly of politicians and bureaucrats. For achieving this, they have to work hard—as much as they worked at nets to get into India team. It is no easy task to dislodge these hard-core politicians. Cricket politicians are harder nut to crack than politicians, who occupy positions in Parliament.

In the end, jungle raj prevails in Indian cricket. Seniors were considered 'disobedient' and were taken to task by the board. But players got a reprieve through PIL (Public Interest Litigation) filed by the Delhi Lawyer in Supreme Court. That was in 1989. Srikkanth was appointed captain to Pakistan. He drew the series there. It was a tremendous achievement because two of his predecessors, Bishan Singh Bedi and Sunil Gavaskar, had lost the series and thereby their throne. The Pakistan tour in 1989-90 seemed to promise a bright future for India with prodigy Sachin Tendulkar giving evidence of his prowess. But, within weeks, Srikkanth was sidelined and young Azharuddin was appointed captain on the tour to New Zealand. Good, bad or indifferent, Indian cricket is as unpredictable as one-day international match.

**K.R. Wadhwaney**

# Content

# 1

# Vengsarkar Deported; Team Enter Sharjah

Money corrupts; it corrupts Indians more easily than many others worldwide. This despicable fact was conclusively established at Dubai Airport 20 years ago on April 1 (Fools Day) 1982.

It was a day of disgrace and shame as Indian cricket players, sporting blazers and ties, abandoned their colleague, comrade and friend for the sake of handful of Darhams. It was a morning when all Indian and, more so, cricket players had to bow their heads for their utter uncricketlike behaviour.

As players trouped in (they landed by Gulf Air flight) the abandoned youngman of proven cricket ability and skill, Dilip Balwant Vengsarkar, tall and graceful, had to cool his heels in the corner of the arrival lounge of the airport and then in transit lounge before he was deported to Mumbai via Cochin by the first available flight. Never before in the history of sports has such an unpardonable incident taken place in any part of the world.

What was Vengsarkar's alleged crime for undergoing such humiliation in presence of his team-mates who unfortunately did not even bat an eyelid? He merely protested against the violation of the age-old 'first come, first served' system.

Had the beneficiary or captain for the Sharjah match been a player from north, east and south, all hell would have broken in Bomaby and defaulting mercenary and other players would have been torn to shreds. While this attitude of Mumbai media—always parochial and conceited—was shocking, what was more disturbing was that the Board of Control for Cricket in India (BCCI) and Bomby Cricket Association (BCA) did not consider it necessary to seek an explanation from the erring beneficiary and players.

Indeed, it was not an official India-Pakistan match. But Indian players were playing and concerned authorities should at least have demanded an explanation from the captain. Sadly, an incident of such magnitude was buried five fathom deep.

**The Incident:**

Asif Iqbal, allegedly accused of selling a series to India in 1979-80, was so agitated and upset over allegations that he chose to migrate to Sharjah-Dubai from Pakistan. In association with Abdul Rehman Bukhatir, who was searching for a business avenue, he floated the 'Cricketers Benefit Fund Series (CBFS)'. Before the Asif-Bukhatir idea became a reality, two benefit matches were staged in 1981 and 1982. It was one such match in which beneficiary was none other than Sunil Manohar Gavaskar, India's cricket God!

The team flew into Dubai where, at airport, Vengsarkar protested against immigration/customs official for clearing first a troupe of film artists who were standing far behind in the queue. He made an observation, which should have been laughed at. The petty-minded immigration official, with typical UAE arrogance on his face, decided to teach this Indian player a lesson. He denied Vengsarkar visa (an entry permit). He sought clearance from his bosses for deporting the Indian player who, according to him, had made a nasty remark in 'Marathi'.

When unprecedented development took place, the entire team, particularly leaders, should have swung into action and sorted out the alleged mess through the good offices of Asif Iqbal and his influential colleagues. In failing, they should have stood by Vengsarkar insisting that they would not enter Dubai, if their colleague was deported. Had the members of the team displayed togetherness and strength of their character, the UAE officials would have had no option except to permit Vengsarkar to enter Dubai for the match.

Had a player of any other country—be it Australia, England, New Zealand, Pakistan, Sri Lanka, South Africa or West Indies—been isolated and insulted like this, the entire side would have staged a walk-out. But Indian players, sadly, considered money more important than respect and dignity of a colleague of high calibre and achievements.

Dilip Doshi, on his form, should have been in the Gavaskar XI. But he was not chosen. He, however, left by the same flight for Dubai on 'business trip'.

"Man proposes, God disposes", it is said. The Indian team fell short of a bowler for the match on April 3. Doshi was requisitioned. He had to borrow 'kit' to play.

Doshi bowled well without being mentally prepared for the match. He took four wickets in the allotted eight overs. He won 'man of the match' award.

Henry Blofeld, who was invited for TV commentary, in his report (The Gulf News—April 3) entitled "Class Cricketers Grace CBFS") in the concluding para on Doshi's bowling, said : "....It was a good piece of spin bowling as I have seen anywhere in the world and it was a real joy to watch".

Doshi, in his book "Spin Punch", says : ".....Organisers of such tournaments as the one in Gulf lay out fabulous hospitality with lavish gifts thrown in, and the elder statesmen of Indian cricket will do well to maintain a sense of proportion about what they accept and what they turn down".

Disturbed at the attitude of his colleagues, Vengsarkar, already an introvert, became more withdrawn. Who would not feel upset when he is accorded such a shabby treatment by his friends?

Upset Vengsarkar was at the ugly incident in which he was not to blame. But this did not disturb his cricketing rhythm. He went from strength to strength amassing runs with precision and skill. He scored 17 centuries (35 fifties) in 6,868 runs (average 42.43) in Test cricket (116 matches).

While uncalled for deportation had led him to become more resolute and determined, Vengsarkar remained wary about criticism, no matter how unbiased. Almost all journalists were unanimous in their observation that Indians lost the first Test at Kanpur against the West Indies by an innings and 83 runs because established batsmen were shying away from rising deliveries. Almost all the wickets were bagged by quickies.

Vengsarkar, among other renowned batsmen, was upset at the reportage. When Vengsarkar ran into Times of India's R. Sriman (he died on December 13, 2000), he surprisingly dared him that he would be dealt with squarely, if he ever came to Bomaby. Sriman was not the one who could be cowed down by such meaningless threats.

On the eve of the second Test at Delhi, Sriman casually raised the topic with the Board chief NKP Salve at an official get-together while discussing India's meek surrender at Kanpur (1983-84). Sriman also told Salve the challenge that Vengsarkar had thrown to him. Salve had a quiet word with the Indian star.

In the Test, Vengsarkar scored 159 and 63 in the drawn match at Kotla. "This is a right kind of expression to mediamen", Salve told Dilip, adding: "Your bat should silence them and not your words". Was it not a sane advise to the star who, despite ill-treatment by his colleagues, continued to be friendly and well-poised to his colleagues, juniors included.

# 2

# Gavaskar's Walk Out At MCG

Success or failure has indeed direct bearing on players' moods. This is a natural human characteristic. But there are some who get too elated in success and too depressed in failure. Such players can be a cause of worry and concern to their teams and team-mates.

Sunil Gavaskar was a player/captain who was pleasant, friendly and witty if the going was good for him. But in failure, he inclined to be withdrawn, if not a loner, to his team-mates. There are innumerable instances that would prove that this observation is correct.

Gavaskar's slide was visible in Australia in 1980-81. He had failed to strike his form in first five innings of the three Tests. He scored zero and 10 in the first Test at Sydney where India lost by an innings and four runs. In the drawn second Test at Adelaide, he could score 25 and five. In the third at Melbourne, he had managed 10 before he was dismissed. He was among runs in the second essay. He had scored a polished 70 when he was declared leg before to Dennis Lillee. The decision was given by a controversial umpire R.A. Whitehead.

Gavaskar felt that he had faintly nicked the ball with his bat before it was deflected on to his pads. He showed his bat to Lillee who dashed down to him and pointed to his pads. There was a commotion for a while.

Disappointed, dejected and dissatisfied, Gavaskar was walking towards pavilion when Lillee reportedly uttered an impious word which, furious as Gavaskar already had been at the decision, led him to lose his shirt. He virtually ordered Chetan Chauhan to return.

Mihir Bose, in his book "A History of Indian Cricket' (Foreword by Gavaskar) says: "As a child, he had got upset and threatened to hit his ,fellow players—now in high dudgeon he decided to concede the match".

India, on the road to earning black spot in its chequered existence, managed to escape from this humiliating situation as manager Wing Commander Salim Durrani ordered Chauhan back and the game continued after a brief drama and excitement.

Gavaskar, in his book 'Idols', says....When the umpire did not reverse his decision a lot of anger was boiling within me but still the idea of walking off did not strike me. When I walked past Chetan, I heard friend Lillee utter one of his profanties which was a very delayed action from Lillee and it was then I lost balance of mind and told Chetan to walk off with me."

It was however beyond comprehension as to why was Gavaskar expecting that Whithead would reverse his decision! He might have changed it if he had any doubt in his mind. But when he was certain that Gavaskar had not snicked the ball onto his pads, why should he make himself a laughing stock at the Melbourne Cricket Ground (MCG) where a huge throng of spectators was present?

India came from behind to win the Test and square the series 1-1. It was a tremendous win which showed that Indians could achieve the impossible.

Gavaskar managed to redeem his reputation to a great extent when he went on record as saying that it was one of the most regrettable incidents in his life. Says Gavaskar: "Whatever may be the provocation and whatever may be the reason, there was no justification for my action and I realise now that I did not behave as a captain and sportsman should. I take all the blame and responsibility for my action and I think that Lillee in his own way forced me to take that action by uttering those words...."

As has always been Gavaskar's wont, his second part of the para contradicts his first part. When he says that he should have stayed cool despite whatever provocation, then why should he accuse Lillee for forcing him to act unlike a captain and a sportsman?

To a question what would he have done if Chauhan had actually been taken off the field, Chappell said : "I would have waited for two minutes, appealed against Chauhan. I would have acted similarly against other incoming batsmen. The entire Indian team would have been dismissed in 20 minutes without any addition to the total".

Of Lillee, Henry Blofeld, in "The Cricketer', said: "I very much doubt if there has ever been a more unpleasant incident in a Test match than that at Perth where Lillee first deliberately blocked the Pakistan captain as he was completing a single and then launched a kick at him when he made his crease. Over the years, Lillee has been involved in probably more unpleasant incidents than any other Test cricketer. He has seemed almost to make a habit of trying to bait and upset his opponents in the most petulant manner".

Durrani had sent a report which was not exactly complimentary to Gavaskar. He was the second manager to have made uncomplimentary observations about a 'little master'. The first was G.S. Ramchand when Gavaskar had made 36 runs while staying at the wicket the full duration of 60 overs in the 1975 World Cup in England.

A friend, Durrani had assured me of a copy of the report. But in his Lucknow letter of July 4, 1986, he says: "It hurt me a lot yesterday hearing from you what you had to say about my report which I suppose you have been expecting from me. I could have retaliated it but decided against it on account of our past close association. Any way I have decided not to make my report public hence my inability to make the same available to you".

It was Durrani who had expressed his desire to provide me a copy of the report before returning to Lucknow. I had undertaken six trips to Lucknow to get a copy of the report but he did not give it to me. If he did not wish to give me a copy, he should have said so instead of making me run about for it.

Following his letter, I wrote him: "....If you had any consideration for past close association, which you so proudly mention in your letter, you certainly would not have made me toss about.

"The humiliation that you have caused me make me consider your exaggerated report no more than an ordinary piece of paper, written by an official without possessing much cricketing knowledge...."

# 3

# Vizzy Hauled Up

It was a contest between a commoner from Kapurthala and a zamindar from sourthern part of the country and a common man won in the battle of attrition. The contesting players were Amarnath and Vizzy.

Amarnath was born to a Pandit family, Bharadwaj. He had a chequred existence but he was a phenomenon of a man who, while being a rolling stone, gathered a valuable mass around him. He was a kind of a gypsy but he always endeavoured to improve his skill, ability and cricketing mind.

A fitness fanatic, Amarnath was fond of good food; he was choosy about quality of food that he ate. He developed a strong body. He was lithe of muscle. He was a kind of a man, who would grab with Fate and get a life out of it. He had only one century in Test cricket but he was a player whose out-cricket should not, rather must not, be judged or evaluated from the number of runs he made and the wickets he obtained. His style of batsmanship and bowling was explosive and extra-ordinary. He would captivate all who had an opportunity to watch him play. His exploits—not from the point of view of runs and wickets—gave credence to the theory of Naville Cardus that "scoreboard is an ass".

Vizzy, thrown out of his state because of personal family feud, settled down in Benaras (Varanasi). He was a sycophant of the Raj and he liked sycophancy and flattery.

He was an articulate politician, and he developed a kind of mastery over intrigues. He accepted "no" from nobody and he had learnt the art of making use of money to his advantage.

A club-class cricket player of no achievements at all, Vizzy was appointed deputy vice-captain of the Indian team that toured England in 1932. He allegedly developed stone in his kidney and pulled out of the team. But he managed a blazer with a monogram "India" and used that jacket more often than his other outfits. He was not capable or competent to lead India to England in 1936 but he succeeded in eliminating all opposition one by one, including Iftikhar Ali Khan Pataudi and C.K. Nayudu.

Yuvraj was also a candidate at one time. He was being promoted by his father. He was appointed captain of the Hindus in preference to C.K. Nayudu, a Mumbai hero, against Australians at Mumbai in 1935-36. The selectors did not appreciate his appointment. He was booed and jeered every time he fielded the ball. He, however, managed 40 runs (five sixes). Even to this brief innings, some motives had been attached. It was alleged that Australians had delivered "Halwa" bowling to him to get among runs. But this short innings could not instal him skipper of the team to England. When time came, Maharaja of Patiala withdrew his candidature.

Vizzy's exploits were not on field but off it. He secured captaincy for reasons other than cricketing ability and skill. He smoked "Hookha" in dressing room even during Test match days, changed his attire after every interval, presented costly gifts to his rivals, his two servants tied his shoe laces, and leg-guards. On the field of play he looked more a "Joker" than a captain. He had carried with him only 36 suitcases!

Amarnath and Vizzy were two totally dissimilar personalities. Amarnath was a brilliant self-made player of sterling qualities, while Vizzy made a handful of runs by presenting gold coins to bowlers to bowl full-tosses or lolly-pops. As both belonged to different school of thought and temperament, there was no love last between them when the team sailed to England.

The Indian team was not a side of players but a kind of mob. There were more than 20 of them. Some were "obliged" because their associations had voted for Vizzy (10 votes) against Nayudu's (five). There were players of varying ages and sizes. There were groups within groups. Those who were 'yes men' of the zamindar-captain got chances to play while men of talent had to stay in pavilion. It was a team in which non-entities stole a decisive march over men of merits.

Amarnath, frank and fearless, was exuberant and brash. He refused to tow the line of the skipper. Although he was in dazzling form (he had scored 613 runs and 32 wickets in 10 matches), he was often treated shabbily. In a match against the Minor Counties, his batting order was shuffled often. He wanted to bat to stay in form before the first Test started. He was eventually sent in at the fag end of the day. He remained unbeaten with one run. He was all fire in the dressing room. He threw his bat and pads and also his 'box' in different corners. Shouting in Punjabi he used words which could do credit to none. Many walked out of the room but a few reported the matter to Vizzy, who was seen shivering. This was not Amarnath's first outburst. He had earlier protested against Vizzy's methods of field-placing.

Vizzy was upset while manager Brittain-Jones was waiting to make a political capital out of Amarnath's behaviour. Brittain-Jones was keen to establish that even a tiny group of Indians was unable to function as a team. He and Vizzy took a spot decision to send Amarnath back home. They stuck to their decision despite appeals made by senior players that Amarnath should be warned and pardoned this time.

There were widespread protests back in India, particularly in Mumbai, then headquarters of Indian cricket. There were agitated people present at harbour when the ship, carrying Amarnath, was anchored. Apprehending trouble, Anthony de Mello hired a boat and smuggled Amarnath out of the ship. He was lodged at Taj hotel where he was forbidden from meeting people or addressing any Press conference. He was rushed to meet Nawab of Bhopal in Bhopal. The mess was being sorted out and he was about to be sent back to England when Nawab got a command not to send Amarnath back.

When Vizzy had returned from England after his prolonged stay, there was a banner head-line. It said: "India's captain unhonoured, unashamed and Unsung returns home".

In the subsequent probe, instituted by the Chief Justice of Mumbai Sir John Beaumont, Amarnath was exonerated, while Vizzy was censored.

We attribute lack of cooperation and coordination to the following causes placed in order of importance:

(1) (a) The conduct of Nayudu in holding himself aloof from the team and his failure to offer any support to the captain.

(b) The policy of the captain in forming his own party and not treating all members of the team with strict impartiality. The policy destroyed any chance there might have been of healing the existing dissensions.

(c) The feeling, whether justified or not but shared by practically the whole team, was that the captaincy in the field was very faulty.

(d) The presence in England of too many idle players.

(2) No blame for any failure of the team is attached to the manager except that the manager should have formulated written directions as to the conduct to be pursued by members engaged in the match. When off the field, for example, and the hour at which the player should return to their hotel, should have been laid down. Nothing of the sort seems to have been done.

(3) There were no breaches of discipline on the field

(4) Amarnath was guilty of ill-mannered and rude conduct in the presence of the captain, but only in a private place. Having regard to the warnings previously given to him, the captain and the manager were right in taking disciplinary action against him, but they committed an error of judgement in the severity of the punishment inflicted.

Amarnath rose to become hero, while Vizzy went underground for more than a decade. He resurfaced soon after India gained independence.

# 4

# Who Axed Bedi

I confirmed doing a 'no-barred' interview of Bishan Singh Bedi on the request (phone call) made by the Sportsworld Associate Editor (A. Sen) from Kolkata. "It should be hard-hitting and factual piece", insisted the Associate Editor, adding: "Quote Bishan extensively".

The interview (Sportsworld) is reproduced below:

A Conspiracy was hatched against me

Bishan Singh Bedi tells K.R. Wadhwaney in an exclusive interview.

"Bishan Singh Bedi, considered the finest exponent of left-hand spin bowling in the world, is a sad and disillusioned man. He has reasons to feel so. He is sad not because he has retired from the first class Indian cricket scene after about two decades' astounding success. He cannot accept the fact that he was axed from Test cricket when he had plenty of guile left in his bowling, through the "sweep" of a player-colleague-captain called Sunil Gavaskar, who allegedly rules the Board of Control for Cricket in India and towers over a five-member selection committee, headed by Polly Umrigar.

"When George Hirst was once left out from the England side, it was said that on the following Sunday there ascended from every pulpit in Yorkshire the fervent prayer that the Lord would remove scales from the eyes of the selectors, and the sermons were based on the story of the man who was blind and was made to see", says Norman Birkett.

"This was the feeling among cricket lovers in India when Bedi, after a reasonably successful tour of England (1979), where he had grabbed the maximum wickets (33 for 847, average 25.66), was on return meted out scant and shabby treatment by the selection committee, which was once again dominated by Gavaskar, who was re-appointed captain. Bedi would not have made it to England had Gavaskar—who had harassed and humiliated him in the three Tests that he played against the West Indies in 1978 by giving him tiny spells from unsuitable ends—continued as skipper instead of Venkataraghavan. This was a well-placed strategy against a gentleman-cricketer, who named his son, Gavasinder about a decade ago when young Gavaskar was on his first tour of West Indies in 1971.

"When asked about the reasons and who were responsible for his exit, Bedi while relaxing in his B-6, Kailash Apartment house said: "I do not know myself why this conspiracy was hatched against me when I had served the team, the cause of cricket and cricket itself devotedly and sincerely." "But let me tell you to set the record right", said Bedi, "even it may sound a little immodest of me, I was still the best bowler, particularly from the viewpoint of experience and skill, and certainly deserved a better deal than I was dished out."

"The critic, if he is to be worth anything, must wear the garb of neutrality, with objectivity as his aim, and impartiality his target." I, therefore, have to write—not without regret—that had Bedi been from Mumbai or Western India, he would have continued for another couple of seasons and would have, in all probability, claimed the remaining 44 wickets to overhaul the existing world record of 309 wickets standing in the name of Lance Gibbs.

"Don't you feel sorry that you have been denied an opportunity to set the world record, which was within your grasp", Bedi replied: "Listen, I have never been after records. I consider cricket as a team game and individual performances are totally secondary. Records just happen. Let me be honest with you. I derive much greater happiness and satisfaction from winning the match or making a grim fight of a losing battle than making records."

"Sir Donald Bradman, the greatest batsman the world has known, was once called by Lord Tennyson: "A little man with no manners". This terse comment, which got world-wide publicity, came in the wake of refusal from Sir Donald to grant an interview to Tennyson, who had played a match against Bradman in pre-war days. Bradman, who was captaining Australia in England in 1948 when the battle royal between the two countries resumed after World War II, mentioned in one of the five exclusive articles he released to The *Times of India* (Mumbai) in 1948 that he did not remember Tennyson's name and that he was amidst hundreds of important "business' letters when he reluctantly expressed his inability to meet Lord Tennyson.

"While Tennyson was unquestionably injudicious and rash in his observation, it should be admitted that Gavaskar, a little man with an exaggerated ego and conceit, chose to "stab Bedi in the back" as he felt extremely uncomfortable in the company of senior players, like Bedi, and Venkataraghavan, on the ground and off it. While seniors have been summarily sacked, Gavaskar has promoted yes-men like Yograj Singh and Ravi Shastri, to form the team. There is no instance in Test history when a substitute has been called for a player (Dilip Doshi) side-lined through injury from a solitary Test. It is an open secret that Shastri was asked by Gavaskar to stay in readiness for the Australia and New Zealand tour. It is also an established fact that it was Gavaskar, and not the manager, Wing Commander S.A.K. Durrani, who trunk-called Mr S.K. Wankhede (he was presiding over the World Cup Tournament meeting at Taj) to send Shastri to New Zealand. The protocol demanded Durrani to initiate communication with the chairman of the selection committee.

"In foreign countries, national sportsmen are honoured and respected. But in this country, national and international sportsmen of the calibre, stature, dedication and selflessness of Bedi are insulted and throttled through utter non-entities who have taken control and management of sports and games.

"There was a time when Mumbai's handful of cricketers, who formed themselves into a well-oiled clique, used to drop catches of bowlers not belonging to their region. Ghulam Ahmed, a fine off-spinner, was a victim of this sordid game of player-politics and he was virtually compelled to relinquish his cricket career, including captaincy, prematurely. In those days and in the pre-Independence days, there was needless emphasis on individualism and groupism. That is why the team seldom fought well despite the presence of such greats, as, Col. C. K. Nayudu, Mohd. Nissar, Amar Singh, Vijay Merchant, Vijay Hazare, Vinoo Mankad, Subash Gupte and Vijay Manjrekar. It should, however, be said here—though I seem to be digressing—that had these players got half as many chances as the present crop of players, who play 12 or more Tests in a year, they would have remained immortal record holders.

"G.S. Ramchand, a seasoned Ranji Trophy player of Sind, was refused admission by many gymkhanas and clubs when he migrated to Mumbai in 1947. He loved cricket and chose to join St Xavier's College to prove his prowess which was then not recognised by Mumbaiites who talk, write and drink about their region. There are in Mumbai, I am sorry to say, cricketers who consider India part of Mumbai. With this environment and atmosphere, Ramchand battled hard to get among the wickets and runs and forced his way into the university, inter-university and Indian team inside of a couple of years.

"This kind of atmosphere persisted since Mumbai was at the helm of affairs. Then Indian cricket was at the cross-roads. But there was a welcome change in the sixties and players began to realise that team-spirit yielded better results than sporadic individual performances. Bedi, the new captain, translated this good work into a reality by building a well-knit combination. This brought laurels to players both at home and abroad. The spirit of never say-die helped India perform creditably against the might of Australia, West Indies and England and the team looked glorious even in defeat.

"Before I took over as a captain, I used to feel very strongly about parochialism", said Bedi. "My single achievement is that, with my sincere and honest approach, I inculcated the spirit of oneness and togetherness among players", added Bedi.

"Except for Maharaja of Porbander, I have had the occasion to meet all Indian Test captains, including Col. C.K. Nayudu. I am convinced that Bedi heads them all on and off the field. He is as shrewd on the field as he is human off it and that is, perhaps, a major reason why every player, young and seasoned (except, of course, Gavaskar) stood loyal and faithful to him in the 22 of the 67 Tests that he captained.

"I daresay that had Bedi been the captain in Australia and New Zealand, India would not have performed so poorly despite an epic victory in Melbourne levelling the series in Australia for the first time. The tragedy is that Gavaskar, compared with Bradman at the start of the tour, was so much wrapped up in his own failure that he did not realise that he was captain and totally neglected the other 15 players. This is, perhaps, one of the reasons "why some young players "socialise" a bit more than they should have.

"Bedi has always been an honest man. By nature an outspoken man and not given to suffering fools and hypocrites, he soon became a thorn to officialdom. Always reacting strongly against injustice, scant and shoddy deals, he took up the cause of players and formed a players' association, as perhaps no one else dared to do against the establishment and he himself stayed on a straight and unfaltering path unlike several other of his contemporaries who were only too willing to bow down to shrewd officialdom. What is most remarkable is that Bedi stood like a rock of Gibraltar not caring about what happened to his cricket and cricket career.

"Bedi's first brush with officialdom was when he questioned the propriety of a Board President, P. M. Rungta, who literally and figuratively threw his weight, by needlessly withholding 50 per cent of the amount granted by the Government specifically for disbursement to players on an English tour. The Board president surprisingly utilised that remaining 50 per cent amount towards the expenses of officials in England. Instead of appreciating Bedi's point of view in the larger interest, the Board president chose to be difficult. So on a filmsy and foolish charge of "not bowling to the field" and "appearing on TV without obtaining permission", Bedi was subjected to an inquiry which was, in a way, the second one in the history of Indian cricket, the first being against Lala Amarnath in 1936 when he was sent back from England.

The enquiry only gave greater status and public image to Bedi. The Education Ministry, which intervened in the episode before it took an ugly turn, considered the charges meaningless and petty and asked the Board president to "play with a straight bat". Bedi, was naturally, reinstated after he was sidelined against West Indies from the first Test at Bangalore.

"Can a bowler bowl against the field set by him?" asked Bedi. "For the minor infringement of providing tips to youngsters on spin bowling on TV in Lodnon, I was taken to task and was even dropped from the Test. Now the wheel has turned a full circle and players, particularly the captain, violate all written and unwritten rules and there is none who can raise a finger at these Johnnies", pointed out Bedi nonchalantly. Now the captain can entertain the TV cameras for ads and interviews or write articles himself—did someone mention that the players and the Board signed a contract before a tour?!! Not only this, but the captain along with his wife often used the manager's double-bed room and the manager was moved into a single-bed room in Australia and New Zealand. All that Gavaskar did on his return from the twin-tour was to say that the manager should be a cricketer! What a reward to Durrani for his magnanimity and generosity! "How can cricket prosper in a country where double standards are being followed with impunity?" observed Bedi.

"The year 1977 was one of disputes, dismissals and departures for Northamptonshire which suddenly sacked Bedi, who played a key role in exposing England and John Lever for using unethical practices of applying vaseline to shine the ball. Called an "unique personality" in Northamptonshire, there were a spate of letters against the County management for providing a raw deal to a bowler who had taken as many as 496 wickets in the short tenure of five years. Described as "joy to watch and true weaver of spells with a six-step shuffle to the wicket", the local newspapers and cricket followers unleashed a barrage of attacks on the County management. Bedi himself thought that the County administrators were "ungrateful and betrayed me".

"Do you think you were dropped from the County because you called a spade a spade in exposing Lever", I asked Bedi. "What is the doubt about it", he replied. "Had I remained non-committal, I would not have been given such a step-motherly treatment by the Northamptonshire County, which had assured me only a few days before I left England that I could play as long as I wished. But let me be frank with you and tell you that I have had no regret for losing the contract, money and benefit match which I would have earned if I had played another couple of seasons there. Patriotism is more important than individual success as I am of the firm belief that the Ship is greater than the Crew", Bedi declared. "What has, however, pained me a great deal is that the English team should have gone scot-free", bemoaned Bedi. "Instead of reporting in detail to the MCC about the shoddy practices of the England team, the Indian authorities were just docile as if they were guilty themselves", observed Bedi.

"Called a master of flight and spin Bedi, who looped the ball towards the batsman and spun it away from him with uncanny accuracy, naturally ran into trouble in Pakistan, as would have happened to any other captain. It was the most ill-advised tour as India had had a gruelling time against Australia and West Indies earlier. But Bedi bore his misfortune philosophically.

"In Pakistan, Bedi was accused of continuing to bowl when he was being punished. "Yes, I admit that I was not effective on those docile wickets and I was thrashed", admitted Bedi without offering any excuse. "But I always felt that I was, apart from being captain, also a main-line bowler", adding "I belong to Bradman's school of thought". When asked to elaborate, Bedi said: "Bradman never shirked his responsibility. He always went to bat at his usual number three, irrespective of score and time. Bradman's argument was that, if he was not equipped to encounter the bowler at such a crucial time of the day, no one else in his team could".

"Bedi lost the series in Pakistan where no visiting team had won before. That was not the first time Bedi had lost the series. But he and his team were exceedingly popular there despite some unwanted incidents. The Maharaja of Baroda, manager, Pakistan Test stars and officials were all praise for Bedi, who was considered a true "ambassador" of India. It was written on the wall that India had no chance against Pakistan then. But Bedi was made the scapegoat and his captaincy was clipped off. "Although I lost the series, as was expected, and captaincy subsequently, I love Pakistan where I have some of my best friends", declared Bedi. "But I must confess that I have enjoyed playing all over the world except in Pakistan where there is lack of proper cricket atmosphere". Elaborating further, Bedi said that lack of atmosphere was, perhaps, the main reason why so may top-notchers like Zaheer Abbas, Mustaq Mohammad, Asif Iqbal, Sadiq Mohammad, Intikhab Alam, Wazir Mohammad, Alimuddin, Khan Mohammad, Naseemul Ghani and others had settled down in the

United Kingdom after saying goodbye to Pakistan. He further said that the majority of our boys on this tour were struggling to apply themselves. "Only after two days of our landing in Pakistan, the boys began asking—how many more days", revealed Bedi.

"There are very few officials who can remain sincere and grateful. There are still fewer who will worship a sun, which has fallen out of favour with the powers that be. As Bedi was deprived of his Indian captaincy, intrigue-ridden local organisers decided to teach this arrogant Sikh a lesson, forgetting that, single-handed, he brought Delhi's and Zone's cricket to the top despite heavy odds and an uncricket-like atmosphere.

"The local authorities, who have received the wrath of the entire country for their misdeeds and malfunctioning, decided to drop him from the captaincy. But the sinister game failed as Madan Lal declined to step into Bedi's shoes and the subsequent leakage of news in a local paper.

"This was the beginning of a battle between the players and local officials, who were using cricket as a platform to prosper in business instead of contributing towards the betterment of cricket and cricketers. All along last season, local cricket was between the grounds and the law courts. The persistent designs and short-sighted and capricious policy of an allegedly money-lending family have reduced Delhi's cricket to a shambles.

Bedi thinks Kolkata's Eden Gardens the best ground where it is always a joy to play Test matches. "The atmosphere is electrifying there, crowds appreciative and wicket sporting," Bedi said. "Chennai, Bangalore and Mumbai (in that order) are other centres where I have enjoyed playing cricket". Continuing, Bedi said: "It is a fallacy to say that a bowler cannot be a good captain. I feel—and I can prove it to the hilt—that a bowler, if he carries a cool and shrewd head over his shoulders, can be as good a captain as a batsman, if not better. The bowler is generally not made captain on the mistaken notion that he either over-bowls or under-bowls. Don't you think a captain-batsman, who is on the threshold of getting his century, will delay declaration and thereby ruin the team's chances of a possible victory", Bedi questioned. "It is totally a batsman's game, let us accept it. A batsman gets all the encouragement from spectators, press and other media for his century while a bowler with a stupendous effort of claiming four or more wickets on a docile strip gets hardly any encouragement", asserted Bedi. "Yet it is the bowlers who win matches and this all-important fact is generally overlooked by all agencies. Is it not unfair to bowlers? Let it be admitted that one can captain as well as one is allowed to," declared Bedi.

"Bedi is one of the three bowler-captains claiming 100 Test wickets. Richie Benaud and Gary Sobers are the other two bowler-captains who have achieved this distinctions. Sobers was, however, an all-rounder not falling in the line of bowlers. The turbaned Sikh, who wore steel-rimmed spectacles and coloured patkas, claimed 100 wickets in a season on two occasions in the County Championship and helped India reign supreme against England in 1971. Yet, strange as it may seem, he has never been honoured or enlisted among Wisden's five any year. "I have no complaints. May be I did not deserve it", said Bedi with all his humility.

"Born in Amritsar on September 25, 1946 and coming of a none-too-affluent family, Bedi began playing cricket when 14. He got some useful hints from Mr Gyan Prakash (Hindu College). (He died recently at Amritsar of Cancer. He was 92). Essentially using fingers to spin the ball, Bedi used his wrist to provide the ball with a little tweak. He worked hard for hours on the famous Gandhi grounds to develop accuracy. "But I must admit that I made a breakthrough in first class cricket, thanks to Khalsa College captain, Gurpal Singh", said Bedi. "Prakash Bhandari is a shrewd cricketing brain and discussion with him when he played for Delhi after semi-retirement for more than a decade was highly rewarding", added Bedi.

"Bedi hit the headlines first when he fashioned almost

single-handedly a thrilling victory for North over redoubtable South in Chennai in 1969-70. South had eight acknowledged Test stars. North, led by Bedi, had only one Test player in Ashok Gandotra. None, not even ardent supporters, hoped that North would prevail over South. The game was so heavily tilted in favour of South on the third day of the match that North's non-cricketing manager, M.L. Mehra, went shopping.

"During the course of the match, Bedi accompanied by a senior jouranalist from North (R. Sriman—He died on December 13, 2000), had a two-hour educative discussion on "using of bowling crease" with an old warrior, A.G. Ram Singh. (He died recently) "I benefitted a great deal from that discussion", said Bedi.

"Bedi had his Test baptism at Kolkata, thanks to the initiative of the so-called less knowledgeable selector, M. Dutta Ray and this really proved a turning point in Bedi's career. There is, however, a former hockey official, who takes pride in saying that he spotted the talent in Bedi and was instrumental in his selection. After an initally wayward start, Bedi soon proved that he was the most effective left-hand spin bowler in the country.

"Winner of Arjuna Award in 1969 and Padma Shree in 1970, Bedi's entry into Test cricket was as meteoric as his retirement was quiet and sedate.

"I have no complaint against umpiring and umpires who, I thought, did their job to the best of their ability and, I suppose, as well as we played", said Bedi, adding, "Let me be honest in saying that Indian umpiring is impartial, but slightly incompetent owing to lack of adequate opportunities". According to him, Delhi's Har Prasad Sharma was one of the finest umpires though he, too, made a few mistakes in Test matches.

"E.W. Swanton, one of the most knowledgeable cricket writers, has said "Cricket is not a pure science and pray Heavens, it never will be this side of the celestial realm, at any rate. It is, however, an expression among other things of character and humour". Since the retirement of MAK

Pataudi and Bedi, I am inclined to admit that 'character and humour' have been at a discount.

"I was not a candidate for the post of a manager for the team of under-19 scheduled to tour England from July to September", asserted Bedi. "It is a pity that my name should have been proposed without consulting me or obtaining my consent.

"Let me make it further clear that I would not have accompanied the team even if I were declared 'elected' because I am required at home for some very important work", Bedi said.

"Bedi was in Lucknow playing in the Sheesh Mahal final and then proceeded to Bangalore to coach the probables for the under-19 team. "You will see that I could not have met any one and it is indeed shocking that some senior officials should be impetuous", said Bedi.

"It came as a shock when Bedi's name was proposed by a representative of Cricket Association of Bengal (CAB). The group, sponsored by the CAB representative, had neither done its homework properly nor assessed the "feeling of the house". Naturally, this group sustained defeat. Many of Bedi's well-wishers in Srinagar, where the Board's special general body meeting was held, felt that if Bedi had such friends, he did not need enemies.

"All senior players have said good bye. But Gavaskar, who is India's best opening batsman, is likely to continue as captain. He should be reminded that "to play cricket" means to be modest in victory, to be resolute in defeat, to work for one's side and not for oneself, to accept the decisions of the umpires without delay and without complaint, to play fair and to keep strictly to the rules. If Gavaskar fails to remember these, the Indian team's performance will take a further nose-drive."

**Gavaskar's point of view was:**

"If Bishan does have a grievance, then I am most surprised

"Sunil Gavaskar, while holidaying in England, spoke

to Ashis Ray to set the record straight about the controversial interview with Bishan Singh Bedi. The interview, which appeared in the issue of Sportsworld dated 22 July, was entitled "Did Gavaskar get Bedi axed?" Gavaskar, in the course of this piece, asserts that the comments attributed to Bedi are nothing but the viewpoints of the author.

"When I first saw the article, I thought *Sportsworld* had started a jokes column. But most magazines have no more than a page of humour. So, I thought, this must be a new fiction series.

"The intriguing thing about the story is that at no stage has Bishan been comprehensively quoted as having said that I got him axed. In the first paragraph, I noticed the suggestion that Bishan was axed through the sweep of a player-colleague-captain called Sunil Gavaskar, where only the sweep is within quotes. Who uttered it no one knows.

"In another passage, Bishan is reported to have said "I do not know myself why this conspriacy was hatched against me," which is within quotes, but that has no reference to me. It appears, in fact, that the comments attributed to Bishan are nothing but the viewpoints of the writer.

"If Bishan does have a grievance then I am most surprised. He has been part of team selection for a long time, and worked with the same members with whom I have been dealing. I can't imagine or even dream of dominating such respected senior cricketers like Polly Umrigar, Dattu Phadkar, M.L. Jaisimha and Chandu Sarwate.

"I think it's quite well known that the captain does not have a vote in a selection committee meeting. All he is empowered to do is to take part in the discussions that precede the picking of a side. Moreover, which captain, I ask, would deliberately choose an inferior player and thereby jeopardise his team's chances?

"There is an accusation that I called the Board president and asked for Ravi Shastri to be sent out to New Zealand. Nothing could be further from the truth. First of all, it was the Manager who made the request. Secondly, what the writer, perhaps, does not know is that the doctor told us that Dilip Doshi would not be available till the final Test at Auckland, while Shivlal Yadav would be fit for the second Test.

"It turned out to be the other way around. But it was on the basis of the initial advice that we sought a left-arm spinner as a replacement.

"It was a collective decision, in which the Manager, the Assistant Manager, the vice-captain and myself were involved.

"In any case, why would I be seeking to purposely weaken the side, if the contributor is trying to say that more deserving candidates were by-passed? Did not Ravi prove himself by taking fifteen wickets in the three Tests?

"However, despite the article, I have the highest possible regard for Bishan as a cricketer. It was a great privilege for me to be playing in the same side as him. He is the finest left-arm spinner I have ever seen.

"But I am disappointed with *Sportsworld* for having carried the piece. I am one of their correspondents, and I did not expect to be blasphemed against in this manner. It's all very well to say "Did Gavaskar get Bedi axed? and put a question mark behind it in the cover. Most people overlook on the punctuation and get the impression that I actually did get Bishan axed. It's not very responsible journalism".

"Sunil Gavaskar reacted violently. In his book "Idols", says Gavaskar: ".....Bishan as a person has been very forthright man not afraid to speak his mind and let the others know exactly what he thought of them and so I do not believe, when people suggest that it was he who had got an article written insinuating that it was I who was responsible for getting him chopped from the Indian team. This is far from truth for the simple reason that if Bishan thought that it was I who was responsible for it, he would have told me on my face and not made someone else write about it though that other person might be his greatest

*chamcha*. Bishan is not a person to fire a gun from some else's shoulder. Another person might have tried that....."
(If the "other person" is Bedi's "chamcha", observers, viewers of TV, readers of newspapers and magazines emphasize that Gavaskar is Sachin Tendulkar's Karchi (Serving Spoon).

"The months rolled by. Then suddenly another unnecessary controversy surfaced. The occasion: The talk between Sunil Gavaskar and Tiger Pataudi in the Gentleman (Mumbai) issue of May 1983.

The relevant dialogue :

Gavaskar : "Have you ever been charged with a defamation case.

Pataudi : "Yes, I have. Somebody wrote something libellous and the editor is always responsible".

Gavaskar : "Well, you have escaped once from me!"

Pataudi : "(Smiles)"

Gavaskar : "Let me give the background. There was an interview with Bishan Bedi in Sportsworld in which a lot of things about me were said. There was this writer who was trying to be more loyal than the King, but to my mind it was just an effort to break up the friendship between Bishan and myself because I personally feel that if Bishan had things to say he wouldn't say it through a third person".

Pataudi: "I agree that it was a terrible piece of journalism".

Gavaskar: "Why did you pass it then".

Pataudi: "Why do you think I'm being sued—it is not possible to see everything that is going into print—one can be abroad, for instance. There are things that are written in my magazine which go straight to Kolkata. But it won't happen again".

"I was least concerned about the contents of the dialogue between two former India captains. But I was extremely shocked at Pataudi's uncalled for accusation. I immediately reacted. I sent the clarification which was published. It is reproduced below:

## Cross-bat

"Tiger Pataudi has made an "unconventional shot" in his dialogue with Sunil Gavaskar in your May 1983 issue which I have just seen. It smacks of bad taste and shows him up as a weak editor, not befitting a magazine of the stature of *Sportsworld*.

"Every word that I wrote in my piece. Did Gavaskar Axe Bedi? which was published by *Sportsworld* was with the complete concurrence of Tiger. He read the piece carefully, suggesting deletion of his name from my write-up before approving it. He also made it clear that the article would appear after 3-4 weeks when he would be in London.

"The exact conversation between us went something like this:

"You've done a thoroughly professional job," said Pataudi after going through the article. And added: "Sunil Gavaskar will stop talking to me after he reads it".

"If that is what you feel, don't publish it or make any changes that you desire," I told him.

"After a little pause, Pat said: "Let it go but, please delete my name wherever you have mentioned it".

"I will revise the copy", I said.

While we were racing down in his sports car from Dupleix Road to Press Enclave, Pat said that the article would appear only when he would be in London.

"In his "dialogue" with Gavaskar in *Gentlemen*, Tiger has called my article a "terribly irresponsible piece of journalism". I am afraid that description fits his inaccurate remark better.

"I am aware that Pat and Sunil came closer to each other in Dubai recently. But it does not speak well of Tiger to make a cross-batted shot on a sticky wicket on which he would be caught more often than he could escape. He should be man enough to admit having seen the "offensive" article instead of shirking his responsibility, in order to maintain good relations with India's current captain.

Nawab was now upset. He was unwilling to accept the

'truthful' position as it stood then. He reacted. The letter reproduced below is self-explanatory:

*Sportsworld--October 19, 1982.*

Dear Mr Wadhwaney:

"This is to inform you that our editor, Mr Mansur Ali Khan Pataudi, has advised us that we can no longer use any articles written by you.

"Since we have accepted the articles already sent to us, we will arrange to pay for them, even if we do not use them.

"Any inconvenience caused is regretted"

With best wishes,
Yours sincerely
**Arijit Sen**
Associate Editor.

**Note:** I was commissioned by Sportsworld to write a series of articles on "cricket umpiring". Majority of them had appeared regularly since April 1982. But only a few remained unpublished.

Despite this minor misunderstaning, I have a very healthy respect for Nawab who, according to me, is an angel among modern-day cricket players. It is always a delight to be in his company. His subtle sense of humour is straight away captivating for those who have been able to understand him. He seldom conceals his emotions. But, at the same time, he is seldom rude to even his detractors. What is remarkable about him is that he is prepared to laugh at himself. He is ever ready to pull someone's leg but he also appreciates if someone chooses to pull his leg. All in all, he is a man of sensitivities. He has values, a trait which has become so uncommon with modern stars who are wrapped up in their conceit and ego. The modern day heroes should be watched from distance. Knowing them from close range will mean nothing but disappointment.

# 5

# Rungta Throws His Weight Around

The Indians were on mat on the tour to England in 1974. There were several unpleasant incidents, which had further tarnished India's already sliding image. Despite dismal performance on and off the field, the Board acceded to players' demand of increasing weekly allowance from £25 to £40 owing to steep escalation in England. Money was brought midway through the tour by the Board president Purshottam Rungta. He gave the good news to the players. But he kept delaying making payment to them.

A sizable amount of money was subsequently spent on the entertainment of the members and officials of the Test and Cricket Board (TCCB). When the players persisted for the additional payment, Rungta reportedly told the captain and others that he would be able to disburse the additional payment for only 10 days instead of for the full duration of the tour. There was resentment among players but most of them were unwilling to cross sword with the heavy-weight pan-chewing Rungta who had the reputation of being revengeful and vindictive.

Bedi, already disillusioned on the tour for many untoward happenings, felt that he could not be a party to the transaction which amounted to a kind of "double deal". He declined to sign the receipt. When asked, he told Rungta that he would either accept payment for full duration or nothing at all. "I will rather bear expenses from the meagre weekly allowance that I have got instead of accepting additional (negligible) part payment", he told Rungta, who was considerably upset at Bedi's firmness and frankness.

When Bedi returned from England, he was served with a charge-sheet comprising two charges, which were both absurd and spoke poorly of the Board and the Board President. One was that he had not bowled to the field set by the captain. Another was that he had violated the contract by appearing on the television.

The more Bedi tried to explain to the Board President that there was absolutely no breach in contract as the programme on the TV pertained to art and subtleties of spin bowling, the less could be understood by Rungta. Eventually the inquiry committee, with Rungta as chairman, dropped a bomb-shell by excluding him from the first Bangalore Test against the mighty West Indies team (1974-75). It was an illogical action against Bedi. There was resentment throughout the country, particularly in Delhi.

The Delhi and District Cricket Association (DDCA) President Ram Prakash Mehra (Lattoo), father-figure for Bedi then, and Times of India sports Editor R. Sriman, waited on deputation to the Education Secretary Shahid Ali. They explained to him the grave injustice done to India's greatest left-hand spinner. Shahid, a bureaucrat with few words, but firm in action, realised that the Board President had done something which was not in the interest of country's cricket.

When Rungta showed disregard to Shahid Ali's messages, he was sent a stern warning that the foreign exchange would not be released if he avoided meeting him. This was enough and Rungta rushed from Jaipur to Delhi next morning to meet the Education Secretary in the Shastri Bhavan.

Shahid Ali pointedly told Rungta that the charge against Bedi for his appearance on TV was flimsy and it was unpardonable to drop a player of the calibre of Bedi from the Test side. Shahid Ali made Rungta realise that Bedi's appearance on TV to provide a few tips to youngsters was not an act of indiscipline, as he had mistakenly thought. Rungta tried to browbeat Shahid Ali, who did not let him have his say. The Board President kept insisting that Bedi would be considered for the second Test if he submitted written apology. Shahid Ali's stand was that the question of apology would have been in order if Bedi had erred. When Rungta found that Shahid Ali was too solid for his bowling, he relented.

# 6

# Shocking Omission of Kapil Dev

Mansur Ali Khan Pataudi has often said—and perhaps rightly—that it is the opening batsmen who create problems for their teams. But in this country sadly the axe falls on other batsmen when the side loses the Test match.

One such glaring instance took place at Delhi in 1984-85 when an all-rounder of the calibre, prowess, dedication and commitment of Kapil Dev was sidelined for one rash stroke in India's second innings against David Gower's English side.

Top-scorer (60) in the first innings, Kapil Dev, as is his wont, went for the big hit, failed to time it properly and was caught. His exit was the signal for collapse and India lost the Test, to the utter delight of Gower, his team-mates and two dozen English mediapersons.

Scores India 307 and 235: England 418 and 127 for two (England won by eight wickets).

The next Test match at Kolkata was scheduled from December 31. The selectors with Chandu Borde as chairman and captain Sunil Gavaskar looked more agitated and upset than players. It was the time to take defeat in its stride because time had always been a big healer. But the committee, including Gavaskar, met at the polluted, Vizzy-constructed Willingdon pavilion. The subject matter was nothing but Kapil Dev's rash stroke. The selectors discussed and debated. Some, who had a gift of the gab, spoke vehemently against Kapil Dev's pre-determined shot, while two selectors were men enough to say that that was his style of batsmanship and he should be told to be more circumspect.

Two selectors were unable to take a charitable viewpoint. They demanded for Kapil Dev's 'head'. Had the meeting been held on some later date, the decision would have been far more balanced than it was. After protracted deliberations, the selectors dropped a bombshell and announced exclusion of Kapil Dev from Kolkata's Test. The reason for his exclusion was 'indiscipline'. The moot point that arose was how could selectors drop a player on the reason of indiscipline? Were they selectors or guardians of discipline or indiscipline? If they could drop a player on charges of indiscipline, what was the role of the Board, its President and other office-bearers?

The exclusion of Kapil Dev caused ripples all over the country. David Gower and many other well-known cricket authorities world over were shocked at the decision. Amidst this confusion worse confounded, Gavaskar went on record as saying that he was unblemished. Could the selectors have dropped Kapil Dev without his concurrence?

Chandu Borde subsequently went on record as saying that it was not only an unanimous decision but it was a very sad decision. He went on to say that along with Kapil Dev, another player Sandip Patil was also sent to gallows. It was because one of the selectors said if Kapil Dev's shot was unpardonable, so was Patil's and he should also be given marching order. Poor Patil, he went out never to return to the Test team! What a sad exit for a player of his talent and wide range of strokes!

The axing of Kapil Dev, the manner of the execution and the reasons for it underlined, yet again, the sordid state of Indian cricket. Whichever way one might look at it, the action showed that mafia was still at work and it was determined to cause further damage to Indian cricket.

When a national daily wrote that Gavaskar had in the

meeting said that he did not want Kapil Dev, he was up in arms. He went on record as saying that it was nothing but fabrication of news. If he was correct in his assertion, could Borde and his four wise men have had courage to drop Kapil Dev without his tacit support?

Kapil Dev accused Gavaskar for his omission. Gavaskar refuted the allegations sayig he was late in the meeting and he did not say a word. This was far from true. He might have been late by a few minutes but the meeting lasted long enough for him to have his say in the deliberations.

All national and regional papers were full of news pertaining to exclusion of Kapil Dev. All media was unanimous that Kapil Dev had been more sinned against than sinning. Consensus was that he had been done in by Gavaskar!

Salve, a shrewd politician, the Board President and leg-spinner when he was a student in Lucknow University, summoned both Gavaskar and Kapil. A.W. Kanmadikar (Judge), secretary of the Board, was also present. He had called them hoping that they would merely say 'yes Minister'. Both did shake each other by the hand and said that they had buried the hatchet after a calculated pep talk by Salve. He impressed upon them India's strength lay in their united approach. Kanmadikar supported his president. The players returned. Salve issued a statement impressing upon selectors to review the position. He "recommended" that the strength of the team should be increased to 15 from 14 meaning Kapil Dev should be included.

The selectors dutifully met at Kolkata three days before the Test. The discussion turned heated among Borde, A.G. Kripal Singh, B.S. Bedi, Hanumant Singh and Ambar Roy. The meeting dragged on for more than 10 hours. Bedi's viewpoint was that it was a collective decision of the committee and president had no role in it. Eventually Salve was spoken to on phone to ascertain from him whether it was his mandate to include Kapil Dev or he had merely made a suggestion. When he said that it was his personal view in his personal capacity, then the temper cooled down a bit and the meeting progressed. But the committee stood by Delhi decision refusing to make any change. In order to impress upon his colleagues, that he was not parochial or regional-minded and that he believed in doing a right thing, Bedi also played his role in keeping Kapil Dev out of the Kolkata Test.

Behind a black cloud, there is always a silver lining. In the exit of Patil, young Azharuddin walked in. Gavaskar seemed in favour of SriKanth. But the selectors stuck to their decision and insisted on the inclusion of Azhar in the playing eleven. Azhar lived up to the confidence reposed in him. He scored a century (110) on his debut and went on to score two more centuries in succession. These two centuries were at Chennai (105) and Kanpur (122). He was 54 unbeaten in the second innings when Gavaskar declared the innings at 97 for one. Though he was still needing 46 for his fourth century, it was within his grasp judging from the manner in which he was batting. No decision was possible and there was enough time for Azharuddin to get on to his fourth century.

# 7

# Probe Was An Eyewash

Money on their minds: Kapil : This was the headline to the news item, an exclusive and sensational interview, written by staffer Pradeep Magazine in Chandigarh's Indian Express on December 16, 1983.

"Indian cricketers are more interested in making money than playing the game seriously". This was how Kapil Dev summed up the debacle against the West Indies in the series (1983) in an interview.

"The attitude of the players and the outbursts of the West Indian Clive Lloyd in the Indian Press are doing a great harm to Indian cricket", felt Kapil Dev.....

Kapil Dev found nothing wrong in the players trying to make a fast buck for a secure future. "But it should not be at the expense of the game. I myself do modelling and such things but whenever I know it will affect my game I put a stop", he said.

He thought that the players should realise that cricket was their full-time occupation and whatever money they were earning was because of the game and not in spite of it.

Sunil Gavaskar reacted sharply. While providing details of the news to N.K.P. Salve on phone, Gavaskar told the Board President that he was contemplating of pulling out of the final Test at Chennai since his skipper had no faith in him and some other players. Salve, conciliatory as always, dissuaded him from taking such a drastic step and organised a meeting between two super stars at his residence at New Delhi. When Kapil Dev said that he had not been quoted 'properly', Salve on his behalf drafted a 'denial' and issued it to the Press. Both listened to Salve's 'pep talk' impressing upon them that 'they should bury the hatchet in the interest of country's cricketing health'. The super stars returned to their respective homes without being fully convinced about the developments. Gavaskar was still in two minds whether to play the Chennai Test or not. Eventually he chose to play the Test.

What Kapil Dev said at Chandigarh was not wholly incorrect but it was a nightmare to substantiate, so intricate was the issue and influence of money on players who were hell-bent on becoming from rags-to-riches. The sordid issue of involvement of stars in betting could have been nipped in the bud had some stars and officials made a sincere attempt to clear the 'dirt and filth' from under the covers of Indian cricket. The bettting then was at its initial stage and cleaning the polluted floor with a strong broom was more than possible. But there were wheels within wheels and, with the passage of time, more people got entangled to money power than their staying clear off it.

What heat and enthusiasm cricket generates now in the sub-continent, it was the case in Australia and England some decades ago. Even judiciary is supportive of cricket and cricket players in the sub-continent now, as it was in Australia years ago.

An article, written by the then Prime Minister Robert Menzies in Wisden, deserves narration.

"....And like all great institutions which are part of our heritence, it gets into the blood, and can invade the seats of judgement. I will illustrate this by an experience I had in my earlier days at the Victorian Bar. The story will be thought scandalous by some, and perhaps it is. But it is true and it makes my point.

"I had been appearing a good deal before an elderly judge who was not a great lawyer but who had for a brief period been a better than average cricketer. He was somewhat pernickety and abhorred slang expressions, but he was always approachable through his three special hobbiess—roses, poultry and cricket. I suppose that purists will say that no advocate should play upon the weakness of foibles of a judge. My reply is that any advocate who does not study and know his judge or judges is going to lose many cases most needlessly.

"Anyhow, my story is this. I was for a defendant in a civil action which arose out of events in the neighbourhood of Ballarat, the famous gold-mining city. My client, as I discovered after a conference with him and his solicitor, was very decent and honest, but a dull man, quite incapable of stating the facts in any coherent or consecutive fashion.

"Right through the first day of the hearing, the plaintiff and his witness were heard. I cross-examined with no particular success. Yet I had a feeling that my bucolic client is right, if he could only register himself with the judge. The plaintiff's evidence closed just on the adjournment. The judge looked at me, kindly enough (he approved of me because he thought I spoke good English) and said: "Mr. Menzies, I think I shall tell you that I find the plaintiff's case and witnesses most impressive".

"I replied: 'I would ask your Honour to suspend the judgement until you have heard my client, who will, I am sure, impress you very much".

"After the adjournment, I led the solicitor and client (we had no other witness) down to my chamber. All efforts to extract coherence from the client failed. I then produced my cards.

M: "Mr X have you ever grown roses?'

X: "I think, the wife has some in the garden".

M: "Can you distinguish a La Balle France from a Frau garl Orpington".

X: "Not for the life of me".

M: "Have you ever played cricket?"

X: "Now, you are talking. I played for Ballarat and District against Ivo Bligh's Eleven!"

M: "Good, conference ended.

"The next morning, I opened my case and called the defendant. He was quite dreadful as a witness. At one stage it became necessary to ask him about a date. Before he could reply I said in the most helpful manner: "Take your time, witness. I know that dates are not always easy to remember. Now, if I were to ask you about the date when you played cricket for Ballarat and District against Ivo Bligh's eleven, that would be much easier".

"The judge, beaming with excitement and delight, switched round his chair and said: "Is that so? Tell me about the match. Who was the fast bowler? How many runs did the defendant get? My client, completely relaxed, had returned to and concluded his evidence. The judge turned to the plaintiff's astonished counsel and said: "Of course, Mr Y, you may cross examine if you like, you have a perfect right to do so. But I think, I should tell you that in all my years on the bench I have never been more favourably impressed by any witness".

"It is hardly necessary to add that the defendant won and, I think, rightly, on the merits. But it was cricket that did it!"

That players, past stars and present heroes, may be involved in amassing riches more through other means than through their exploits on the field, may not be untrue. Concrete proof may be difficult to obtain. But there are 'circumstantial evidences' which point to their involvement in betting and gambling.

No one is a witness to seeing a man and a woman together on a bed in an intimate posture. But a child is born is a conclusive enough proof. Similarly, in this betting scenario, it may be one person's word against another person's denial. It will be difficult to prove who is telling the truth. But indirect evidences prove beyond doubt that the players are involved. Can there be smoke without fire?

The betting culture in Indian cricket is at least two decades old. It started with little money at stake. As following increased and sponsors joined, the quantum of betting and gambling increased beyond one's expectations. Now sky is the limit and crores of rupees are at stake. Life in major cities revolves around betting centres and bucket shops.

Many awesome stories on betting have appeared from time to time. But one mentioned by N.K.P. Salve, in his book 'The Story of the Reliance Cup', is worth reproducing here. Writes Salve: "....Came the Test match between India and West Indies in Kolkata. Sunil Gavaskar played a very clumsy stroke on the first ball and it snicked into the hands of the wicket-keeper. The wicket-keeper made no mistake and Gavaskar was back in the pavilion with a duck. Having got out to a most inelegant un-Gavaskar-like stroke every one was disappointed. But this is correct and except that Gavaskar played a rank bad shot, to say anything else about his character with refernece to the stroke was sheer vulgarity and ribeldry of the most heinous variety.

"I had gone to witness the Kolkata Test and after I returned to Delhi someone told me that Mr. Gavaskar's father had taken a bet and to enable him to win the bet Sunil had snicked the ball on the very first delivery into the hands of the wicket-keeper.

"I went to attend a meeting of the Cabinet Committee. Before the agenda is taken, normally the Prime Minister has an informal chat with the ministers present and the officials. Cricket was discussed for a few minutes and, to my sheer amusement, one of the ministers mentioned about the rumour of Gavaskar's getting out on the first ball to enable his father to earn a bet of Rs. 10 lakh.

"Later, Ms Gandhi hardly knew the subtle points of the cricket but her reaction was: "What nonsense...."

Whether such accusations made non-sense or sense, it was an appropriate time for Salve and others to undertake a wide-range probe to prevent Indian cricket from degenerating into a 'gambling den'. The officials continued to be in deep slumber and suffered from hang-over after winning the 1983 Prudential World Cup.

Board's general apathy and callousness as also Supreme

Court's reprieve to the players in 1989 led to situation going from bad to worse. What was a minor injury in early 1980s, assumed canceric magnitude by mid 1995. Amidst this vex scenario, Manoj Prabhakar, after quitting from competitive cricket and after sustaining an ignoble defeat in general elections, threw a sensational story through a weekly magazine saying that he was offered Rs. 25 lakh by a team-mate (Kapil Dev) to sabotage a match in favour of Pakistan during the Singer Cup in Sri Lanka in 1994.

Prabhakar, never a dreamer or a schemer, could not have 'manufactured such a story. It required judicious handling and dispassionate probe to reach at the bottom of what Delhi star had alleged. He was not a gainer by releasing such a news. He was morally unloading himself after receiving a harsh treatment from authorities who were governing Indian cricket. Prabhakar was "too straight' a player to level such a serious charge against team-mate. But the Board once again bungled adding more problems to the already raging controversy of betting, bribery and match-fixing.

As Prabhakar accusations had engulfed entire country, there came a disclosure in a daily paper of a Journalist's chance meeting with a Delhi-based influential and wealthy bookie in the West Indies. The bookie reportedly offered him a huge amount of money for providing him an innocuous type of information on wickets, availability and form of players as also organising meetings with the Indian stars.

A keen follower of cricket and races (horses), Yashwant Vishnu Chandrachud, a seasoned jurist, was appointed by Board to investigate the matter. No one knew what his terms of reference were and no one knew what discussion was held with him by the Board officials. From all accounts of all those who were examined or interviewed by him, the probe was nothing but an eyewash.

The manner in which the investigation was made by the established jurist, it seemed Chandrachud had made up his mind to exonerate players. He tossed the ball into the court of Prabhakar and a journalist. Might be, the players were not guilty. But the Board should have released officially his 194-page findings to the Press. Suffice it to say, "a mountain was long in labour and produced a proverbial mouse." While exonerating stars, he came down heavily on Prabhakar whom he virtually called as a "liar". He went on to say: "It is indeed an easy exercise. Make any unfounded allegation against the team-mates, officials and others and then try to get away with it by saying that the names of the culprits cannot be disclosed because there is danger to his life and fear of litigation". According to one-man commission, "Prabhakar has no regard for truth whatsoever".

If the commission failed to get any concrete proof of players' involveement, it also could not secure concrete proof that they were not involved.

Subsequently, Pradeep Magazine wrote a book entitled 'Not quite Cricket'. His contents were no better than Chandrachud's probe. He said nothing more than what he had written in a daily paper (Pioneer) or what others had said. His book threw no new light. The truth of the book was that Magazine was narrating a 'cricket fiction' in his own language. Had he chosen to provide details about the bookie, he perhaps would have done a lot of service to the cause of cricket in India. Unquestionably knowledgeable and a good writer, with his laid-back style, he should have been more forthright in his observation than providing "consolidated" information under the cover.

The Board, in its wisdom, filed a defamation suit in Mumbai High Court against Prabhakar and Outlook weekly magazine for Rs. 5 crores in early 1998. The Board's move was extremely intriguing as legal tangle on betting scandal would only cause further embarrassment to the parent body.

Nobody knows how the case stands although it was filed more than four years ago. The suit, unique in the history of cricket, will provide all the opportunities to both Prabhakar and Vinod Mehta (Editor) to take the lid off the alleged 'betting and match-fixing racket'. There are many skeletons in the cupboard and the Outlook-Prabhakar team will succeed in their match, should Board decide to go ahead with the case.

# 8

# Vengsarkar Banned

Rivalry among newspapers was as intense as competition among players for selection in the Indian team. Aware that cricket generated a lot of enthusiasm and following, they began commissioning Test stars to write for their newspapers by offering them a huge amount.

Except for handful of players, who could write or could provide a befitting tape-recorded version, many said nothing but their reports or comments appeared under their names.

There are several instances. But one that needs mentioning is: An Indian newspaper engaged Imran Khan to air his views for three days of the five-day Test between India and Pakistan in Pakistan. For a day or two, the correspondent contacted him on phone. Then the deal was struck: "Write whatever you want but, please, do not write any controversial stuff". This was done not because Imran Khan could not pen down his views but he had no time to write, so engrossed was he with many other engagements off the field.

Some enterprising youngmen, who styled themselves as 'promoters', engaged junior reporters on negligible remuneration to handle Test stars' syndicated columns. Some stars got more money for one column, actually written by a reporter, than what reporter earned in a month by way of his salary.

All this holy or unholy arrangement continued--and it still continues in some cases—as ill-informed editors felt that their circulation would increase with the reports appearing under the names of Test players.

There was time when foreign captains/players were engaged to write for newspapers. They earned enough from newspapers to meet their out-of-pocket expenses, including shopping, as they saved entire amount of foreign exchange earnings from the tour. This was not the cause enough for complaint. But shrewd and calculative as these foreign captains were, they started lambasting umpiring and umpires. This brought about additional pressure on Indian umpires who had no defence for themselves as they were forbidden by the Board to air their views. Under pressure from foreign captains on the play-field and also in newspapers, they started humming visiting teams' tune instead of umpiring impartially, as it ought to have been. There were numerous occasions when their judgements did no credit to them. The Board should have stepped in. While discussing of guarantee money, perks and other facilities on tour, the Board should have added a clause forbidding them from writing in newspaper columns while on tour. But the spineless Board did nothing of that sort providing them needless advantage.

The Board showed little wisdom in dealing with such vex situations. It allowed foreign captains to write, but it banned Indian stars from doing the similar kind of reportage. The more they were impressed upon by the Indian players and captains, the less they were prepared to understand. These weakling Board officials were more over-awed by Clive Lloyd, for example, than Indian batsmen or bowlers.

When the Indian stars started writing, the Board showed its disapproval but did nothing beyond it. Amidst this ticklish scenario, another problem pertaining to wearing of logos surfaced. The Board slapped a fine of Rs. 5,000 each on nine players, including Kapil Dev and vice-captain

Ravi Shastri for wearing sponsors' logos without obtaining approval.

Srikanth faced another problem. In his defence, he had stated that his column in a Mumbai eveninger had been used in the previous series without obtaining his consent. This was considered in violation of the contract. He was asked to secure a 'regret' letter from the publishers. The Board's letter further said that he would have to pay another sum of Rs. 5,000 in case he was unable to obtain a letter of 'regret' from the newspaper management.

This trouble had erupted a few months before the 1987 World Cup which was being hosted jointly by India and Pakistan. The Board had prepared a new contract for players to sign. The players, not a united bunch, refused to oblige. "There is no problem and the players will duly sign the new contract", emphasised the Board spokesman. While saying all this, the Board official also said that standbys were ready, should players show their stubbornness.

Captain Kapil Dev and some other players were painfully disturbed at Board's double standards. While the stars were being prevented from wearing the logo of their own sponsors, they were being vehemently asked to wear 'Reliance' logo—sponsors of the World Cup. This was not a happy augury on the part of the Board, argued players.

The Board was, for once, duly stumped. They found the players were united and also what they were saying had a lot of logic. What compelled the Board to yield was that it did not want to fail in organising the World Cup. The Board President N.K.P. Salve had earned the right to stage the championship after encountering many problems, initiated by Englishmen who were unwilling to realise the reality that sun was after all setting on their Empire.

A fresh contract was made after discussing with some legal luminaries. It was handed over to 14 selected players. The Indian stars were happy that their points of view were incorporated in the contract.

"Illogical" was the word that players vehemently

pronounced for Udaipur, which did not have bare minimum facilities for the conditioning camp. Following complaints, the camp was shifted to Delhi where, even after signing the contract, there were some rough edges to be sorted out between players and the Board.

Two problems surfaced. One was players' right to write. Another was the subtle difference between logo and language inscription and what would be displayed by players on the ground and what they were not obliged to display.

Despite sincere efforts, the problems actually could not be sorted out as players had now tested 'blood (lure of money) and they did not want lucrative cake to be cut at any cost.

Amidst this scenario, India failed to qualify for the World Cup Semi-final. In fact, both favourite teams, India and Pakistan, were eliminated.

The authorities in India, in fact in sub-continent, are governed by funny and foolish instincts. They think that the team that wins is great and the side that loses, no matter how well players perform or fight, is bad. As is universally accepted, winner has many fathers and loser is an orphan. This foolish attitude came into play.

To Board's show cause notice during the third Test at Kolkata, Vengsarkar had drafted his reply. But before he could hand it over, he was hurt. He could not play in the remaining part of the Test. He also missed the fourth Test at Chennai where, under Ravi Shastri, India won the Test.

Vengsarkar eventually sent his reply, which was not accepted by the Board. He was debarred on February 3, 1988 from playing for his country and state (Mumbai) for six months. He was also fined Rs. 10,000. It was as much a 'historical' decision as it was illogical. The decision was taken at Board's working committee meeting. It was announced that it was 'unanimous' but it was not so as meeting became a platform for heated debate.

The Board spokesman said that Vengsarkar, who was served with two show cause notices, was also dissuaded from writing by senior Board officials but he was unwilling to see any point of view other than his.

The Board apprehended trouble as players, according to newspaper reports, were united. To counter it, the Board issued an order that a player refusing to play for the country, except for reasons that were considered proper by the Board, he would not be considered for a period of one year.

The decision of the special committee of the Board did not go well with many former players and well known critics. The former selection committee chairman Bapu Nadkarni reportedly said that Vengsarkar was unlucky to have been punished while some of his predecessors had gone scot-free. He reportedly added that it was a case of a good player getting a bad decision.

Vengsarkar, in the meantime, consulted an eminent legal expert. After examining the case, he told Vengsarkar: "You will certainly win the case but that is about all". While telling him all this, he asked Vengsarkar that he should get along with his game.

After weighing pros and cons, Vengsarkar felt that he should not jeopardise chances of others, some of them youngsters. He took the ban philosophically. He subsequently revealed: "My whole team wanted to boycott the game till I was reinstated", he said adding: "The players had given me a signed letter but I did not want to involve any one of them".

When Vengsarkar asked for permission to play in local competitions, the Board immediately granted it.

# 9

# Supreme Court's Unholy Ruling

Various rumblings were being whispered even when the 1987 World Cup was in progress. Rumblings became serious controversies as India crashed out of the contest at the semi-final stage. Without any justifiable reason, Kapil Dev was dumped as a captain. Did he captain badly? Did he fail to motivate his players? Was he not popular with players? The selectors, always mysterious, did not consider it necessary to explain reasons for his removal. They also did not specify as to why was change necessary in the leadership?

Kapil Dev deserved to continue as he was a popular choice with the players, who mattered the most. But if he had to be changed, for the sake of the change, the responsibility should have been entrusted to Ravi Shastri, a deputy to Kapil Dev. An extrovert and a very fine student of the game and its finer points, his claims were bypassed. Why was Shastri, who hailed from Mangalore, ignored? Many thought that he would have been a good choice.

Kapil Dev axed and Shastri bypassed, in came Dilip Vengsarkar as a captain. He had only recently become captain of Mumbai. His doings for the Mumbai team were not extra-ordinary. He was not ready yet for the arduous responsibilities of captaincy as he was not, in essentiality, a man endowed with qualities of stirring up men under his charge.

Vengsarkar's climb to Everest was not smooth. There

was a Hitchcock-like drama which was being enacted behind the cover in Chandigarh. The Board authorities had prepared a new contract. They were unsure whether Vengsarkar, who always had his independent views, would sign it. Uncertain as they were, they invited Mohinder to reach Chandigarh. He was given to understand that he would be the captain. Actually, it was a very injudicious handling by the powers that-be. He should, in fact, have been given the correct picture, as the situation stood then. But, by the time, Mohinder reached Chandigarh, the issue with Vengsarkar had been sorted out and he was chosen captain. Naturally Mohinder was offended. Any one would have felt as such. This was yet another example of Board's faulty functioning.

When Vengsarkar took over, Indian team was in total disarray. Gavaskar had retired from Test cricket and India had to learn to do without a master batsman opening the innings. Three senior players, Kapil Dev, Ravi Shastri, and Mohinder were extremely unhappy with the Board's functioning which, according to them, lacked in sense of direction. The Board's judgement was uncanny and, above all, its doings smacked of victimisation.

When the first Test against West Indies at Delhi was about to start, there was more depressing news. Azharuddin's groin trouble had aggravated during World Cup and he was hardly able to run. He expressed his doubts about playing. He was prevailed upon to play even without being 100 per cent fit after he missed the first Test.

Vengsarkar's first innings as a captain was not a failure. He scored centuries at Delhi and Kolkata. He saw India draw the four-Test series against West Indies 1-1. The drawn series was not a true index of the strengths of two teams. The visitors were far superior. 'Wisden said: ".....
2-1 in favour of the West Indies would have been more appropriate as a solitary Indian victory in the last Test on a wicket that made a mockery of Test Cricket. Narender Hirwani with his leg-breaks and googly bowling was the destroyer. The wicket at Chennai was a paradise for

spinners. Bespectacled, short and stocky with casual walk, Hirwani, like Jasu Patel at Kanpur against Kangaroos decades ago, was inducted. He turned the ball viciously. He had eight wickets in the first innings and another eight in the second innings, (match figures 16 for 136). When he took eight wickets on debut, he became the fourth bowler in history to achieve this feat. Vivian Richards, however, did not consider much about his bowling. He went on record to say: "One swallow does not summer make".

Vengsarkar was banned for six months for writing a newspaper column when his contract prohibited him. He also had problem in Mumbai where he had a heated argument with umpires.

It was vehemently said that Vengsarkar's ban was a wishy-washy exercise as he did not miss any international match. As the ban period ended, he was prompty appointed captain for the Champions Trophy in Sharjah and Asia Cup in Dhaka. The action-futile as it was—was to establish who the boss of Indian cricket was! Vengsarkar failed to make the most of these twin engagements as he ran into problems with senior players, including Azharuddin.

First Shastri returned from Dhaka under the plea that he needed 'rest'. How could a player be permitted to leave on the ground that he required rest? Were there no terms and conditions? Obviously, there was no discipline. It was a fit case for the management to have reported to the Board against him. According to inside story, he returned because he came to know that he might be dropped from the team and he did not want to take it.

This was bad. What was worse was that Vengsarkar started screaming at Azharuddin from the pavilion when the match was in progress against Sri Lanka at Dhaka. How could Vengsarkar do this? Was he playing a club match? Vengsarkar's screaming was shocking. He was upset as India was lagging behind in run-rate. But there was a method to handle the situation instead of screaming. Azharuddin, a senior player and a recognised batsman, felt upset at the treatment meted out to him by his skipper.

The consensus among players was that 'captaincy had gone into the head of Vengsarkar'.

This and many other incidents had led to two senior batsmen, Vengsarkar and Azharuddin, drifting away from each other. It was not a happy augury since many seniors had already left the scene of the international cricket.

The selectors' faith in Vengsarkar continued. He was the captain to the West Indies in 1988-89. The team was thoroughly thrashed (0-3). An accomplished batsman for 3-4 years, Vengsarkar could not find his form. He could make only 110 runs from six innings. He seemed totally frustrated at his performance. He was also disillusioned with the doings of his team-mates. While this might be understandable, his lashing out at players was not.

When a Sportsworld correspondent interviewed Vengsarkar, he was raging in fury. Among many harsh remarks, he said: "If people are frightened of fast bowling, they should not play Test cricket". Quite a bit of criticism was levelled against Azharuddin who, according to Vengsarkar, was not a good batsman to negotiate short-pitched deliveries.

The team, beaten in West Indies, returned home via USA disunited, disillusioned and disappointed.

To call some of them "cowards" did not do credit to the captain of the side. Was he not he who was up in arms against a senior journalist when he had accused him of shying away from the ball at Kanpur against the same West Indians? To say that the batsmen surrendered 'wilfully' was more a sign of complete frustration than his candid observations. He did not endear himself with players and cricket following public.

Vengsarkar's outbursts were being discussed threadbare when Board dropped a bombshell on August 6, 1989, by banning six leading stars for one year. They were Vengsarkar, Kapil Dev, Ravi Shastri, Arun Lal, Kiran More and Mohd. Azharuddin. They were also fined along with other junior players.

The players were punished for violating the contract.

Despite contract and despite repeated requests by the Board president B.N. Dutt to return home, they stopped over in the United States to make a few quick bucks. This was considered a gross defiance and the committee consisting of Dutt (Chairman), I.S. Bindra, P.M. Rungta, Madhav Mantri and A.W. Kanmadikar handed out this extreme punishment.

The players were considerably shaken at the extreme step taken by the Board. They met but could not decide any course of action. Just when all seemed lost, a college-level player Vineet Kumar, an advocate, now filed a PIL (Public Interest Litigation) in the Supreme Court. The case generated such a heat and interest that the court used to be jam-packed with players, officials and promoters in addition to legal experts.

India's Chief Justice E.S. Venkataramaiah scrutinised papers, contracts and also constitution of the Board. A hard-core lover of cricket and players, he came down heavily upon the Board officials pointing out several loop-holes. Such were harsh observations of the Chief Justice that the Board got disturbed although it was also being defended by a few senior legal luminaries.

When Justice Venkataramaiah told Board to 'set its own house in order' and it would be 'in the interest of the Board to undertake a mutual agreement with the players', the Board had no option except to heed the Justice's observations. Had the case proceeded, the Board might have run into a lot of unforseen problems.

N.K.P. Salve, a former Board President, had gone on record as saying that no other single person had done as much disservice to cricket and Board as the Chief Justice of India. These were harsh remarks but nevertheless Venkataramaiah had given a reprieve to the players who were growing indisciplined and arrogant.

In a bid to strengthen arms of the Board, several affiliated units had filed petitions seeking intervention in the case. Their contention was that disciplinary action taken by a parent body against players was essential for the health and welfare of cricket (sports) in the country. This was the pattern followed worldwide. If the parent body does not take action against erring players, who would? Their contention also was that such matters were beyond the jurisdiction of the court.

Against this view was observations of some senior journalists, particularly of Kuldip Nayyar, who held the view that an unjust action by the parent body could only be challenged by players through court.

Kapil Dev accused Sunil Gavaskar for his dubious role. He also accused Jagmohan Dalmiya for masterminding the Board's action plan to 'silence' players. Kapil Dev blamed Gavaskar for his effort to disown his role in planning some matches in USA and Canada.

On September 12, 1989, the Supreme Court issued an ultimatum to the Board to dispose of the case within a week. The court also ordered that the ban should not be implemented until the next hearing on September 25.

The issue of Mohinder became alive. The court granted him permission to prefer an appeal and the Board was directed to dispose it of in a week.

The players' advocate Soli Sorabji launched a frontal attack on the Board and its working. The contract was considered one-sided and the players had no voice or choice in accepting or rejecting it. Mr. Justice K.N. Singh observed that even captain had no choice to refuse to sign the contract. The Chief Justice observed: "A player who refuses to sign the contract cannot even play in Ranji Trophy matches. According to him, it was nothing short of violation of a citizen's right to freedom of action.

When Sorabji pointed out that the contract denied players the right to write about the game or Board officials, Mr. Justice Singh wanted to know whether "they (Officials) are beyond criticism and in a much more exalted position than the Prime Minister". "Even we judges are being criticised every day," he added.

The truth of the matter was that the officials were being criticised every day by media and others. The point was whether it was in order for players to criticise Board's functioning. The argument, as advanced by some senior lawyers, was how would the Chief Justice or any Justice for that matter, react if his stenographer or secretary criticised his judgement?

The Chief Justice cautioned the Board that it would be 'doing harm to itself by claiming itself to a private body without anything to do with public conscience'. He advised the Board to claim itself as a public body open to judicial scrutiny instead of holding itself above law.

The Attorney-General of India K. Parasaran, appearing on behalf of the Government, gave his ruling that the Board was open to judiciary scrutiny.

# 10

# Merchant's Claims Bypassed

Iftikhar Ali Khan Pataudi, a fine ball player, was a candidate to captain India on tours to England in 1932 and 1936. But he was against a lobby of Maharajahs, princes and zamindars who, because of their excellence in sychophancy, generally had their say with the ruling clique of Britishers. His credentials of batsmanship were such that he could be considered to lead the country. He was, however, stumped on both occasions by non-entity of cricket players, Maharajah of Porbander in 1932 and Zamindar Vizzy in 1936. Porbander was luckily man enough to realise his deficiencies and stood down for C.K. Nayudu to lead the team in the only Test played at Lord's in 1932.

Iftikhar, who had also functioned as a selector in 1932 and in 1936, continued to play his competitive cricket in England. He was in a reasonably good form before his health deteriorated.

When it became certain that India would undertake a full tour of England in 1946 to provide a much-needed practice to English players, starved of competitive cricket because of World War II, Iftikhar resurfaced for Indian captaincy. C.K. Nayudu, still fighting fit at a ripe age, was not a strong candidate as he had suffered in popularity with his contemporary players.

Iftikhar had rigorous nets and physical training at Kotla for a few days before he represented South Punjab against Delhi. It was January 10, 1946 when the match began. He did not have much success against Delhi and against Baroda in the next match but in the brief knocks that he played, the sparks of his brilliant batsmanship were visible.

With Nayudu out of favour, three candidates were in fray. They were Iftikhar, Yuvraj, now full-fledged Maharajah of Patiala and Vijay Merchant. Sensing that he had a little chance to secure sufficient support, Yuvraj pulled out of the contest leaving Iftikhar and Merchant in the field for a straight fight.

On form and commitment to cricket, Merchant should have been preferred to Iftikhar. But Merchant had earned the wrath of Dr. Subbaroyan, who was then the president of the Board. In the tiff, Merchant was totally right and Dr. Subbaroyan wrong. But Dr. Subbaroyan had felt insulted and being a politician he wanted to have a pound of flesh.

## The Incident

In the Mumbai-Holkar match in March 1945 there were reportedly a few umpiring aberrations. Both teams were on receiving end. But Dr. Subbaroyan was upset at certain lbw decisions which had gone against Holkar. He rushed to the Mumbai dressing room where umpires were having a cup of tea. He fired the umpires. Merchant did not appreciate it and asked Dr. Subbaroyan to leave the room. If the presence of umpires in Mumbai dressing room was incorrect, it was absolutely wrong for Dr. Subbaroyan to dash there to rebuke the umpires. The dressing room is a private room and no one, no matter how important, is entitled to enter unless he has been explicitly invited by the captain or the manager. What was wrong that Dr. Subbaroyan was providing rough treatment to the umpires in presence of Mumbai players.

Dr. Subbaroyan was now openly canvassing against Merchant and was supporting the candidature of Iftikhar. The plea he was making was that Iftikhar had known the English conditions and hence he would be an ideal choice for the captaincy.

As the captaincy issue hotted up, some Congress politicians also started canvassing for Iftikhar. It was then rumoured that Pandit Jawaharlal Nehru also secretly put in a word in favour of Iftikhar because of his good relations with the Nawab of Bhopal.

When the elections took place in the Board's annual meeting at Connemara Hotel (Chennai), Iftikhar scraped through 10-8. Pankaj Gupta (Bengal) was elected Manager instead of favourite Homi Contractor.

Following this coupe, there were many adverse reports against Iftikhar throughout the country, particularly in Mumbai, which was all for Merchant. While Times of India screamed advising Mumbai to break away from the Board, there were rumours that Merchant might withdraw from the team. But he did not saying that he was a "disciplined soldier". He said that he would abide by the decision taken by the Board. Iftikhar stayed unperturbed. He went on record as saying that: "It will do no harm if a lot of dirty linen is washed in public in India. It will help us to go to England with clean shirts."

(In the pre-tour match at Mumbai, Brabourne Stadium), East Zone were skittled out by Fazal Mehamood for 65 runs. (Fazal was not chosen for the tour.) Pataudi (North zone captain) kept himself at number eight in batting order. When he came in to bat, he just played one ball and declared. As he returned to dressing room, Duleepsinhji told him : "So you 'shirked' playing". Pat did not appreciate Duleep's outbursts. He told him sternly: "'Go to the Ganges, recover ashes of your uncle Ranji and ask him what he thought of me".

A few years earlier, Iftikhar had stated that Indian captaincy was a nightmare as the captain was saddled with the responsibility of pleasing players from different communities, from different states and from different affiliated units for the sake of votes.

# 11

# UnMerchant Like Shot

Two wrongs do not make one right. Vijay Merchant, of all persons, did not realise this. He used his casting vote in the five-member selection committee and installed Ajit Wadekar as captain and dislodged Mansur Ali Khan Pataudi.

Many ardent lovers of the game thought that Merchant had resorted to taking revenge as Mansur's father Iftikhar had deprived him from India's captaincy on tour to England in 1946. Indeed he deserved the honour then but why should he have held son responsible for father's lapses, if any? Merchant, who had been inducted in the selection committee as chairman after years of inactivity, had until then enjoyed the reputation of playing with a straight bat. His colleagues in the committee were: M.M. Jagdale, M. Datta Ray, H.T. Dani, and C.D. Gopinath. Only Dani supported Vijay Merchant for the candidature of Wadekar, while Datta Ray and Gopinath were for Pataudi as skipper. Jagdale abstained. Stalemate continued for awhile when Merchant utilised his casting vote.

When the selection committee met on January 8, 1971, there were three for the coveted post of captain. Pataudi was the sitting captain. Chandu Borde had been in the running for long, while new player was Wadekar. Borde was quickly discarded on the plea that he was already 36 and there was no point in saddling him with an additional responsibility of the captaincy. The choice narrowed down to two.

Now Merchant miscalculated. He thought that Jagdale, for old times sake, would go along with him and it would make 3-2. But Jagdale had his own ideas. He thought that Pataudi had done a yeoman's service in building the side and that Wadekar still had a long way to go.

Pataudi's captaincy record in 36 Tests—the longest reign in India's history until then—was not particularly impressive. Nor had he batted as consistently as many had expected from him. But he weighed his weight in gold as a fielder. His style of fielding inspired many others to rise to the occasion. Eknath Solkar, for example, drew a leaf out of his book.

All in all, Pataudi as a batsman-captain was far from outstanding. But his contribution, which was unparalled in the history of Indian cricket, was that he, despite his usual aloofness, saw to it that the players buried their regional affinities and played as a cohesive unit. He provided players faith and respect. He imposed no curfew on players who were generally fit on the field judging from their exploits in fielding. India might not have won many Tests under his captaincy but team's ascendancy in international cricket began with his leadership. Wadekar, Bedi, Gavaskar, Kapil Dev and Azharuddin then lent stability and durability to the team. Gone are the days when the fielders dropped catches deliberately to deprive a bowler from another region of legitimate wickets. Such a player deserved better treatment than removed by the casting vote of Merchant.

Pataudi's first innings of captaincy was not a bed of roses. When Mike Smith's England team in 1963-64 came, his place in the team was doubtful. But he scored a century in domestic cricket and he was appointed captain for the first two Tests. Prior to appointing him captain, for the third Test at Kolkata, he was asked by selectors : "Will you have your eye checked, because we are not sure whether you can see so well"? "I have had the same bad eye for the last ten years and I feel I am seeing just as well", said Pat adding: "It is just that I am not getting good scores at present". When they insisted, he said, "O.K. if that's the way you want it". Seeing Pat's reaction and displeasure, they dropped the issue.

Wadekar was visibly taken aback on his elevation. He did not expect it even in his wildest dreams. So sure was he of Pataudi's continuation that he had even requested him for putting a favourable word for his selection.

Pataudi should have taken his removal from captaincy gracefully. But he did not. He sent a pre-dated telegram saying that he would not be available for the tour. He did not play for the South Zone against the East Zone. He then announced that he was contesting general elections from Haryana.

Following loss of one eye in England in road accident, Pataudi had shifted to Delhi where he played for Delhi and captained the side for some years. Here also he stayed aloof from the players. He arrived at Kotla at the nick of the time and left soon after day's play was over. But the team did well and the players enjoyed playing under him. He moved to Hyderabad as he thought that the atmosphere in Delhi was no longer homogeneous. Many thought he had a reason to feel so. There were currents and cross-currents, including a tinge of communal bias against him.

# 12

# Contractor Felled

Charlie Griffith, of Barbados, was an extremely quick bowler whose action was typical. There were some who considered his action 'doubtful'. He was called for chucking by Cortez Jordan. But he was a bowler who was endowed with very strong shoulders and, with a little effort, he could get the ball stand up. He was not a mean fellow, as some of his countrymen were. He did make use of the bumper within a frame-work of laws without trying to injure or maim a batsman. While he generated a lot of speed and wore a determined look on his face, he was a likeable person off the field.

Nari Contractor, skipper, was one of the finest left-hand opening batsmen the country had produced. His on-side play, particularly between fine-leg and mid-wicket, was seen to be believed. With a subtle drop of wrists and movement of his nimble feet, he was in a position to alter the direction of the ball. He was a batsman, who could pierce the field or find gaps to get boundaries behind. His batsmanship on the on-side region was a joy to behold.

As usual, Contractor opened an Indian innings against Barbados, a colony side. Griffith, with a longish run-in, delivered the ball which from his action looked a bouncer. In fact, it was not exactly a bouncer. Contractor misread it on March 16, 1962. He hunched his shoulders. The ball crashed on his person.

Says Wisden: ....."Could not judge the height to which

it would fly, bent back from the waist in a desperate, split-second attempt to avoid it and was hit just above the right ear".

It was a terrible blow, the sound of it could be heard in the pavilion. Contractor was dazed, but he stood up giving the impression that nothing had happened. In a few seconds, he found he was unable to stand up. He wobbled at the crease before he sank to the ground. He was escorted to the dressing room.

Seated on the chair, Contractor suddenly started screaming loudly. Obviously he was in great pain. Blood oozed out of his ears and nose. He was rushed in an ambulance to the hospital where, an X-ray examination revealed a fractured skull and clotting of blood at the vital area around brain. Another X-ray was taken. Specialists were summoned. The examination showed that the damaged area was a critical one. Any delay could be suicidal. There was no time for consultation or procrastination. The surgeons were authorised to undertake an emergency operation by the manager Ghulam Ahmed. Frank Worrell, who came to hospital, donated his blood. So did many others. The entire team was in the hospital praying for his recovery. His family was informed in the meantime. Griffith also came to the hospital. He was visibly shaken. He kept muttering that he did not mean to hurt him. "It was just one of those accidents", he said, "God willing, every thing will be alright".

It was an agonising day for all Indians. Luckily, surgeons walked out of the theatre and happily pronounced that the operation was a success. "But next 12 hours are still critical until he regains his consciousness", said one surgeon. Another operation became essential to remove clotting of blood.

Contractor recovered. He was flown back to his home along with his wife who had by this time arrived in Barbados. After months of resting, Contractor regained his health. He walked about. He started jogging. He began his work-out. He did play cricket but he was not the Contractor he was. It was a great loss to the country as he was a batsman of exceptional technique, skill and competence.

There were some who said that Contractor actually ducked into the ball. Peter Lashly, who was fielding at short-leg, raised his arms giving the indication that he was appealing for leg before. This was a very far-fetched argument as Contractor was quite tall and could not have gone down to the level of stumps height.

Vijay Manjrekar, technically as sound as Vijay Mechant, was also hit by Griffith's rising delivey. He took the ball on the bridge of his nose. He also retired. As he entered he shouted: "I have been blinded, I cannot see a thing". The atmosphere in the Indian dressing room was tense. Going in to bat seemed going for the "gallows".

Manjerakar was undaunted by the injury. He batted superbly in the second innings. He scored a century. It was great.

Following this near fatal accident, laws pertaining to bumpers have been amended. Following initiation of one-day version, further amendments have been made. There are however many who feel that bumper is a legitimate weapon in the armoury of fast bowlers since the game is heavily weighed towards batsmen. This is truism as most of the laws are in favour of batsmen.

For West Indians, it is "war on the pitch". They believe and thrive on it. Pain is the name of the game. Their quickies bowl to achieve their end even if they have to maim batsmen. There was time when it was said that they maimed one for every three Tests they played. In 1970s and 1980s their bowlers left batsmen with bruised, battered and broken bones.

Mohinder, among Indian batsmen, was the only one who stood up to a 'battery' of four quickies. He showed them (a) he was not afraid of them, (b) that he could bear a few knocks on his person, (c) that he could bat for a long time and (d) he would not play a 'stupid' shot because of fear.

With Contractor out, Pat became India's captain when he was 21 years, two months and 18 days.

# 13

# Sidhu Errs,
# Goes Almost Scot Free

Navjot Singh Sidhu, highly religious and staunch believer in God, and left-handed Saurav Ganguly, extremely talented but yet to descend on Indian cricket firmament, became friends as they were clubbed together on the tour of England in 1996. Both poured their hearts out to each other for several days in the confines of the hotel rooms.

Both Sidhu and Ganguly had their minds loaded with complaints and grouses against the powers that-be. While Sidhu, senior-most in the team, was constantly tossed about from one berth to another and was dubbed as an injury prone batsman, Ganguly was accused of securing his berth in the team through rich contacts in the corridors of the Board.

In the first one-dayer against England at Oval, Sidhu, batting at number four, was bowled by Lewis for three and in the second at Leeds he was run out for 20. In this match he batted at number three. Despite his expreience and quite a bit of consistency, he was never sure as to what number he would be called upon to bat. Azharuddin and manager Sandeep Patil did not consider it necessary to have a word with him.

If there was no result in the first match because of rain, the second India had lost conclusively. Sidhu getting run out was held against him by the management. It was said that he was a poor runner between wicket and missed many singles, which were there. On this plea he was sidelined from the third Test at Old Trafford. India again lost the match losing series 0-2.

That Sidhu was a poor runner between wickets did not cause him much worry. But when he was accused of letting down the side, he felt upset. It caused him concern and anguish. He kept revolting within himself on his bed. Eventually, he opened his mind to room-partner Ganguly saying that he was leaving the team mid-way through the tour. Ganguly reportedly asked him to reconsider his decision. He also reportedly suggested him that he should defer the decision as time was a great healer. But when 'sardar' had made up his mind, there was no one who could make him see reason.

Sidhu expressed his desire to return home to both Azharuddin and Patil. It was here where fire could have been extinguished with a careful and judicious handling. But it was Azhar, who did not like Sidhu. Patil had no opinion. Both lacked in maturity to handle such an explosive situation.

Sidhu needed a subtle counselling and not condemnation. What was shocking was that both Azhar and Patil did not care to study Sidhu's mind. They thought he was threatening and he was questioning their decision in sidelining him from the third match. Unable to get judicious handling and proper justice, Sidhu, with suitcases already packed, walked out of the tour. This raised an unprecedented uproar in England and in India.

Most of the officials, critics and former players blamed Sidhu for walking out of the burning ship' while being stationed at the deck. They thought Sidhu's action had brought further blot on the Indian cricket, which continued to have a chequered existence.

On arrival back home, Sidhu had a detailed discussion with Inderjit Singh Bindra, President of the Punjab Cricket Association. He advised him to 'stay quiet' and should not give any interview. He was asked to stay away from the media glare and should lie low in case he wished to continue with his international cricket.

What was the cause for a fall out between Azhar and Sidhu? When Manoj Prabhakar (along with Mongia) was suspended for two matches, Azhar sought opinion of other members of the team whether Prabhakar should be reinstated. Most of the players did not give their opinion. But Sidhu was categorical. He opposed Azhar's thinking. Following this, Sidhu was harassed. He was dropped from both one-dayer and Test against touring New Zealand team.

When Sidhu 'deserted' the ship, anchored in England, most of the stars, past and present, expressed sympathy with the Patiala-player. There were a few who said against Sidhu. One of them was Bedi. He said that whatever provocation he should have fought there instead of running home.

While almost all the seniors, including team managers Patil and Nagraj, pleaded with Sidhu to give up 'rigid stand', skipper Azharuddin said : "No player is above the game. The game is greater than the players. If they are not capable of learning, what can I do", he questioned.

Sidhu, however, said that his decision was 'irrevocable'.

The three-member probe committee comprising Rajsingh Dungarpur, Sunil Gavaskar and Jaywant Lele was of the view that it was 'no more than frivolous' for Sidhu to have walked out of the tour. The committee held the view that it was a case of 'needless over-reaction' by Sidhu. The committee, at the behest of the Board, took a very 'soft' view of the unusual incident although on paper he had been served with 'show cause notice'.

By banning Sidhu until October 14, 1996, the Board's disciplinary committee, headed by I.J.S. Bindra, succeeded in making a mockery of the issue of 'discipline'.

The Bindra Committee said that Sidhu had been banned for 50 days. He was actually rested for 45 days when there was no cricket in progress and banned for only five days from October 10 to 14 when the India-Australia Test was played at Kotla. It was nothing but an eyewash. Thus far and no further.

Four or five persons were struggling to lift the dead body, so heavy it was. A youngster whispered to the head of the family: "Shave off his hair".

"Soft" punishment, so to say, over, Sidhu re-established himself as an outstanding batsman.

Sidhu's unwarranted walk-out did earn him a lot of negative publicity. But his action proved a blessing in disguise for Indian cricket. His walk out led to installing, in no uncertain manner, Ganguly as one of most polished batsmen. His achievements in England and subsequent style of batsmanship silenced all critics. But, like Sidhu, he was also being tossed about for a while.

# 14

# Salve Outwits Englishmen

Conservation is the hallmark of Englishmen. They are sporting and generous only after they have safeguarded their own interest. They believe in receiving every thing from every one and giving nothing to nobody. They indeed make fair rules and regulations but they draft constitutions of the associations retaining over-riding powers or advantages for themselves.

When Imperial (now International) Cricket Conference (now Council ) constitution was drafted, the Englishmen saw to it that they along with their brothers-in-arms Australians had the veto voting power. They were styled as 'founding members', in other words 'founding fathers'. There were full members, who had two votes each. while associate members had one vote each.

The functioning of the ICC along with the association of the Test and County Cricket Board (TCCB) was dictatorial. Only once in 1930s a volatile clash surfaced between two founder members when Douglas Jardine resorted to body-line bowling to 'silence' Don Bradman. Diplomatic relations between the two countries were about to be broken. Stiff cables were exchanged but good sense prevailed on both and the ugly situation was brought under control.

The World Cup was born out of necessity of paucity of funds in England counties. That was in 1975. The Cup was a success. Another Cup, also held in England, was a grand success with funds pouring into the kitty of the ICC and TCCB. Staging counties and other counties were also gainers. Both the Cups were won by the West Indies, a suprme power then. Came the 1983 third chapter. It was again staged in England. West Indies were the favourites to make a hat-trick of titles. But Kapil Dev's India came from behind to get into the final. The odds were 1 to 19 in favour of West Indies.

An unexpected Indian entry into the final led to tremendous interest among Indians. The Board President N.K.P. Salve, already in England, needed four tickets against payment for his guests, including Siddharth Shankar Ray, Governor of Punjab, and his wife, Maya. The Board Secretary A.W. (Judge) Kanmadikar tried his best to get tickets. The organisers were in no mood to oblige. The more, Kanmadikar impressed upon them the urgency of those tickets, the less they were willing to help. Salve was naturally upset at the total discourteous attitude of the organisers. It was this incident that made him resolve that monopoly of Englishmen must be broken. India then went on to shock West Indies and became the new champions. It was a tumultuous victory. That was June 25, 1983.

The following day (June 26) Salve's brother-in-law C.P. Srivastava was hosting a lunch for the team and a few guests. It was there that Salve in association with Pakistan Supremo Air Marshal (Retd) Noor Khan made a plan to bid for the 1987 World Cup in India and Pakistan.

The task of hosting jointly (India and Pakistan) was arduous but both Salve and Noor Khan were determined that the dominance of the Englishmen in staging the World Cup had to be broken in the interest of cricket.

Back home, both Salve and Noor Khan obtained permission for staging the mega event from their respective Governments. Sponsors were secured. Hindujas agreed to help for the prestigious event. All hurdles on domestic front had been sorted out. Salve had to overcome problems, including legal, in the ICC. The Queen's Counsel was arguing for the ICC while India's legal luminaries, such as N.A. Palkhiwala, P.N. Bhagwati, retired Chief Justice of India, and Soli Sorabji were engaged on the question of interpretation of the rules of the ICC.

India won the first round on veto ruling. That was a great achievement. Then the crucial meeting took place at Lord's on July 19, 1983. The ICC Chairman Dribbs showed his impartiality in announcing that a simple majority would apply for deciding the venue for the 1987 World Cup. Already actively supported by Sri Lanka and West Indies in addition to two hosts, India and Pakistan won the bid 16-12. It was a miracle achieved by Salve and Noor Khan. Salve had shown his ability as lawyer, politician and diplomat although he was, by profession, a chartered accountant. Because of his splendid work, he was re-elected Board President for another year although his two-year term had already ended. He had actually stepped in place of his family-friend S.K. Wankhede, who had still one year to continue in the office. But the term of the President was reduced from three years to two so that Wankhede did not feel disappointed and hurt. The same Board officials went back on their decision giving an extra year to Salve. Such are the doings of the Board and Board Officials!

In politics, nothing is fair or foul. Egged on by Bindra and Dalmiya, who had an eye for their own piece of cake, Salve unseated Wankhede. It was morally incorrect. But Salve, a hard-core politician, smelt power and threw friendship to wayside. Salve , however, kept conveying the impression that he reluctantly stepped in the Board in the interest of Indian cricket.

# 15

# Varanasi Money Episode

The wound caused to nation by the assassination of Indira Gandhi, then Prime Minister, had not healed when an unofficial single-wicket competition, comprising past and present stars, was staged in Varanasi. The 'brain' behind the match was a cricket-crazy youngman Ashok, son of Shyamlal Yadav, deputy Chairman of Rajya Sabha.

The day was November 18, 1984. The organisers had originally agreed to pay Rs. 50,000 to players in the form of prize-money. Following request by players' spokesman, the prize-money was increased to Rs. 75,000. Actually, on the day of the match, threats were issued to the organisers that the players would not take the field, if the prize-money had not been further increased.

No player knew what the terms and conditions for the match were. All were telephonically told that the terms were 'lucrative' and that they should reach Varanasi.

The ground was jam-packed with spectators. Apart from sale of tickets, huge amount was collected from wealthy people and firms as 'donations'. They had assembled in cricket-starved city which had once produced many renowned Ranji and Zonal players. Varanasi was once headquarters of UP cricket as Vizzy had stayed there. The match, more a 'tamasha' than a competition, ended with some lusty hitting and improvised batting.

The prize money was not distributed equally. It was

not given on the basis of performance. It was distributed on the basis of seniority. Yashpal Sharma won it but he was handed over Rs. 3,500. Kapil Dev, who was runner-up, was given Rs. 7,000. Some players, eliminated in early rounds, were paid Rs. 4,000 each, while Balwinder Singh Sandhu, a fine gentleman, was given merely Rs. 2,000. No one knew why discrimination was made in distributing prize-moey. Even the hosts were upset as they were told that prize-money would be distributed equally.

Kapil Dev considered it an act of 'Dadagiri (high-handedness). When asked, Sunil Gavaskar merely gave him a huge grin and walked away. There were many players who felt that the distribution of the prize money was not done with 'straight bat'.

Considering it unjust and unfair, some were heard saying that this kind of tactics promoted differences and divisiveness among players. Kapil Dev indeed was the most vocal on the subject.

According to players at Kotla, where they had assembled for nets, only Rs. 36,000 were distributed. No one could know what happened to the rest of the money.

Kapil Dev's painful observations first appeared in Delhi's national daily. They were then carried by Mumbai's eveninger. The correspondent was subsequently taken to task by an affected star, who wanted him to spell out as to who said and what. This controversy led to two super stars, Kapil Dev and Gavaskar, further drifting away from each other. Kapil Dev had already felt offended on Gavaskar's assertions in public that the Haryana all-rounder would never get a century.

While Gavaskar maintained a 'Gandhian' silence over this sordid affair, Sandip Patil, one of the participants, reportedly said that there was nothing wrong in the method of distribution of money. He said that one who initiated in collecting players through his good offices and influence had every reason to retain more money than others.

Recalling that the negotiations were held in the Nirlon

office (Worli), Patil said: "We players share the entire prize-money that is generated in such matches".

Agitated, Kapil Dev asked even Board President Salve to intervene in the interest of the togetherness of players. "I will donate entire share of money for charity, but I should not be deprived of what is my due", Kapil Dev told Salve. "I do not think, Gavaskar will cheat anyone", was the reaction of Salve. After hearing Kapil Dev patiently, Salve asked Kapil Dev that he should be magnanimous enough to forget the entire incident. Salve also made clear to Kapil Dev that it would not be proper for him to intervene since it was a festival match, played without the consent and concurrence of the Board. Kapil Dev left but he did not seem happy about it. "However, I did not know that his hurt was far deeper than that I had realised", said Salve.

Says Patil in Shatkaar (Marathi paper that he edited): "Craze for money is bad, but worse is in keeping an eye on somebody else's money! He (meaning Kapil Dev) did not have any need to be chambhar-chookshi (Cobblers' gossip) about what Gavaskar got and what we got....To accept it in the first place and then spread discontentment is like stabbing someone in the back". Patil adds: "The most despicable thing was to give this news on the eve of the Test against England. That was done deliberately to promote differencess...At least Kapil Dev should not have dared to provoke the Mumbai players who would do anything for Gavaskar without any charges".

Patil had made a futile attempt to defend the indefensible. Whether Gavaskar was to blame or Kapil Dev was indiscreet, the fact remained that no one knew for a long time as to how much was received and how much was distributed among players.

# 16

# Vaseline Debate

An average Englishman in olden days was extremely sensitive; he was equally meticulous. He had values; he cared for them. He believed in fairplay strictly adhering to the code of conduct both in victory and in defeat. He exercised moderation all the time. He was a symbol of etiquette. He did nothing that could undermine the spirit of cricket, once a noble game. While describing characteristic of a typical Englishman, someone said that a person standing last in the long queue for a bus or a train would invariably be an Englishman. He chose to stand at the tail-end of the queue because he did not want to jostle nor did he want to draw anybody's attention. While standing in the queue, he would be busy reading an eveninger or a magazine or a book. Those were the palmy days in England when even taxi drivers were extremely courteous, honest and helpful to tourists or visitors unlike taxiwallahs elsewhere in the world.

Sea-change has taken place in the characteristics of an average Englishman. The change is as steep as decline of country's cricket strandard. The cycle has taken a full circle. The originators of the game and masters once have been reduced to the level of orphans. The time may not be far off when Asians, settled in the United Kingdom, will be drafted into the team. They will wear an English cap, ascrew and with aplomb! That will be the day.

When India's captain Bishan Singh Bedi, an extrovert,

frank and fearless, protested loudly against England's left-hand medium-pacer John Lever for an alleged unethical use of vaseline on the tour to India in 1976-77, the Northomptonshire authorities (1977) should have been sporting enough to see the reality. But the English authorities, irked at being accused of cheating, chose to sack the pro who had given the best years of his cricketing life to enhance the prestige and reputation of the county. To dismiss and thereby deprive him of earning a 'benefit match' for his loyal and robust services for the county in the English League was certainly 'not cricket'.

Lever, in Tony Greig's England team for his stubborn batting and less prone to injury, had certainly come to India without the pre-knowledge or an attemps of making dubious use of vaseline for the ball to swerve more alarmingly and for longer duration than he was usually capable of. But when he found it advantageous in smuggy Delhi weather in late December 1976, he made use of vaseline with vergeance. He saw his skipper win the first Test hands down.

The details: The weather was cold, as usual in Delhi in December. England made 381, the total that many experts thought was beyond them. The home team made a sober start through Gavaskar and Anshuman Gaekwad. Then the bowlers and Greig complained about the shape of the ball which was replaced. The changed ball acquired the name of 'rogue ball' (it was presented to Lever) as Lever became a destroyer-in-chief. The ball, made in India, was being used for the first time for the India-England Tests. To their utter surprise, they found that it moved through air more than the ball, made in England. It suited them as they had better medium pacers than India could boast of them. Lever was not very pacy. He was a natural mover of the ball, like Gary Sobers and Kapil Dev later.

Lever was wearing a string of gauze around his forehead so that sweat did not disturb him in his run-in. He did caress the tape, rubbed and rolled the ball with his fingers. He ran into an unexpected success with the ball swerving and standing up to cause worry to the batsmen. Wickets kept falling in his lap. The more wickets fell, the more vigorously he caressed the vaseline tape. He went on to claim career-best seven wickets for 46 from 23 overs as India slid from 43 for no loss to 122. Even English mediapersons, present in a large number, were visibly surprised at Lever's unexpected success. There were discussions and debates for the cause or causes that led to ball swerving so deep.

Following-on, Lever had another three wickets as India were dismissed for 234 losing the Test by an innings and 25 runs. There was nothing wrong with the pitch. But the mystery of the unpredictable behaviour of the ball remained unsolved. Bedi did point out to Lever's alleged unethical use of vaseline but the Board officials did not consider it advisable to pursue the matter in the absence of adequate evidence.

India lost the second Test by 10 wickets at Kolkata. The teams then moved to Chennai where vaseline episode resurfaced. The weather was sultry and humid when the Test started. England made 262. When they fielded, all eyes from the pavilion and from the two umpires were carefully trained on Lever and his movements. Accurate indeed Lever was, but he was warned by umpire Judah Reuben for allegedly using vaseline on the ball. His success (5 for 56) was linked with his unethical practice.

As India lost the third Test by 10 wickets and thereby rubber 0-3, Bedi accused England management of 'not playing cricket'. There were arguments and counter-arguments. England authorities stood by Lever and Greig. It was not so with the Indian Board. The officials were lukewarm. They left Bedi high and dry. This was the saddest part of the vaseline racket.

John Woodcock termed the allegation as "ridiculous". He went on record as saying that it had all the signs of stupidity and none of corruption. Greig called it "Vaseline non-sense". Former England Captain Ray Illingworth and John Snow (Daily Mirror-February 6, 1977) admitted "some greasy substance like vaseline and lip ice had been used by the past Englishmen. The players cited were Geoff Arnold, Tony Greig and Basil D'Oliveira. Chemical analysis would later confirm the use of vaseline in the India series....."

BBC commentator Martin-Jenkins in his book "MCC in India" says: "Lest there be any doubt it was very clear to me and most who were able to view the matter objectively that Lever was entirely innocent and that suggestions about England shining the ball by illegal methods at Delhi ignored the fact that the early destruction of India's first innings was achieved by Lever with virtually a new ball which swung freakily from the outset."

Martin-Jenkins was not objective in his observation. It was the "changed" ball which swung after India were 43 for no loss.

The Board Secretary Ghulam Ahmed said that the MCC had agreed that there had been an infringement of the rules, but there being no provisions in the experimental law about penalties, no action could be taken. He said the ICC would discuss the issue.

There is an amusing story about the changed ball in the series between India and New Zealand in 1969. It was the third day of the Test. The venue was Mumbai. Pataudi led the side to the ground and asked Bedi to bowl from the pavilion end. Sathyaji Rao was at bolwer's end, while A.M. Mamsa on the square-leg position. After completing the over, Bedi told his skipper that the ball with which he completed his over was not the 'match ball'. The fielding side had brought the ball with them on the ground while the match ball was lying in Rao's coat. The ball was changed and the match progressed wth the correct ball. Mamsa asked Rao to let the wrong ball stay in his pocket. Had he thrown the ball to the pavilion, the mistake might have become public and there could have been criticism against the umpires. As it was, only Pataudi and Bedi knew about the mistake made by Rao.

In the following summer, it was England who were on the receiving end at the Oval . Mark Walker (Australia) swung the ball alarmingly. Says Jim Laker: "Walker breaks the rules by smearing suntar cream from his face on to the ball". Richie Benaud on TV said: "Maxie, you can't do that". The umpires did not take any action as they had reportedly not noticed it. Skipper Greg Chappell thought it was nothing but "rubbish".

# 17

# Team Insulted

The Indians, like typical West Indians, can win a match by a mile and lose it by a mile. They can score 400 plus runs in the fourth innings to claim the Test and surrender the match lying in their pockets. They are capable of achieving an impossibility on either side.

The wicket at Lord's (1974) was a sleeping beauty. To England's huge total of 629, India could reply with 302. They still had in them to force a draw. But, following-on, they once again batted casually and recklessly and were shot out for 42 desultory total.

The players were disappointed and dejected at their pathetic batting. They were cursing themselves. Their state of mind was understandable. But Indian mediapersons, based in England and visiting journalists, were more upset than the players. They were in wild and vicious mood. They needlessly got into an argument with the players and words, hard to digest, were exchanged. The mediapersons were free to write what they wanted. But why should they be rude to players, who were already down and out? They accused the team members of arguing among themselves, spending time in drinking and many other misdemeanours. The Players told them to "shut up". Peeved at players lashing, they wrote stories which did no credit to them.

The team was invited for two receptions after the Lord's Test. One was at the State Bank of India (5.45 p.m. to 6.15 p.m). As skipper Wadekar and his seven other players were on the rolls of the bank, the team was invited to accord farewell to the London-based manager and to welcome the new incumbent. The reception was in the city.

The heated exchange of words with the journalists delayed the departure of the team from the SBI reception. When the team got into the bus, it was already 6.30 p.m.— the time for the High Commissioner's get-together. The High Commissioner's residence was situated at Kensington Garden. The driving distance of about 15 minutes became longish because of evening traffic.

Adhikari and B.C. Mohanty (treasurer) had already reached the High Commissioner's residence to explain to him the variety of reasons for the delay, including Sudhir Naik's shop-lifting episode. The team reached 40 minutes behind schedule at 7.10 p.m. B.K. Nehru, irked at dismal display of the team as also the Naik incident, was in an unfriendly mood, and asked Ajit Wadekar and a few others to 'go away'. Crestfallen and disturbed at the harsh treatment meted out to the players, they trooped back into the bus.

Some were visibly upset at High Commissioner's undiplomatic behaviour. Most of them were insisting that the team should return to the hotel after this insult. As the players were discussing the issue threadbare, Adhikari kept insisting on the players 'to be sport and attend the party'. Eventually, the team went back to the function where Nehru was man enough to apologise for losing his cool. He hugged Wadekar and told him: "I am sorry for losing my temper". In saying these few words, he enhanced his own image. After initial hesitation, all players calmed down and most of them had drinks and snacks, as it should have been.

Despite all this, some reports appeared saying that the players did insult the High Commissioner and declined to partake drinks and refreshment. If this was wrong, it was equally injudicious on the part of Gavaskar to say in his book "Sunny Days: "....I suppose having to stay in London, they could not afford to write against the High Commissioner". Journalists, with convictions, have written against even Prime Minister and President. Just as Gavaskar cannot be accused of shirking his responsibility, known and established journalists cannot afford to supress facts. But in this particular case, journalists took a negative viewpoint. They accused players for snubbing and insulting the High Commissioner.

Bishan Bedi was accused of saying uncomplimentary words about Nehru. This was far from the truth. What he did say in his own typical style was: If we had won, even if we had turned up late, there would not have been any problem. But just because we lost, we were given the stick." He was right in his observation. But this is what happens worldwide. A child, who fails in his examination, gets the stick and another child, who gets first class first, is applauded! He himself would do the same thing.

The important reason for all the trouble that surfaced on the tour was that there was a poison in the air. There was no trouble-shooter to handle the players of different ages and temperament. Adhikari and Mohanty were too meak to handle them. At the initial stages of the tour, there was a clash of personality between Wadekar and Bedi. The incident, ugly as it was, took place at a private party (during match against Derrick Robins XI). This was all the more shocking because there were guests and junior players. Both Wadekar and Bedi were on different wave lengths. Following a heated discussion, Wadekar retorted: "You all are Pataudi's men". This was enough for Bedi to take off. They were pacified but Bedi wanted Wadekar to apologise. Peace was however restored. Both did try their best but their display as also of others fell short of lofty reputation with which the team had flown into London. What became clear was that glass once broken could not be mended into new. Wadekar and Bedi could not be made great friends: This had some kind of effect on other members of the team. The side was now split into two or more groups.

When the team returned, Wadekar's house was stoned.

All members of the team got a hostile reception. It was more so in the case of Wadekar as he was the captain. Wadekar became so indignant that he announced his retirement, although he had atleast 4-5 years of international cricket left in him. He walked out of international cricket not because of public misbehaviour but because he was dropped from even Zonal (West) side. This was unthinkable that country's captain should be sidelined from the zonal outfit.

# 18

# Naik Accused Of Shop-Lifting

Sudhir Naik, one of the few gentleman-players from Mumbai, nearly ended his young life as he was unable to bear any more stigma of shop-lifting in London in 1974. But some of his good friends, who knew him intimately, and Sunil Gavaskar talked him out of this utter depression impressing upon him that truth would eventually prevail and that he was too good a human being to cut short his precious and young life. Luckily, he did not take the extreme step but sadly he went out of competitive cricket when there was much left in him. It was a pity that he could not be persuaded into continuing with his cricket. It was sad that a player of his talent, temperament and commitment should have gone out of cricket for reasons other than merit and skill.

Indepth investigations reveal that Naik was a victim of circumstances. He was not, in reality, guilty of shop-lifting. But Lt Col Hemu Adhikari, more a weak man than a peace-loving manager, coaxed him into pleading guilty before the magistrate in the mistaken hope that the incident would not become a major issue. This was a complete miscalculation as the incident, with added 'Mirch and Masala' was flashed in England, India and outside.

Had the manager been a Pakistani or an official from any other country, he would have fought out in the court of law and Naik would have returned home unscathed.

The marks and Spencer authorities could not have conclusively proved that Naik had intentionally hidden two pairs of socks after paying for 20 pairs and many other costlier articles. But Indian officials always believe in compromising not realising that such compromise is a sure sign of weakness.

What added credence to the ugly incident was that even some members of the team were happy at the predicament of Naik. They chose to give publicity to the incident instead of trying to ascertain the facts. This kind of uncalled for situation obtained because there were breaches and dissensions among team members belonging to different regions. It was pathetic and deplorable to see members of the team letting down each other. Some players even suggested that Naik should be sent back home without listening to his side of version.

## The incident

Naik chose not to rest or relax or go to a movie as his colleagues had done. Instead he volunteered to shop for them essential articles, like under-garments.

Naik had done a lot of shopping for himself and his colleagues from one or two departmental stores before stepping on to Marks and Spencer at Oxford Street. He purchased several small articles as also socks. He kept all the articles on counter for payment that he had purchased from Mark and Spencer when the sales girl found two pairs of socks lying under trouser. She felt that he had deliberately concealed them. She called her supervisor who without listening him accused him of shop-lifting. The more Naik tried to explain to them that it was a sheer lapse, the less they were willing to listen to him.

The charge against Naik was framed. The matter was reported and Adhikari summoned. He should have vehemently argued with the authorities that the allegation was totally absurd. But he sadly accepted their line of argument instead of defending his own man.

The Indian managers on tours to England, Australia,

New Zealand and to other countries seldom put their hands into their pockets even when expenses incurred are borne by the Board. Adhikari should have engaged a good lawyer and fought the case and claimed reimbursement of expenses from the Board. Instead of doing this, he advised Naik to plead guilty not realising that such a step would jeopardise his career and reputation.

As Naik was extremely dejected and disturbed, he was placed in the room with Sunil Gavaskar for the rest of the tour. It was a sensible step. Gavaskar played his role admirably trying to keep Naik in a good humour. In fact Ajit Wadekar (captain) and other senior players should have stood by him and he should have been made to play most of the matches instead of his sulking in the pavilion or dressing room. But in this country, we do not believe in togetherness; we practice regionalism. What a sad state of affairs.

# 19

# Vizzy's Unscrupulous Move

On the eve of the first Test against England in 1936, Vijay Merchant asked his skipper Vizzy that he should be man enough to stand down in the interest of the country. He also told him that he did not deserve to be in the side. As if this was not enough, Merchant told Vizzy that C.K. Nayudu would be the right choice to captain, as was the case in 1932 when Maharajah of Porbandar stood down for Nayudu to captain the side at Lord's.

This candid observation infuriated Vizzy. They never could become friends since then. Vizzy's disliking against Merchant grew so intense that he never visited Mumbai for any official or unofficial cricket assignment. When he chose to cover Tests for Indian Express and other papers, he wrote his reports from Varanasi while listening radio commentary on matches played in Mumbai.

Mushtaq Ali and Merchant got associated for a long and enduring opening wicket stand in the second innings of the second Test at Old Trafford (Manchester) in July 1936. Mushtaq was first to complete his century while Merchant was batting with 75.

While showering praise on Mushtaq Ali for his superb century, Vizzy presented him a golden wrist watch. The skipper then asked him to run Merchant out before he could get to his century.

Vizzy wanted to take his revenge for Merchant's

remarks which, the skipper thought, were rude. Can there be another example in which a captain of the side manoeuvers to get his main-line, settled batsman run out to satisfy his ego? Vizzy's plea to Mushtaq was that Merchant had got him run out in the first innings. But Mushtaq Ali went on record as saying that he was run out because of his own mistake. Says Mushtaq Ali: "Merchant hit a shot which straight came on to me and rebounded off my pads. But I hastily ran for a single and got run out (13)".

Stunned as Mushtaq Ali was at Vizzy's unpatriotic attitude, he mustered his courage to tell him that it was beyond him to resort to such mean tactics. "I am playing for the country and not to please whims and fancies of others", said Mushtaq Ali to Vizzy.

Next day as Mushtaq Ali and Merchant were walking in to resume their innings, Mushtaq Ali told his partner that he was supposed to run him out. Mushtaq Ali did not elaborate this at that point of time but gave details to Merchant subsequently. Merchant duly completed his century and Mushtaq Ali was among many who were happy at Merchant's feat. Vizzy was however seen sulking in the pavilion.

Says Mushtaq: ...."I was in a very disturbed frame of mind that day. While the captain's words kept ringing in my ears to run him out, Merchant, on the other hand, was telling me—Mushtaq we have to break the record of Jack Hobbs and Wilfred Rhodes of 323. Don't throw your wicket. Play safe".

Unlike Vizzy, Porbander was realistic. He allowed C.K. Nayudu to captain in the only Test at Lord's in 1932. But, dressed in his princely robes and a pink turban, he presented his team to King George V. Then also there were groups within groups. CK was called: "Bahar se Kala, Andar se Kala, Bara Badmash Hai Yeh Indorewala". Some disgruntled players went on record as saying that India could have won the Test but for C.K's captaincy. Accusing him of making several mistakes in bowling changes and field placings, they had the temerity to say that there were "at least two" who would have served India's cause better. There were occasional fist-fightings and heated arguments and angry remarks against C.K.

# 20

# Barbarism At Kingston

The tour to the West Indies in 1975-76 was full of controversies and acrimonies as Bishan Bedi failed to handle some of irksome situations with the same finesse as he bowled his left-hand spinners. Some of the spot decisions that he took there were more from his heart than from his mind resulting in strained relations between him and West Indian skipper Clive Lloyd and players.

India lost the first Bridgetown Test rather tamely. The Indians could not translate a distinct advantageous position into a victory at Port of Spain's Queen Park Oval in the second Test. The Test petered out into a draw. But it was the venue for the first of many incidents that unfolded against the normal code of accepted conduct.

Vivian Richards had sprained his leg muscle. He was not on the field most of the day on previous day. But when his turn came to bat, he did come in. It could easily be noticed that he was not his usual self. On the final day of the Test, he had slipped and had fallen down. He aggravated his injury. He asked for Bedi's permission to retire. Bedi suggested him that he should have a runner instead. When Richards insisted, Bedi said that he might but he would exercise his right when he could resume his innings. This was in accordance to the law. The matter was discussed with umpires who, in turn, summoned Lloyd in the middle. The mess could not be sorted out as Bedi, quoting the law, stuck to his decision. Bedi's insistence caused an anguish and annoyance to Lloyd.

Richards eventually retired. He returned to bat after the fall of the next wicket. Bedi's reasoning was that injured Richards' quick dismissal might swung the Test into India's favour.

Richards was soon run out as he had a misunderstanding with Lloyd. Richards' dismissal did not have any demoralising effect on other batsmen who stayed long enough for the match to end in a draw.

When Gavaskar, in his light vein, asked Lloyd when was he declaring the innings, he angrily replied: "You want me to declare when your captain does not play ball, as cricket match should be played. If he is such a stickler for rules, I could have claimed the wicket of Mohinder who took more than two minutes to walk in". Bedi, on the other hand, was fuming in anger because Gosein had shown utter partiality in pronouncing his decisions. It was felt that had the umpiring been impartial, as it should have been, India might have won the Test.

The third Test, scheduled for Georgetown, had to be shifted to Port of Spain because of torrent of rain. The change of the venue became a blessing in disguise for Indians who came from behind to score 400 plus runs in the fourth innings to win the Test and make it 1-all. This was the second occasion when the team, chasing 400 plus runs, had achieved the target. The first instance was at Leeds in 1948 when Bradman's all-conquering team had done it against England.

Lloyd was now hell-bent on winning the fourth Test at Kingston (Sabina Park). It was mainly because his team had lost 1-5 to Australia that year (1975-76). He did not want to lose to India. He resorted to tactics which could be termed as 'uncricketlike'. Gavaskar called the match 'Barbarism at Kingston'. It was downright cricket war. Lloyd achieved the 10-wicket victory and won the series 2-1 but he did not look glorious in triumph. The West Indians also did not enhance their reputation and image in their own country. Sir Frank Worrell would not have endorsed Lloyd's tactics.

The galleries were packed. There were clouds around blue mountains. While the spectators in "blood thirsty mood yelled before the start of the match, there was camel-coloured square in the center.

Put into bat, India were 62 without loss at lunch on a very bouncy wicket. It was now that Lloyd directed his quickies (Holding, Daniel, Julien and Holder) to bowl bouncers and beamers. There were occasions when Holding bowled four bouncers in an over and the umpires did not even warn him. What Holding was doing was unethical, but what spectators did was even worse. They kept on egging the bowlers to 'bash him mann and kill him mann'. Gavaskar was so upset at the tactics that he went on record as saying: "All this proved beyond a shadow of doubt that these people still belonged to the jungle and forests instead of civilised country". Many thought it was too harsh an observation and Gavaskar of all batsmen should have exercised restraint.

Bedi and Gavaskar did speak to umpires, Dougles Seng Hue and Ralph Gosein. Bedi did lodge official protest against frequent use of bumpers. This was against law 46.

India rose from 178 for one to 306 for six wickets when Bedi decided to declare instead of tail-enders facing barrage of bumpers. Amarnath was first to go deflecting a bouncer. Vishwanath fended away a delivery which crashed on his knuckles resulting in fracture of his finger. Gaekwad, who had manfully withstood repeated blows on his person, was eventually hit behind the left ear and he had to retire.

The Indian dressing room resembled to "wounded soldiers' room". Gaekwad remained unattended in the pavilion for awhile as manager Polly Umrigar had accompanied Vishwanath to the hospital. Soon Gaekwad was transported to the hospital where Brijesh Patel also joined him with a mouth injury.

Vengsarkar batted defiantly dealing with rising

deliveries by weaving away from them instead of ducking. He fell to Holding after scoring 39.

Lloyd did not think that his tactics were objectionable. He gave the impression that a kind of "ridge" had developed on the wicket and this was making the bounce uneven.

At the Governor General's reception, an uneasy lull hung over the brightly lit lawns of massive monsoon. In the subsequent Press conference, Bedi, Umrigar and others decried the tactics adopted by Lloyd.

Bedi was injured (finger) while attempting a return catch and Chandrasekhar fractured his thumb. The situation became so alarming that all 17 players fielded at one time or the other.

As if all these casualities were not enough, the 12th man Surinder had to be rushed to hospital with appendicitis. The West Indies were dismissed for 391.

When substitute Solkar came on field, umpire Rowe objected to his fielding at backward short-leg. He had to be relocated. What was a minor violation was objected to by the umpires, but major violations were ignored.

India, 85 runs in arrears, had only a few fit soldiers to handle the bat. As many as five players were injured. India's second innings terminated at 97 for five wickets. It could not be termed as declaration as there was no batsman who could walk in to bat. The West Indies got the 13 required runs to win the Test, which was termed as 'the most disreputable' match.

There were accusations and counter-accusations in the subsequent Press conference. Each blamed the other. The West Indies accused Indians for shying away from rising deliveries, while Bedi and his men said that the West Indies had made use of the bumpers and beamers illegitimately. "Bumper may be a legitimate weapon", said Indians, adding: "But bowling to injure batsmen was utterly unethical and objectionable".

The consensus was that Lloyd did exceed in his limits but Bedi should have displayed more diplomacy than he did. The starting point was Bedi's refusal to give permission to Richards to retire under the garb of laws. Lloyd also took advantage of laws and local umpires to trouble and torment the Indian batsmen.

The Indians, bruised and battered, returned home. Said Wisden "They looked like Nepoleon's troups on the retreat from Moscow". Some of them wore plasters and bandages even on their arrival in India. As the time went up their wounds healed, but they stayed hurt 'for a long time'. They felt—some thought rightly—that they had been cheated and bounced out of the series which they should have won.

To Pakistan's 205 for seven in the Sahiwal one-dayer in 1978, India were 183 for two when Pakistan bowlers resorted to "total negative tactics'. In the 38th over Sarfraz Nawaz bowled all four bouner-wides which were beyond the reach of batsmen. Bedi protested. The umpires ignored his protests. Disgusted with umpires and Pakistani bowlers, Bedi asked his batsmen to return conceding the match to Pakistan.

# 21

# Board Official Errs

Mohinder Amarnath was an automatic choice for a berth in the Indian team against New Zealand in 1988-89 series in India in view of his outstanding performances in matches at home and abroad. But the selection committee, with Raj Singh Dungarpur as chairman, was contemplating seriously to rebuild the side since Kiwis were certainly not rated as a very strong combination. In view of this thinking, the committee, meeting at Faridabad, decided that Navjot Singh Sidhu should be inducted in the team as one-drop batsman and Mohinder rested.

The decision was understandable and the chairman himself should have briefed at the Nahar Stadium (Faridabad). But the Board spokesman shocked all mediapersons when he said that Mohinder had been dropped on account of his cricketing performance.

When Mohinder read that he had been sidelined from Bangalore's first Test, he naturally was furious. He thought that he was in no position to suffer any more insults from the committee after his recent stupendous doings. He had a reason to feel so.

Upset and angry, Mohinder took a flight to Bangalore and rushed to the Karnataka Stadium where electronic mediapersons were busy making preparations for the coverage of the match. One over-zealous TV reporter went on record as announcing that Mohinder had been drafted into the team without talking to him or team captain Vengsarkar.

After Indian team's nets were over, Mohinder summoned a Press conference where he said: "Enough was enough". He then called selectors a "bunch of jokers". His remarks were made at the West End Hotel where the two teams were staying.

All mediapersons in the Press conference were unanimous in their thinking that a grave injustice had been done to Mohinder. Statistics were in favour of the defiant batsman who had done superbly in Sharjah and Bangladesh. He had headed the batting average in Asia Cup (1988-89). He helped India outplay Pakistan by scoring an unbeaten 74 and also played two grand innings against New Zealand in March-April 1988.

When asked, Raj Singh was candid in saying that Mohinder's exclusion was 'temporary'. He also said that he was 'rested' in view of 'building process' and that he was automatic choice for the ensuing West Indies tour. That indeed was the correct position as it stood then. He was needlessly maligned. He was paying the penalty for allowing the Board official to address the Press conference.

Mohinder was rightly upset. But his father Lala was more furious than even his son. He held a Press conference at his residence and called selectors as "bunch of trump card jokers".

This was 12th time Mohinder was sidelined since his debut against Bill Lawry's Australia team at Chennai in 1969 as 19-year-old boy. He had then impressed selection committee chairman Vijay Merchant at the Kolkata nets.

Mohinder's outbursts did not go well with the Board. There were officials who said that there was nothing more important than discipline. He was served with show-cause notice. A five-member committee comprising Board president B.N. Dutt, Madhavrao Scindia, Ghulam Ahmed, Abbas Ali Baig and Ashok Mankad was formed. He was given 10 days to explain.

Mohinder's reply to the show cause notice through his

advocate Haresh M Jagtiani was: The manner in which his client Mohinder had been excluded was most hurtful....With his performances, he reasonably expected to be selected as a member of the Indian team against New Zealand. What added insult to injury was that the reply appeared in one national daily before it reached the Board president.

Most of the disciplinary committee members were in the heart of hearts convinced that Mohinder had been dropped wrongly. They wanted to help him but they were not supportive of his subsequent actions, including attending the meeting with his advocate and walking out of the meeting. Yet the committee took a very lenient view and imposed merely a fine of Rs. 20,000 without fixing any date for the payment of it.

Mohinder was eligible for selection for the tour to West Indies in February 1989. But he was not chosen. No reason was advanced for his exclusion. He was recalled for the Sharjah Cup and Nehru Centenary Cup but that was about all as he was not subsequently chosen for the national side. When he was not selected for the 1989 Pakistan tour, his remarkable and valiant international career came to an end.

# 22

# Riot In Kolkata (1967)

It was a series between Indian youth and world-beater West Indies team in 1967 and the visitors won the three-Test contest 2-0. Poor fielding led to India losing the first Test by six wickets at Wankhede Stadium where an affair between Gary Sobers and Anju Mahendru, a film star, gained currency. The Test was a memorable match for Chandrasekhar, who claimed 11 wickets in two innings in a marathon bowling effort of 93 overs.

Kolkata wore a bright and glamorous look as it was Chirstmas and new year's time. The city and Eden Gardens got an added colour and brightness, as the mighty West Indies were to provide demonstration of their superb and classic out-cricket.

There was hope among Indian players who had begun to think that the West Indies team were not invincible. They thought that they could win the Test and could go to Chennai with the series score of 1-1. But it turned out to be a wishful thinking and Indians were swamped by an innings and 45 runs. That indeed were disappointing show. But what caused dismay to players and brought disgrace to the country was unethical and unprofessional doings of the officials of the Cricket Association of Bengal (CAB). The capacity, though increased, was for 59,000 spectators while the tickets sold were for 80,000 spectators. In addition facilities were grossly inadequate.

There were allegations against officials for selling

duplicate tickets. There were charges against officials for indulging in black-marketing. There were accusations that important office-bearers were guilty of selling even complimentary tickets meant for VIPs, players and their guests. Aware that there was an unprecedented craze to watch the West Indians in action, the office-bearers had stooped low to have duplicate tickets printed for unreserved enclosures to make a quick buck. Here the organisers showed that they cared a damn for their reputation and Kolkata's image as long as they were able to have their pound of flesh. All in all it was a disgraceful affair.

Ray Robinson (Australia), one of the most reputed writers, was given altogether wrong information by William Walker. The information was that "if a Bengali and a Cobra confront one on a road, one should kill the more dangerous one first—the Bengali". This was what Robinson stated in his book: "The Wildest Test".

The original proverb said the same thing about a Punjabi and Cobra. But Babu Rao Patel in Film India, one of the most widely read magazines for decades, twisted it to say: "If one encounters a Sindhi and a Cobra, one should kill a Sindhi first and then Cobra, if at all". (Patel, a resident of Mumbai' had written all this because Sindhis had outclassed local businessmen following partition in 1947).

At least 20,000 more spectators than the Eden Gardens could hold secured admittance on New Year's day (Second day). Unable to secure even elbow's room in various enclosures much before the scheduled time for the day's play to start, a sizeable number of spectators spilled on to the lawns. The teams were on the ground but the play could not start until spectators had been cleared from the ground. It was a difficult situation for the authorities to handle. The occasion was tense: it required judicious and intelligent handling. But the organisers played truant, while police, with lathis and batons, and Home Guard personnels resorted to rough and tough methods. It was a shocking spectacle to see authorities trying to crush the spectators, who had paid to watch their heroes in action. Now it was free for all, a full-fledged riot. Spectators started throwing stones, bricks and whatever was available on the ground. Police resorted to tear gas. One spectator Sitesh Roy was beaten. The city, always edgy, became volatile. It was now beyond the control of existing police force on the ground. Reinforcement came but, by that time, mob had invaded the whole field, dug up the ground and set fire on the stands. There was panic among players who, though in their dressing rooms, were frightened, so desperate was the situation.

As tear gas engulfed dressing rooms, the West Indies players dashed out of their rooms for their lives. The mob was furious but not against players who were unblemished. The spectators shouting slogans were looking for officials who had indulged in cheating for over-selling the tickets. While some West Indies players like Lloyd and Griffith were stranded before reaching their hotel, some small officials managed shelter inside the Indian team's coach. Luckily, they could not be spotted by spectators. Had they been seen, they would have been dragged out and burnt alive.

P.N. Sunderesan, in Indian Cricket, wrote: "What followed was like hell being let loose and the whole Eden Gardens was swallowed up in flames".

The West Indies refused to resume the Test despite assurances given to them for their security. But timely intervention by legendary figure Frank Worrell, who was in Kolkata on his personal visit, helped resume the Test. The West Indies players were also assured of bonus of about £45 each. India lost the Test by an innings and 45 runs and Kolkata surrendered its pride and prestige.

In the inquiry conducted by Mr Justice Kamlesh Chandra Sen, the CAB officials were squarely blamed for the mis-management and riots that broke at the Eden Gardens. There were several strictures passed against CAB and Justice Sen, in his 400-page report, gave many suggestions as how to run the Test match in future.

There was no TV in 1967. The All-India Radio commentators shocked by announcing that the play had been held up because of fog. Such a lie would not have done credit to even Vizzy who, when the proceedings were dull and drab, would say that they were lively and absorbing.

# 23

# Mumbai Blots Its Copy Book

Commentators in an idiot box, among many dos and dont's, are advised that they should exercise restraint while talking about umpiring and their decisions. One commentator, sufficiently experienced, erred in adhering to this golden advice. He criticised the decision. This led to a riot and the name of Mumbai, a cricket loving city, was sullied in the opening Test against Australia at Brabourne Stadium in November 1969.

There was no justification for the riot as India were on the verge of defeat fairly and squarely by Bill Lawry's team. Venkataraghavan flashed at a delivery outside the off-stump from paceman Alan Connolly, who appealed half-heartedly. The close-in fielders did not join the bowler. Wicketkeeper Brian Taber threw the ball to Stackpole at second slip. When Sambhu Pan raised his finger Venkat was aghast. Wadekar, at non-striker's end, also had a word with the umpire. But when commentator (Devraj Puri) criticised the umpire Pan for declaring Venkataraghavan caught at the wicket, the East stand spectators were up in arms. There was no plausible reason as to why spectators felt so agitated.

The umpires, Pan and I. Gopalakrishnan, were both Indians but that was the time when players and spectators did not have much faith in them. It was a love's labour lost because remuneration for standing in five days' Test was negligible. But umpires often favoured a visiting team in order to get a favourable report from the foreign captain. The Board sadly attached greater importance to visiting captain's observations than remarks by the Indian captain.

Mumbai had always looked down upon spectators from Kanpur and Kolkata. But riots in Mumbai proved that the mentality of the mob was the same all over the country.

A section of spectators first threw stones and missiles on the ground. Then they marched out and set on fire an area surrounding the tennis courts behind the East stand.

As strong sea breeze was blowing across, the black smoke soon engulfed the ground. But Lawry stayed put at the centre. He insisted for the match to continue. He was a captain who was unwilling to yield under pressure. For about an hour the game continued as bottles and chairs were being hurled on the ground. With about 30 minutes left, the scorer (Jahangir Patel) protested saying he was unable to follow the game from the press box. As the scorer walked in to explain his difficulty to umpires, G.K Menon, a journalist, dashed in. "Stop the game," shouted Menon adding "we cannot watch the game"? The umpires asked him to leave. Heated words were exchanged between him and Lawry. Why should a journalist have dashed in? The incident ignited the situation further in stands.

The umpires and Indians seemed disiclined to continue with the match but Lawry had felt it was a very calculated ploy by spectators to help India save the match.

India, who had conceded a lead of 75 runs, were again out for a miserable total of 137. Australia had a little problem in romping home by eight wickets.

It was a day of infamy for Indian cricket. It was a black day for Mumbai. But Lawry was complimented for his firmess which saw him win the Test for Australia. In ultimate analysis India lost both Test and reputation.

Transistors then and TV sets now have always acted as villains. They promote trouble through their commentators. Some of whom are as excitable and biased as section of spectators. Just as a penalty is imposed on players for dissent, there should be some kind of restrictions imposed on commentators for inciting spectators. There are some knowledgeable critics who feel TV sets should not be installed in dressing rooms and press boxes. Let players and mediapersons watch umpires, (their) doings though their naked eyes instead of watching slow motion replays and then showering their wrath on the umpires. What is the big deal in showing their knowledge after watching TV replays?

# 24

# England Bad Losers

Raman Subba Row is one of the nicest souls living in England. He is an excellent human being. An outstanding personality in man-management affairs, he was as readily available to Indian mediapersons as he was ready to share information with his media people. Above all, he was fair and impartial. Had he not been at the helm of England team, the India-England series in 1981-82 would have degenerated into one of the worst ever series played any where.

Before the team flew to India, there were apartheid problems facing the England side. Geoff Boycott and Geoff Cook were blacklisted as they had played in South Africa. The Gleneagles Agreement was clear-cut. It said that Commonwealth countries would discourage their sportspersons to have any contact with players of South Africa. It was however not very clear that if a team included players who had been to South Africa, the team should be banned.

The concerned authorities in Government could not clear the tour as Prime Minister Indira Gandhi was in Mexico for an official conference. Hectic diplomatic negotiation followed. The time was running out. Just then she cleared the tour, to the delight of all cricket loving people in the country.

In a low scoring and bowlers dominated Test at Mumbai, England lost on a wearing wicket. Now all hell broke loose.

Fletcher, Botham and Emburey blamed partisan umpiring for their defeat. The English press sensationalised accusing umpires all the way. Actually, the trouble began when David Gower was given run out in the first innings. The British Press—more temperamental than the players— went on record as saying—very close decisions. What did they mean by this? If it was a close call, it could go either way. Why should it go in favour of England? But how did they know that it was a close decision? The umpires went on saying that Gower was a clear run out. If there was any doubt, it was perhaps in the minds and pens of the English media.

Scyld Berry has been a brilliant writer. He is also a pleasant conversationist. But he is more partial to his team than even England's ardent admirers could be. Sample what he says in his tour book 'Cricketwallah.... It is improbable that two long established Test batsmen in skipper Fletcher and Botham, and one good exponent of the sweep shot in Emburey, would all make fatal mistakes in the space of only five overs. Could the umpire truly have had no doubts in his mind in every instance? On the other hand, by playing the sweep shot and not hitting the ball cleanly, these batsmen had all tempted fate in the form of Ramaswamy's finger".

How did he feel that the umpire had any doubt? The pitch was worn out and the ball was turning. It was all the more prudent for batsmen not to attempt a shot that could be their undoing. If three batsmen commit mistakes inside of five overs, should they be condoned for their indiscretion? Scyld is a seasoned correspondent and should have shown his impartiality and finesse in dealing with the imaginary problem.

To call Ramaswamy the 'Butcher of Mumbai' and referred to the umpires as 'The little and large show', a sort of Laurel and Hardy comic strip, did not do justice to the writer who has covered Test cricket world over. After-all both Swarup Kishan and Ramaswamy were experienced umpires and they deserved a better deal from Scyld.

Fletcher and his men were prevented from filing an official complaint against umpiring by Subba Row. But Fletcher blotted his copy-book when he hit his wicket after being caught at wicket. For making a faulty shot, should he have broken his own stumps? There was a deflection. It was unfortunate that he should have thought that he had been done to death by the umpire. Following this ugly incident, he had to submit his apology.

In the Delhi Test, Boycott overtook Sobers's record of 8,032 runs. He had a reason to feel happy. But his happiness was short-lived as his total was overtaken by Gavaskar.

As Boycott achieved this milestone, he seemed disinterested in the remaining series. He said that he was not enjoying playing cricket in India. His attitude was disturbing and behaviour was causing concern to his management. He did not play fourth Test saying that he was not feeling 100 per cent fit. While his team mates were roughing it out at Eden Gardens, he was busy playing a round of golf. He was unfit for Test but fit for golf.

This and many other incidents compelled the management to send him back home or did he return on his own? The news of his returning home leaked out when English mediapersons were fast asleep in Jamshedpur. It was dead of night when correspondents made a beeline for Central Telegraph office. All operators were asleep. No phone or message could go as telegraph staff showed little interest in tackling the situation. The more English journalists were keen, the less they were bothered. Luckily a Reuter stringer (an author of this book) was able to send a para or two which Delhi office transmitted to London. Those were the days when communication facilities at certain centres were miserable.

Back home, Boycott got busy organising a 'rebel' party's tour to South Africa. Those who accompanied him, among others, were Gooch, Emburey and Underwood.

In the final, drawn Test at Mumbai, Gavaskar was called upon to open the attack in England's second innings. The England openers, particularly Amiss, alleged that

Gavaskar was deliberately following through on the pitch to make an attempt to create a spot for his spinners. This was a far-fetched argument as to how Gavaskar, of all bowlers, without spikes, could create a spot with his kind of bowling and weight. He bowled only one over. This was yet another example of Englishmen who could be fussy on trifles when the going for them was rough.

The partition of the country came about 16 years later. But Churchill's words have come true! England is not only a minor power, but it is also a minor cricket power! Be it as it is, all English teams have denounced Indian crowds as "Partisan". This may be true as spectators world over are inclined to support their own team. But English mediapersons are much more partisan than Indian crowds! Looking at the state of affairs prevailing in England, one is inclined to say how absolutely right was Winston Churchill. When Mahatma Gandhi's agitation for Indian independence was gaining ground, Sir Winston had said : "The loss of India would be final and fatal for us. It could not fail to be part of a process that would reduce us to the scale of a minor power." This was sometime in 1931.

# 25

# Boycott's Vulgarism

Geoff Boycott was relaxed and jovial in the dressing room where he was quick in exchanging pleasantries with his colleagues. He would drop his 'box' and wear all his parapharnelia quickly. Unlike Sunil Gavaskar, his preparations for going in to start his innings were precise. His walk to the wicket was brisk and confident with measured steps. After obtaining his guard from the umpire, he would discreetly survey the field like a seasoned general. His stance was upright without any bend in his knees. He was well poised with one foot inside the crease. He was a batsman who played his shots late and very close to his body. He revelled in his footwork which provided him enough scope and opportunity to alter the direction of his shot. His eye-sight was hawk-like and concentration rapt. He scrutinised bowler's action as also read movement of the seam and the ball. His technique was sound bordering on copy-book. He had a very wide range of strokes but he brought them into play only after assessing the wicket and bowling. A thorough professional he believed in eliminating or minimising his mistakes while batting. He believed in going in and not getting out. He believed in tormenting the bowlers. He was slow but steady in compiling his runs which he loved as dearly as gold. When the going was good, he was a brilliant conversationist (his TV commentary is a positive proof). But when his tenure at the wicket was brief and when he felt that he had been 'umpired' out, he could be tense, imtemperate and volatile. All in all, he was a man of many moods.

When Boycott arrived in Hyderabad for his team's engagement with the South Zone in 1981-82, he appeared in a rough mood. When the Chief Minister of Andhra Pradesh T. Anjiah presented him a blooming rose, he quietly placed it in his 'fly'. He acted vulgarly in presence of many officials and a team of journalists.

Hardly had Anjiah settled down when a brilliant left-hand batsman David Gower made a very inelegant shot by telling the dignitary: "old man, we have been waiting for you for the last 45 minutes". Anjiah fielded this fiery shot with the poise of a seasoned politician by ignoring the remark.

When the English team was being introduced to one of the senior ministers, he asked Boycott: "May I know your name"? Boycott retorted: "If you don't know my name, why have you invited me here?". The minister negotiated this bouncer with customary ease leaving it alone.

Boycott had two packets neatly wrapped. They were books. When he was entering the Jubilee Hall for dinner, a sweet-looking receptionist asked him: "Sir, why don't you leave these packets here so that you may have dinner in comfort"? Boycott's reaction was : "No, no I shall not. The packets will disappear and so will you".

These were the incidents which should have been reported to the Test and Country Cricket Board (TCCB) through the manager Raman Subha Row. But our weakling Board pocketed all these insults without a murmur.

Why was Boycott in such hostile mood? His mind was set on a tour to South Africa, an outlawed country then. In addition, he was not enjoying cricket in India where, according to him and some other English cricket players, cricket was boring and negative, umpiring partisan and evenings dull.

England team were touring Australia. At one of the functions, there were a few who were not talking in complimentary terms about the Queen. The players walked out of the function immediately.

When the English players display so much regard and respect for their dignitaries, why should they act so boorishly while on an official tour to India? It did no good to them and their country.

When Boycott was on TV commentary assignment in Pakistan in 1998, he slapped a scorer, who stood up and blocked his view. He reportedly tendered his apology for his crude stroke.

Despite his occassional odd behaviour, Boycott is unquestionably one of the finest TV commentators. He is fair and frank in his observations and comments. He is also occassionally witty.

Most of the modern English people, journalists included, are demanding, coneited, inhospitable, egoistic and unreasonable. This is the characteristic of present-day Englishmen who will enjoy all the hospitality on tour in India and provide virtually nothing when Indians are on tour to their country. They will generally be unavailable. But if a few are available, they will be gracious enough to take an Indian to a pub. Soon, the Englishman will say: "My pound is over, what about yours"? If an Indian suggests that he (Englishman) whould provide him lunch or dinner, the Englishman will quietly, though politely, say: "But that's your habit".

When Keith Fletcher's England was on tour to India in 1981-82, says Graham Gooch, in his book : "Out of the wilderness": "Boredom gets the blame for many of modern society's problems. We are told it causes to become soccer louts, the unemployed to become depressants and the elderly to feel suicidal. All of which makes my claims to sympathy look pretty thin. With that said, however, I must also concede that I might never have gone to the outlawed country if the 1981-82 trip to India had been stimulating, successful or preferably both. Instead, it came as a dire disillusionment to one who had felt he would never tire of international cricket. During that winter of unspeakably tedious cricket and endless dull evenings, I slipped into the type of depression I would not have considered possible while playing for England. So I went to South Africa".

The fact of the matter is that much before undertaking the tour to India, many of England players were actively considering the trip to South Africa because of lure of money. Why then take refute in the plea of 'boredom' that led Gooch and others to go to the 'outlawed' country ? Granting that India connot be England because of acute problems of population, poverty and pollution, but what is left in England ? Its cricket standards have declined to the depth of depression and its cricketing values and traditions are getting buried five fathom deep. Can Gooch deny this ?

Contrary to what Gooch and some other Englishmen may have to say, just read what manager Raman Subha Row has to say :

"It was a memorable tour, and I must thank all our hosts for their hospitality which exceeded even what I had anticipated. Quite the hardest job of the tour was to have to decline so many kind invitations and I only hope that those people understood the pressures on time. I am also very grateful to all the local managers who helped us so much and put up with my aggressive behaviour in times of stress. And to all the local associations who gave us such wonderful presents. I hope they realise that most England players say that India is the best tour to go on.

"If I have any regrets over the trip, they relate to the cricket. After being beaten fairly and squarely in the first interesting Test match at Mumbai, I think that most people were bored by the remaining Tests in India. Such a slow over-rate by both sides was pathetic in my view and I really can only applaud the patience of the crowds.

"In contrast, the five one-day matches were great fun and any one who went to any of them could not fail to have been excited by the stroke-play. Some people may deplore it, but I found it delightful to watch".

# 26

# Australians' Crude Behaviour

Indeed, many centres in the country lack in bare minimum facilities essential for teams, particularly for visiting teams, to give off their best. It is also true that most of the stadia are over-crowded because organisers, in their greed to make money, sell more tickets than the stadia can hold. There have been loud protests but the thick-skinned officials have shown little concern because they essentially have no reputation to lose. It is also true that ill-informed and uncouth spectators, in their over-zealousness, act in uncivilised manner causing annoynace to players, who are already tense and edgy because of importance attached to a Test match and a one-day international.

When the going is good, players take even hardships in their stridess. But when the going is rough, they tend to make a mountain of a molehill. The players are international heroes and they have got to take smooth with the rough.

Among Australian teams that have visited this country, Benaud's team got famously with the Indian authorities, while Allan Border's team in 1986-87 encountered many problems and gave several problems to the organisers. The visitors' behaviour deteriorated considerably as they reached Ahmedabad and Rajkot for their fifth and sixth one-dayers. When Craig McDermott was given out stumped by Pandit off Shastri, he expressed his dissatisfaction in the middle and damaged furniture in the dressing room. This was bad. What was worse was that some of the members of the team peed into the swimming pool outside the Ahmedabad stadium.

At Rajkot, the manager Alan Crompton lost his cool with the District Commissioner in full view of the Chief Minister Amarsingh Chaudhry. When some officials tried to pacify McDermott, he used words which would have put even drill sergeant to shame.

The trouble started when Australian players tried to occupy seats meant for the Government dignitaries and guests. When District Commissioner told him that the seats were occupied, the Australian manager crossed all bounds of decency and pushed aside the commissioner. The situation deteriorated to such an extent that some district administration officials wanted to detain the rampaging Australian. But the Board officials intervened and the unpleasant situation was averted.

There were several other members whose behaviour on and off the field left much to be desired. There were instances when a batsman would hit a four and, while running, he would ask the bowler how did he like the shot. There were instances when they made indecent gestures while playing. They were also guilty of passing vulgar remarks while hostesses were serving them snacks and meals. There were instances when players flung ice-cream down the aisle. This Australian side failed to uphold high traditions of cricket and maintain impeccable reputation of their country.

# 27

# No Act Of Patriotism

A report in the Times of London, dated July 29, 1990 caused concern in all cricket playing circles. Even Lord's Press box took notice of it. Pakistan journalist Qamar Ahmed, settled in London, in the exclusive news said that India's former captain Sunil Gavaskar had declined to accept the honorary life membership of the MCC.

Gavaskar had reportedly refused to accept the membership because he was refused admittance at Lord's for the Bicentenary match in August 1987. In June 1987, he had met with the same treatment at the hands of a steward. The occasion was the Pakistan-England match. In 1990, he had problems with the supervisory staff on the first day of the opening Test between India and England.

Gavaskar's point of view was : "On no ground in the world have I encountered such rudeness and ruthless behaviour by the stewards—they should have people at the gate who can at least recognise the current Test players and the ones playing in the match on the day".

Col J.R. Stephenson, secretary of the MCC, said "It is virtually impossible to employ stewards who could recognise every famous cricketer".

Let the case be examined threadbare dispassionately:

Admittance to a stadium for a match is by an invitation or a ticket purchased. Was he carrying the pass ? If he was, why did he decline to display it? Would he have become small if he had shown it to the steward ? If he was not, he should have asked for one from the authorities?

If Gavaskar had, by mistake, left it behind in a hotel room, he should have requested the steward to phone the concerned person, who could have come to the gate to escort him.

Indeed Gavaskar was an important cricketing personality and the steward should have shown the courtesy and let him enter without a pass. But, this he could have done on his own discretion. He could have been penalised by the authorities for allowing a player, renowend or otherwise, without the admittance card. There are innumerable instances when players of the stature of Denis Compton have been refused admittance in stadiam in London. If this is correct, Gavaskar should have been man enough to accept the functioning of the steward instead of getting peeved or agitated.

During these three years from 1987 to 1990, did Gavaskar at any stage lodge a protest or complaint with the MCC authorities against stewards uncooperative attitude? Why was he feeling shy of writing to the MCC authorities or Lord's authorities against steward's difficult posture? May be, the MCC authorities would have issued instructions to the steward or stewards that renowned Test stars of England and other countries could be permitted to enter even if they were not armed with requisite passes or tickets. This would have been his service to MCC ! There was yet another question. Was the steward on all these three occasions the same official? If there were different stewards, he should have all the more appreciated that they were merely doing their duties, as they ought to be.

In the end, granting that the steward or stewards had erred, should he have refused MCC membership when the officialdom was in no way to blame? Gavaskar would have been well within his rights, if any official of the MCC had, at any stage, failed to display proper courtesies to him at any time and at any place. There was no patriotism in refusing to accept membership nor did he grow tall in his otherwise lofty standards for declining membership.

Many of Gavaskar's ardent admirers felt that he had over-reacted to the entire situation. He should have accepted membership there and then and, while doing so, he might have brought to the notice of the secretary that he had been refused admittance by a steward or stewards in the past.

Gavaskar is reported to have accepted the membership after initial refusal or hesitancy. But even now he will have to display his honorary membership card before he gets inside the Lord's. Would he refuse to show that precious piece of paper now?

If Gavaskar's refusal to accept membership was termed as 'injudicious act', Bishan Singh Bedi's open letter to him in 1990 was shocking. Some of the paras from his letter are: 'I felt I must write to show how shocked and ashamed I am at your decision. In September 1989, you were offered an honorary membership of the MCC to which you did not reply. In November, you refused it for personal reasons. You have undone all your deeds with one stroke by ridiculing the greatest institution in the cricketing world. You have proved that only the mighty can be petty. I feel personally quite disgusted and ashamed. I even played cricket with you. You have let down the Indian cricket team, world cricket and more importantly, the Indian people in Britain".

These were Bedi's personal views. Why should he have written an open letter to Gavaskar on the letter-head of 'manager, Indian cricket team'?

# 28

# Amarnath Faces Ups And Downs

Two highly strung personalities, Anthony de mello and Amarnath, once on the same wave length, were on loggerheads before the 1948 tour of the West Indies ended at Mumbai. Words hard to forget were spoken at the Cricket Club of India (CCI) room in presence of many, including some junior players. It was a scene as shocking as the one enacted by Ajit Wadekar and Bishan Singh Bedi in England in mid 1970s.

De Mello was hell-bent on teaching Amarnath a lesson for his loud-mouthed and arregance. Amarnath, in turn, was determined: "Who the hell was he?" de Mello reportedly said that he had picked Amar from gutter to instal him as India's captain, while Amarnath's assertion was that Tony would not have been what he was without his support and assistance.

The controversy took a drastic turn as Amarnath's interview (National Herald) had appeared quoting him against de Mello. Taking that as a handle, de Mello suspended Amarnath. India's stormy petrel threatened to sue the Lucknow paper saying that he had been misquoted. But Amarnath did not seek legal redress for certain reasons.

Amarnath did not figure in the matches played by the Commonwealth teams in India in 1949-51. He stood suspended. Vijay Hazare captained India against England in 1951-52 and also led India on a tour to England in 1952.

The wheel of politics in Indian Board was now moving towards Amarnath's way and de Mello was losing his dominance. This was the beginning for Amarnath to resurface on the firmament of Indian scene. A lobby, influential enough, started circulating that Amarnath would be an ideal choice to captain India against Pakistan on their maiden tour to India in 1952. While shouting this from house-top, the lobby was also vocal in saying that Vijay Hazare was 'too gentlemanly' to lead the side. In other words they were projecting that a thorn could be removed with only by thorn and Amarnath, a hard-core Punjabi, would be a fitting answer to deal with articulate and shrewd Abdul Hafiz Kardar's Pakistanis.

Rival factions were at work. Mumbai and allies were pro-Hazare, while a powerful faction from Kolkata was pro-Amarnath. Votes were sold and bought. In those days, the captain was elected by the Board and not by the four-five-member selection committee. When the Board met, Amarnath scraped through 12-11. It was a trmendous victory for him. Nayudu, who was aligned with de Mello, lost both elections for vice-president and selector. For the post of selector, he could manage 11 to Ramaswami's 12.

The venue for the second Test was Lucknow and not Kanpur. UP's zamindar-monarch, called Vizzy, had fallen out with the Kanpur industrialists and he had the match shifted from Green Park to Lucknow.

The search for the ground was made. There was no stadium, no worthwhile ground. La Martiniere College ground, where UP Governor verses Commonwealth XI was staged earlier was not considered good enough for such an important Test match. Cricket in Lucknow was then run by the Lucknow Sports Association (LSA), which was virtually in the grasp of two hockey-knowing persons, N.N. (Habul) Mukerjee and Dr A.C. Chattarjee. They had a legal support of B.N. Roy, who was a fine advocate.

Eventually, LSA and Vizzy chose Lucknow University ground, outside the campus. It was known as Gomati ground. Now it is a bed of river Gomati, which has changed its course with the passage of time.

Man proposes and God disposes. Vizzy in particular and Amarnath in general had planned that gravel (Bajri) pitch with jute matting spread over it would be a good strategy to pin down Pakistan. Pitch was laid by Sita Ram, a known curator and a fine exponent of seam bowling at Roshanara Club and then for Delhi in Ranji matches. Jute matting was specially made and brought from South. Temporary stands, like at La Martiniere ground, were put up. As luck would have it, the jute matting wicket was fully exploited by Fazal for Pakistan as India lost the Test as badly as Pakistan had lost the first Test at Delhi.

The selectors in general and Amarnath in particulalr were to blame for this ignominy of defeat. Amarnath impressed upon the selectors that Hazare, Mankad and Adhikari would not be useful on jute matting. They were shockingly left out of the Test. Had Hazare and Mankad been there, India might not have sustained such a huge defeat.

As Indian team was on the receiving end, there were stream of cat-calls against Vizzy, Mustafa, UPCA Secretary, and others. As the match ended on the fourth day, there were jeers and booing for Amarnath. Shaken by the defeat, he lost his shirt and was about to dash out of the bus with a bat in his hand to attack the agitated section of spectators. But policemen, standing nearby, prevented the situation from deteriorating any further.

India won the third Test of Mumbai and were leading the series 2-1. They had Pakistan in jitters on the opening day of the fourth Test at Chennai. The visitors crumbled to 240 for nine wickets. Amarnath prevented his bowlers from taking the last wicket as he did not want his team to bat at the fag end of the day. But Amarnath's gamble misfired. The pair of Zulfiqar and Amir Elahi could not be dislodged for a long time. The pair raised the total to 344 before Elahi (47) was eventually bowled by Amarnath.

The Test however petered out into a tame draw as rain played a spoilsport.

Another furious controversy surfaced at Chennai where selectors named Hazare as captain for the tour to West Indies. The selection was to be a 'secret'. Even president of the Board J.C. Mukherjea did not know about it. But Amarnath came to know of it through a journalist-friend. He was furious. He thought Board and selectors had played 'dirty' with him.

When official get-together was in progress at Chennai, Amarnath rose to say: "I congratulate Hazare on his being appointed captain". He went on to say that it would be in fitness of things that he should lead the side in the fifth and final Test at Kolkata. "I will gladly play under him", he said. But Hazare pulled out of the Test. Amarnath, however, continued to captain the side.

Amarnath accused Vizzy for this unexpected coup. In the post-dinner speech, he said: ".....I know Vizzy is a responsible man, but he plays other games to cricket on the board". There were some, who said that C.K. Nayudu had joined Vizzy in dislodging Amarnath from the captaincy of the team to the West Indies.

# 29

# Vizzy's Controversial "Shikar"

Vizzy's cricketing life—whatever it might have been—was nothing but a saga of controversies. Nothing that he did was not controversial. When he played cricket, he was wrapped up in controversies. When he resurfaced after a long lay-off, he was involved in controversies in the Board politics and the U.P. Cricket Association. He was governed by dictatorial instincts and he functioned on his personal whims and fancies. He would demand from the Board allotment of matches for UP and single-handedly would decide which would be the venue—Allahabad, Kanpur or Lucknow. He was virtually law unto himself. When he was doing commentary on radio (there was no TV then), he was involved in controversies. Once a panel of judges decided to get rid off him from the commentary box. He came to know of it. He went to Prime Minister's office and asked Pandit Jawaharlal Nehru's secretary to fix an appointment with the All-India Radio Director-General. This call was enough. As he stepped into DG's office, he was told: "Sir, don't worry, you are continuing on the panel of commentators".!

Vizzy wore the label of a sharp shooter. His Palace in Varanasi had tiger heads and tiger skins all over. He was a Member of Parliament (MP). Without obtaining clearance, he carried with him a group of Pakistanis in the Nailani jungle (Lakhimpur-Kheri district) for a big game shoot. It was forbidden to go on 'big game' shikar with foreigners without obtaining permission from an appropriate authority. A mishap took place in April 1962. Vizzy was on an elephant. Foreigners were following him. Suddenly a tigress appeared. The tigress was shot and injured.

She disappeared in thick bushes. Out of blue, she made frontal attack on Vizzy's elephant. Vizzy fell down. His gun lay nearby. Luckily for him, tigress picked up his sola topi and disappeared again in the bushes.

Vizzy was rushed from Lakhimpur to Lucknow (Balrampur Hospital) for an emergent operation. He had sustained a fracture of a pelvic bone and urinary bladder had been punctured. The operation, which lasted for about two hours, was a success. But Vizzy's condition stayed serious. He had only one kidney and that too with a stone in it. The other kidney had been removed a long time ago.

Delhi's well known surgeon Dr S.K. Sen had, in the meantime, arrived in Lucknow. He approved of the post-operation treatment, advised by Dr R. V. Singh who had performed the operation.

After a prolonged rest, Vizzy began moving about. But he was not the Vizzy he was. He, however, continued to have a pie in every finger where U.P. cricket was concerned.

There was an amusing story about Vizzy's ability and skill as a sharp-shooter. A youngster, while lunching at Varanasi Palace, posed a question whether Vizzy was such an accurate shooter. Vijay Manjrekar quickly replied: "Vizzy carries in jungle his tape-recorded cricket commentary and plays it. Tigers go to sleep. He then bowls them out".

# 30

# Rift Between Bosom Friend

"Whom I best love, I cross". These are famous words of a world renowned poet, Shakespeare. Inderjit Singh Bindra and Jagmohan Dalmiya were great friends for years. They were considered to have had one soul in two bodies.

Together Bindra and Dalmiya waged many battles against groups in power. Initially dislodging incumbents in office and in power proved a nightmare for them. They kept fighting. Their tenacity worked. They eventually succeeded winning a battle of attrition. They gained control over the Board. They went from strength to strength. Also they exercised their judgement and practiced public relations in winning friends and influencing people. The time came when they could do what they wanted and other members merely nodded their heads in appreciation.

The Board began to lay golden eggs during their tenure. Power, it is said, corrupts; absolute power corrupts absolutely. Money, always an evil, fell in their coffers. More money and unlimited power led to their falling apart. The drift, between the two, led to cracks. The time was when they were inseparable and they were in constant touch although they stayed 1,000 miles away from each other at Chandigarh and Kolkata. The cycle turned full circle. They became so averse to each other, that they could no longer see the sight of each other.

When Bindra and Dalmiya were at the helm of affairs, they indeed bettered Board's financial health. But they could also be accused of destroying the very fibre of Indian cricket. The very hand that fed them was being bitten by them.

Who was to blame for this blatant ugly situation obtaining in the Board? Suffice it to say that both were allegedly guilty. There were charges and counter-charges. Each blamed the other. The situation was complex and complicated that it was virtually impossible to pinpoint as to who, in reality, was the villian in this sordid drama.

Bindra's term ended and in came Rajsingh Dungarpur as President. Dalmiya crossed over from Board to International Cricket Council (ICC) making way for Jaywant Lele to take over as secretary. The situation did not improve. Lele often put his foot in his mouth causing more problems to the Board instead of sorting them out.

What were the causes of their fall out? Main among them were:

1. When the ICC (in session) broke for lunch after heated debate some 'whites' mischievously told Bindra within the hearing of Dalmiya that they would vote for him to take over as president. To the utter surprise of Dalmiya, Bindra consented to become president. (Bindra denied there was any truth in this).

Before this offer, there was a seven-hour debate. The England-Australia-New Zealand representatives, who have always showed their bias against sub-continent nominess, insisted on adhering to two-third majority (nine members) vote for the election of the president. The Asia representatives stood for simple majority rule. Eventually the rule of simple majority was followed and Dalmiya was elected President. In the first round of voting Dalmiya got 16 votes (three full members and 10 associated members), Malcolm Gray (Australia) got 15 (4 full members and seven associate members), Krish Mackerdhuj (South Africa) got 9 (2 full members and 5 associate members). In the second round Mackerdhuj withdrew. Dalmiya polled four votes of full members and 17 of associate members (25 votes) while Gray got 13 votes (4 full members and 5 associate members). In the crucial election meeting, sitting president Sir Clyde Walcott (West Indies) did not function as impartially and independently as he ought to have. He was "supportive of Whites" as he nurtured personal ambitions of continuing in ICC.

The opinion of Sir Michael Beloff, Queen's counsel, and Justice R.S. Pathak, the former Chief Justice of Supreme Court, held the view that the ICC rules did not specify that the election of chairman to be governed by special majority of full members and that any contrary action was illegal and against the rules.

Until this crucial meeting, the ICC meetings were attended by "locals" as associate members. They all followed the line of England and Australia. This was the most unethical practice followed by two founder-members.

2. When CBI proceedings were initiated against Bindra for alleged misuse of funds for the construction of the stadium (Mohali), he allegedly accused Dalmiya for playing a 'sinister role'. (Dalmiya laughed at Bindra's accusations).

3. It was alleged that Dalmiya played a key role in bringing about division between Bindra and World Tel's bigwig Mark Mascrenhas.

4. Before Bindra relinquished his office as president, he was promised of chairmanship of Marketing and Sponsorship Committee. But Dalmiya and Rajsingh went back on their assurance.

With Bindra out of the Board, Dalmiya and Rajsingh secured all the powers and won over member-affiliated units through shrewd distribution of 'loaves'. Bindra was totally isolated. Once Bindra sent a letter to members of the ICC pointing out certain deficiencies and irregularities in the functioning of the Board. Bindra's ardent admirers felt that he should not have washed 'dirty linen' in public (ICC). Bindra got peeved at this and expressed his desire to walk out of the working committee meeting at Delhi. Rajshingh was in chair. Bindra rose in a bid to leave. He changed his mind and told Rajsingh that he was continuing sitting in the meeting. Rajsingh replied: "I did not ask you to leave and I will not ask you to sit down".

Now engaged on two different paths, the Bindra faction held a lavish get-together. It was decided there that D.C. Agashe (Pune) would opposite Rajsingh (CCI), sitting president. It was also decided that the Bindra group would field a candidate for each post of the office-bearer.

In love and war, it is said, there is nothing fair or foul. It was Bindra who, while holding a proxy from West, defeated Agashe in the elections at Gwalior. Rajsingh became president on the proxy of Rajasthan (Central). Now the same Bindra had befriended Agashe, a sugar heavy weight from Pune. Politics can indeed turn friends into foes and enemies into friends.

Came crucial annual meeting, 68th edition, at Chennai on September 21, 1997. Efforts for compromise failed. In the 30-member house, the groups were evenly matched with the Dalmiya faction enjoying a wee-bit advantage. But neither group seemed certain of its victory. When the Bindra faction objected to non-circulation of the amended minutes of the previous meeting, it was decided to go by the constitution and provide 21-day notice to members to study the minute before calling the meeting again.

During the meeting, there was a heated discussion, over the candidature of the Railways and Jammu and Kashmir.

The Railways Sports Control Board (RSCB) secretary Balkar Singh had flown to Chennai from Poland to attend the meeting. But the Chennai-based RSCB vice-president issued a letter authorising another official (R. Ananth) to attend the meeting.

Similar kind of thing had happened some years ago at the Kolkata meeting. It was sad that the Government units and officials should be reduced to virtual 'pawns' in the hands of the politicians. In the Kolkata meeting, Madhavrao

Scindia just prevailed upon Bindra by a solitary vote.

What the RSCB official did was bad. But what sitting president did was worse. Rajsingh ruled against RSCB secretary Balkar Singh. It was in direct violation of the constitution, which said that the affiliated units would be represented by presidents or secretaries. The constitution further said that in case president or secretary could not attend, the president would nominate a representative to attend the meeting.

Ajay Shatru, son of Dr Karan Singh, was nominated by the Jammu and Kashmir Cricket Association president Farooq Abdullah, who is also the Chief Minister, to attend the meeting. Also present was S.D.A. Drabu. He claimed that he was the rightful representative. But the presiding official, Rajsingh, allowed Shatru to attend the meeting.

Following that unruly, abortive annual general meeting at Chennai, Bindra on September 25 dashed off a long letter to Rajsingh, which is reproduced here:

"I am writing this letter with a deep sense of anguish, a feeling of personal hurt and veritable sense of shock and disbelief in the manner in which the last AGM was conducted. These feelings have further been aggravated by the subsequent happenings, including the Press briefing, done by J.Y. Lele, secretary, after the meeting.

"You may recollect that during the course of the abandoned meeting, I had spoken to you during the many short adjournments, about the glorious traditions of the Board and the role played by the past presidents who had always been treated in high esteem and dignity by the members, even at times when the Board was vertically divided into two groups. Even at those times the presidents had always acted impartially, objectively and in a fair manner.

"During my 22 years of association with the Board, at no point of time has the office of president been accused of being subjective. You will recall that during the last 20 years, three elections were fiercely contested and in some cases won with slimmest of majority but, at no point, the glorious traditions, conventions of the Board and rules of fairplay and objectivity were given a go-by. N.K.P. Salve was elected at Bangalore and at that time Board was vertically divided. Salve, with his esteemed leadership, rare objectivity and deep sense of fairplay, helped in cementing the cracks and schisms and, during his tenure, the Board was totally united. Those three years were a glorious chapter in the annals of the Board, the biggest milestone being victory in the World Cup at Lord's in 1983, allotment of Reliance Cup and its subsequent conduct and the effective and meaningful role played by India in the corridors of the ICC.

"After Salve, Scindia's elevation as Board president was again preceded by an extremely bitter campaign, a fairly contested election and a debate on the floor of the house which at times was highly acrimonious. However, after these elections, Scindia also carried all sections with him and provided tremendous leadership and the Board became a cohesive unit. Scindia succeeded in bringing the World Cup to the sub-continent for the second time in a decade. Also during that period, India successfully created a solid block of like-minded members in ICC and was successful in democratisation of ICC and repealing of some of the antiquated outdated feudal and colonial provisions relating to veto etc. in the ICC constitution. It was due to his efforts that the first democratically elected chairman was installed.

"In November 1993 when I took over at Gwalior, again there was a keenly contested election. Even though I may not have provided the kind of leadership which predecessors had but in my humble way I succeeded in carrying the entire Board together. With the support and commitment of all members, we achieved reasonable success in terms of innovative marketing and spread of the game and in 1996 handed over to you at Mohali a Board which was vibrant, united and transparent in all its dealings. Mohali witnessed unanimous elections—a true vindication of its unity.

"During last one year you have, for reasons best known

to you, allowed situation to deteriorate to the extent of the impasse of the AGM. This was one of the saddest days in the history of the Board.

"Your rulings in respect of representatives of two member-associations, namely, Railways and Jammu and Kashmir, were, to say the least, totally subjective, arbitrary, contrary to the provisions of rules and regulations of the Board and all established conventions. In the case of Balkar Singh (Railways), he was duly nominated by the president besides being the secretary and was totally competent to represent Railways in the AGM. You had categorically stated that in case he gave in writing that he was duly nominated by the Railways to attend the meeting, you would allow him to represent the member association. When he gave the same in writing, to our utter shock and disbelief, you changed your ruling and declared that the person nominated by the vice-president would represent the Railways.

"A large number of members had pointed the inherent contradictions; the apparent illegalities and the likely consequences which would flow from your arbitrary ruling. It was pointed out that in case the vice-presidents of respective associations could nominate, it could lead to chaos with multiple-nominations, thereby creating impossible situations which would jeopardise cohesive and unity of the Board and its administrative structure. It would also lead to ridiculous consequences whereby the electoral college comprising the representatives of the various member-associations could be manipulated by the chairman of the meeting to suit his convenience and of the convenience of his faction or the group. It was all the more unfortunate because you had declared your candidature for the post of president in the group meeting held the previous day.

"A greater shock was reserved for us in terms of your ruling in respect of representative from Jammu and Kashmir. Whereas in the first case you had said that letter from vice-president could nullify the authority given by the president and conferred by the constitution rules and regulations of RSCB, in the second case you gave a ruling that (two authority letters were issued, one by Farooq Abdullah, president of Jammu and Kashmir in favour of Ajay Shatru, the other by the secretary in favour of Drabhu) both could attend the meeting.

"For casting of vote in case of subsequent vote you ruled that both representatives shall have the right to vote and their votes would be kept in a sealed cover. This ruling was not only in contravention of the rules and regulations of the Board, the regulations governing administration of J and K association but was totally contradictory to your own earlier ruling in respect of the representative of the Railways. In first case, you authorised the representative nominated by the vice-president to attend even though the secretary was totally authorised in terms of the constitution of the RSCB. You over-ruled all the arguments made by a large number of members on the floor of the house and gave an arbitrary ruling. We had requested that in both cases the votes should be kept in a sealed cover so that to have consistency in two rulings. Subsequently after two hours of heated discussion, good sense and wisdom prevailed upon you and you over-ruled your earlier ruling and allowed Shatru to attend and vote at the meeting. In respect of the Railway representative, however, you persisted with your arbitrary and totally illegal ruling which may well create a precedence which will eventually make the working of the Board impossible.

"The news item appearing in the next day's newspaper based on the official briefing given by the secretary Lele further compounded the shocking state of affairs by giving a totally erroneous and distorted version of what actually took place in the meeting both in respect of your ruling pertaining to representatives from J and K and Railways and also in respect of circumstances leading to postponement of the meeting on grounds of notice being in contravention of rules and regulations of the Board.

'1. When notice for the meeting was read, I got up and

raised an objection that the minutes which had been circulated along with the notice had not been approved by me in my captaincy as the then president and chairman of the last AGM held on September 25 and 26, 1996 at Mohali.

"At this point of time some of the members sought a short adjournment to enable them to go through the minutes which were tabled only after I had raised the objection. A strong objection was taken to this by one of the vice-presidents and effort was made to shout down the representatives who had sought a short adjournment. When the request for short adjournment was turned down, I had got up and said that, even though technically notice for the meeting was defective, in the interest of smooth working of the Board, its public image and the resultant implications, we did not wish to raise technical points. At this point of time, Dalmiya representing Cricket Association of Bengal specifically sought postponement on the ground that the notice was illegal and that a fresh clear 21 days notice to be issued. In the official briefing, as appeared in newspapers, Lele has tried to confuse the issue and even gone to the extent of saying that a large number of members had sought abandonment whereas actually brief adjournment had been sought.

2. While postponing the meeting, it was categorically stated that the meeting would be re-convened within the shortest possible time by giving 21 days' clear notice. It was also decided that the actual date would be between Dussehra and Deepavali.

3. Subsequently, Lele in a statement from Mumbai has stated that the meeting would be held some time in November. This is not only contrary to what had been decided at the time of postponing the meeting at Chennai on September 21, 1997 but is also against the interest of the Board and the member-associations. The motives for such an act will obviously be suspect. Lele has already received and duly

approved minutes on September 23, and if he had issued a notice on September 24, the meeting could have been convened by October 15, 1997 as was intended at Chennai. I see no reason why the meeting cannot be convened between Dussehra and Diwali. Postponing it beyond Diwali is once again arbitrary and against the interest of the Board and can jeopardise its working.

4. Technically speaking, after September 30, 1997, all office-bearers, committee and sub-committees seize to exist but we did not wish to create a vacuum in the Board and the members had agreed that till the middle of October routine decisions may be taken by the concerned committees.

I, therefore, request you to please direct the secretary to convene the meeting forthwith by giving 21 days' notice. Any delay will not only be contrary to the understanding and the decision arrived at Chennai but will be totally suspect in the eyes of members and the public at large and could have consequences detrimental to the interest of the Board.

"I do hope that you will take this letter in the spirit in which I have written it. Keeping in view of the glorious traditions of the Board, the sanctity of its conventions and the pristine heritage, I would request you to correct the distortions and not allow the matter to drift further.

"Keeping in view the gravity of the issues involved, I am taking the liberty of endorsing a copy of this letter to all affiliated member-associations and office-bearers".

The Board's meeting was reconvened at Chennai where a no-hold barred elections took place. It was one of the bitterest contests in which Inderjit Singh Bindra was caught by Jagmohan Dalmiya and bowled by Nalini Chidambaram, wife of the Finance Minister P. Chidambaram.

Dalmiya's manipulative ability and Nalini's legal acuemen were subtly handled by the Finance Minister for Rajsingh Dungapur to retain his office of the president defeating D.C. Agashe 17/13 in a straight contest.

It was not a battle of mere attrition but it was a war in which traditions of fair-play and ethics were given a go-by. Neither faction played 'cricket'. One faction resorted to all kinds of tactics to maintain its stranglehold in the Board, while opposition group did every thing in its control to unseat the sitting incumbents.

It will be difficult to say who was more guilty in resorting to methods which brought a huge blot on the wealthiest Indian sports body. The tactics adopted were so crude and foul that the Indian Board and cricket would not be the same in years to come.

If September 21 was a 'black day' in the annals of Board's chequered existence, the reconvened meeting on November 6, 1997 was the 'most disastrous day' for Board. Cricket was buried five fathom deep never to emerge out of the claws and clutches of people who could not be termed worthy enough to control this game, which was once a noble discipline.

On the eve of the meeting at Taj Coromandal hotel, both Bindra and Dalmiya were certain of their victory. Both, however, were certain that the margin of victory would be very thin. Then Dalmiya played a trump card through a seasoned politician who, with his influence and ministerial weight, succeeded in 'snatching away' two institutional votes of the Railways and Services from the grasp of the Bindra faction.

Both senior institutional officials, Agarwal (Railways) and Air Vice Marshal A.V. Pasricha (Services) received mandates from their bosses that they should vote for the Dalmiya faction regardless of their loyalties or personal commitments. A seasoned advocate Nalini ran the elections from here hotel room 503. She fashioned a win for the Dalmiya faction. No one knows what fees were paid to her.

If politician saw two representatives of the Railways and the Services cross over from the Bindra group to Dalmiya faction, the Bindra side tried to prevent Lele from attending the meeting. They had brought the influence of customs and excise officials. But this move boomeranged.

In the politics-ridden Board, a gentleman-cricket player Agashe was the sufferer. A soft-spoken and deserving official, Agashe lost to Bindra a few years ago at Gwalior. It was his legitimate turn then but he became a pawn in subtle manoeuvrings of Bindra-Dalmiya, who were then together. In the 1997 elections, he again went down fighting spending a sizeable amount. The analysts felt that Bindra brought about his own downfall through his needless loud talking. Had he played his cards discreetly instead of shouting from house-top, he would have emerged winner with Agashe at the helm of affairs.

As some one said it was a fight between a northern official and a Marwari. While northern official was loud-mouthed, aggressive and showy in whatever he did; Marwari was a 'miser' in his strategy.

Lele retained his post of the secretary defeating Delhi's Sunil Dev, who was talkative and assertive as his mentor. Lele won by a heavier margin than Rajsingh Dungarpur had won.

The Dalmiya faction did try its level best to dislodge M.P. Pandov from the office of the selector. But northerns, for once, stayed united and Pandov retained his post.

A former Railways official, Mati Lal Phalguni seemed beholden to the Bindra faction. He should have stayed away from the elections since he could not officially represent Railways nor did he have sponsorship from any other unit. Yet he was in Chennai where he had filed a Public Interest Litigation when the meeting was scheduled on September 21. This led to Chennai High Court appointing an observer, an advocate.

For this crucial meeting, there were one or two 'professional' voters, who were known for attending all kinds of voting-meetings from cricket to Kabaddi.

# 31

# Virginity Of Pitch Questioned

India's cricketing image was further slackened and pride, if any, punctured as for the first time in more than 100 years of international competitions, an official match against Sri Lanka had to be called off as the 'virgin strip' at Indore was declared unoperational for play on December 27, 1997.

Full house—some of the spectators had bought tickets from black market—were humming with excitement and enthusiasm when the announcement for 'cancellation' of the match was made as players, umpires and officials felt that the pitch was 'dangerous' for play.

That this should have happened at Indore, playing home town of C.K. Nayudu (he was born in Nagpur) was deplorable. Mushtaq Ali, eldest living Indian player, and C.T. Sarvate among many others of the Holkar-era had to bow their head in shame. It was indeed shocking that it should have happened after Board had spent more than Rs. 30 lakh in inviting a team from New Zealand to educate the Indian curators on the art and subtleties of laying wickets.

All this drama had been enacted after India had been in international cricket for 65 years. During these 65 years, foreign teams had dreaded to play in India because they found the wickets were too placid to get the Indian team dismissed twice to win a Test. Now the one-day match had to be called off after merely 18 balls had been bowled because the 'virgin wicket' was after all not so 'virgin'. The batsmen and bowlers felt that there was no 'virginity' in the pitch and it was not worth making use of it. What a fall!

Charity, it is said, "begins at home". The BCCI has a member, K.B. Pawar, who is a leading geologist. Indeed he is not a cricket knowing person, but he is one who knows about the soil as much as any in New Zealand. Yet he was not even consulted and a foreign team was invited. Does not this show how stupid Indians and Indian Board authorities can be? The objection by the Sri Lankan batsmen about the 'dangerous designs' of the pitch was not exactly understandable as only 18 balls had been bowled and one wicket had fallen. Pitches world over behave unpredictably before settling down. The objection should have been ruled out by the umpires without any reference to the match referee.

The complete situation got further complicated as India's captain Sachin Tendulkar also said 'wolf' in the pitch. The two captains hummed the same tune and the match referee Justice Ahmed Ebrahim ruled for abandonment of the match. The decision was shocking and unheard of.

The wicket was prepared under the supervision of Narendra Menon. A fine cricket player, an umpire and a curator, he had prepared a 'strip' good enough for the one-day match.

Several allegations surfaced following the abandonement of the match. Some of them are.

1. A senior Board member, at the behest of the team management, had allegedly asked Menon to prepare an under-prepared wicket as Sri Lankan batting was too good for Indian bowlers to contain them on a placid wicket,

2. Why did India agree to the abandonment when they were sitting pretty after bagging one wicket for 17 and after being one up in the series?

3. Did the match referee Justice Ebrahim (Zimbabwe) and the umpires Subroto Porel and Devender Sharma take the decision on thier own or were they guided by rival captains?
4. Were Indian specialist batsmen worried to play Sri Lanka bowlers on this wicket which certainly was not docile?

An eyewash 25-over match was organised. It was a meaningless contest. The spectators were not refunded money for many months. Who bore the losses for the unplayed match? Was Sri Lanka Board paid 'guarantee money" for the match that did not take place?

The pitch problem at Indore took place only after New Zealand team of "expert curators" visited India. For more than 65 years (since 1932), no such problem surfaced. Was there any need to invite Kiwi soil team? Many thought it was an exercise in futility!

It is again Indore where statue of "CK" showed him as a left-handed batsman.

# 32

# Prabhakar Quits In Disgust

There are players, who do right thing at wrong time. There are some others who do wrong thing at right time. But Manoj Prabhakar, one of the most tenacious and dedicated players in modern Indian cricket, was unfortunately one who was credited with doing a wrong thing at a wrong time. His exit from international cricket was one of the saddest chapters in Indian cricket.

Essentially self-made, Prabhakar played more with his in-born instincts than with any bookish technique or skill. His competence lay in his robust character. Never over-awed by any opposition, he gave of his best when the going was rough and tough. Physically fit, his mental strength came from the determination of 'never to say die'. His century against West Indies at fast Mohali wicket was a proof of his guts. He was hit on his face, yet he did not lose his courage. No other specialist batsman faced fast bowling with tenacity.

There was absolutely no justification for Prabhakar to have announced his retirement from international cricket. It was a rash and uncalled for step undertaken more through his emotional outbursts than because of shrewd and calculating thinking. Indeed he was not treated well during the Wills World Cup in 1996. But it was not cause enough for him to have announced his retirement. He needlessly played into the hands of selectors. Had he deferred his retirement announcement, he would have been an automatic choice to tour South Africa and West Indies in addition to playing a few matches on the domestic circuit.

In early 1996 (May) Prabhakar said: "I have decided to call it a day. I have no motivation left to continue after the treatment I received from some of the esteemed men who run cricket in this country.....Today, I feel sad at the manner in which I have to go. I am not being a coward by quitting but being wise considering the events of the recent past. For all my hard work, all my sacrifices on and off the field, I did not receive a second chance from the same people who would rave about my contribution not long ago....."

As if this announcement was not enough, Prabhakar needlessly got involved in yet another controversy with the DDCA officials. Here again he was misled by his so-called colleagues.

The matter was trifle. Instigated by some self-seeking senior players, Prabhakar took upon himself the responsibility of demanding gradation payment for Delhi team in Ranji Trophy. The move was first initiated by Sunil Gavaskar when Indian team was in Pakistan in 1982. Fatehsingh Rao Gaekwad, then manager, undertook two trips to India to discuss with the Board officials before he carefully "spiked" Gavaskar's suggestion.

Prabhakar and his team-mates should have had discussion with the DDCA officials instead of resorting to 'show of strength'. Egged by fenceg-sitting players, Prabhakar defied the logo contract until gradation payment was initiated. As the controversy raged, one by one all his colleagues 'deserted' him. This was not the first time nor would it be the last for players sommersaulting and leaving one or two players in lurch. As a result of players double-deal and double-talk, poor Prabhakar was on the mat.

**Dear friends.....**

"Cricket was my first love and I shall always remember

the nice life this game gave me. I owe everything that I have and everything I have achieved in life to cricket.

"Today, I feel sad at the manner in which I have to go. "I was always honest in my approach. True, I have had a few tiffs with the media and a few with fellow cricketers, but then such things are bound to happen in a world of fierce competition. Believe me, I have no enemies as I leave the cricketing scene today and I hold no grudge against anyone.

"Though I feel I could have contributed more, the selectors obviously feel otherwise. It is good that they have become so demanding and I hope they follow the same yardstick in the future too. The selectors have a very tough task and I can only wish them well. Indian cricket is heading for great times and I will be happy if my mates maintain the high standards set in the last few years.

"Looking back I think I can take pride in the act that I lasted 12 years in international cricket. I never had any great talent and I had to strive to improve under coach Tarak Sinha and keep my place in the side. I can say that I am satisfied with my career. There is no point in sulking over some of the sore moments in life...."

Prabhakar suddenly switched over to politics. He now wore a white Kurta-Pyjama. When asked why was he getting into 'dirty game of politics, he said: "I want to teach a lesson to people who run cricket". There was threat in his reply.

Essentially, Prabhakar suffered from persecution-mania. Fighter he was, but he fought more often against himself than against others. His behaviour even in dressing room was odd. No wonder, most of his mates kept safe distance from him. He, in fact, had one or two quarrels with his colleagues in dressing room and against his rivals in the middle. But he could not care less. He refused to learn. Add to it, his sharp temper, an acid tongue, and thoughtless statement, he was not a popular man.

# 33

## Merchant Out, Pat In

Upset Mansur Ali Khan Pataudi was when he was axed from the captaincy through the casting vote of Vijay Merchant in 1970-71. He resorted to playing hide and seek. He missed some domestic matches and even sent a telegram (purported to have been pre-dated) that he would not be available for the West Indies tour. He even announced that he was contesting general elections from Gurgaon (Haryana). To this Chief Minister of Haryana Bansi Lal, father of Ranbir Singh, whose last assignment with the Board was secretary, reportedly said: "...You want to vote for Pataudi. What good can he do for you, if he wins this election? It will be hazardous for you to meet him. If you decide to meet him at the stadium, you will be required to queue up for hours to get inside the stadium. When inside, it will be difficult for you to meet him. Granting that you met him, he would at least provide you a ball and a bat"!

Subsequently Pat predicted that he would return to India's captaincy at his terms. He proved he was right in his calculations as he was named captain unopposed. This was after he had stayed away from captaincy for about five years. He had, however, made three appearances against England in 1972-73 in home series. All this happened immediately after Vijay Merchant relinquished his office of the chairman of the selection committee.

During this long lay-off period, Pat was not playing

domestic cricket as keenly and enthusiastically, as he ought to have been. But he maintained his physical sharpness. He was, however, not a player who believed much in 'nets'. His philosophy was that the match-play was more important than practice in nets. This was unlike his father Iftikhar, who had tremendous faith in rigorous 'nets'. Those, who had seen both Iftikhar and Mansur in their prime, were quick to say that younger Pataudi was more natural player than his father. Fielding and striking the ball regardless of position of his feet were imbedded in his system.

As soon as Merchant laid down his office, Pat decided that it was the time to re-enter the arena of Indian cricket.

England, on tour to India under A.R. (Tony) Lewis, were scheduled to play against South Zone at Bangalore. Pat made the most of this match as he notched up a fine century. His knock spoke highly of his skill and ability, even after such a long disassociation from international cricket. His strokes had the same authority that he had displayed some years ago. The new chairman, C.D. Gopinath, was at the stadium when Pat was in the middle making strokes and taking uncanny singles. His team of selectors was also present. Gopinath asked Pat whether he would be available to play at Chennai, if chosen. He said that he was most willing to play under Wadekar although in the first two Tests at Delhi and Kolkata he worked as a journalist from the Press box.

Following Pat's consent, he was duly chosen and he moved to the Chennai dressing room. Reserved he was, but he had many friends in the team and he mixed with them as if he was back at his rightful place.

Wadekar had then gone on record as saying that Pat returned to Indian team on his insistence. "I offered him to join the team to tour England in the summer of 1974", said Wadekar, adding: "I even offered him to lead the side and I would stand down in his favour". But he reportedly declined saying that he was not available for tours.

Pat started his innings in the third Chennai Test against

Lewis's England in a whirlwind style. He hit six fours in his 50 and made 73 before he was caught by Old off Pocock. Says Wisden: "....Coming in to a royal and tumultuous welcome from fine crowd, he straightaway attacked the bowling with an array of glittering strokes". He was unbeaten with 14 in the second innings. He had another good knock of 54 in the fourth Test at Kanpur.

Pat was "invited" to lead India against West Indies in 1974-75. Pat could not make a 'Nawabi' start in the first Test at Bangalore where he could score 22 and India lost the match by 267 runs. When he dislocated his finger while attempting a difficult catch, he had to rush indoors. No one knew who his deputy was. Gavaskar was told that he was vice-captain but he was told to 'keep it a secret'. Naturally he did not assume his role of captaincy until a substitute Rajinder Goel came on the field to tell him that he should lead the side.

Gavaskar was appointed captain for the second Test at Delhi but he could not as he was hurt while playing a match in domestic competition. A lot of confusion prevailed before Venkataraghavan was made captain a few minutes before the start of the match. Then as Pat returned to lead, Venkat was dropped from the team at Kolkata's third Test!

India trailing 1-2 made it 2-2 before losing the final Test.

Pat's captaincy was appreciated. "The measure of his success as captain lies in the fact that the series restored India's prestige in international cricket which rose to a remarkable, if not to the full extent", said P.N. Sunderesan.

# 34

# Clash Of Personalities

None, not even Sunil Gavaskar or Mohammad Azharuddin or any one else, can dare doubt Bishan Singh Bedi's commitment to cricket. His love for cricket is simply infectious. He respects veteran players, who have been forgotten by this wicked, mercenary world of cricket. He took a flight from Delhi to Chennai to attend A.G. Ramsingh's "Bhog" ceremony and returned the same evening. But that is one part of Bedi. The other side is harsh and his firm style of functioning. He saw Delhi win Ranji Trophy in 1979, he helped Punjab claim national championship in March 1993. But in doing a yeoman's service to Delhi and Punjab, he lost two dear friends— Ram Prakash Mehra and Inderjit Singh Bindra. In both controversies, which became acrimonious, Bedi was much less to blame than Mehra and Bindra.

When Punjab became Ranji champion, every Punjabi folk was proud. It was an occasion to rejoice. Players received "shabash" from all quarters. Presents in cash and kind were awarded to them for the splendid job well done. Bedi was also winner of awards, rewards and appreciation for translating an average side into a champion material. What Bedi instilled into players was to "have faith in themselves". This did wonders and Punjab defeated Maharashtra by 120 runs in the Ranji final at Ludhiana. It was a great day for Punjab.

The `Punjab Cricket Association made some

presentations (also cash) to Bedi. The association's decisions were to stay only on files. But the secretary M.P. Pandov indiscreetly released details to media. Chandigarh's Tribune carried an innocuous news item. There was nothig much to be read in it. But Bedi took an offence to it. He thought there was a breach of contract. He felt that it was a calculated attempt by Pandov to place a blot on his high image. He had a confrontation with Pandov and also with Bindra, who was his great admirer for his tremendous commitment to the game.

In those days, Bedi had a weekly column in 'Tribune'. He launched a frontal attack on Pandov. There were many personal references against Pandov, PCA and Bindra. Situation deteriorated to such an extent that Pandov wrote a rebuttal. The controversy took an unseeming turn. The editor had no option except to put a stop by saying that the controversy had been closed.

In this fall out, Daljit Singh played a role of a "Chanakiya". A smart wicket-keeper of some ability and skill, he knew that his importance in the team as a curator and administrator would be minimal as long as Bedi was at the helm of affairs. He saw to it that the rift between Bedi and PCA bigwigs did not get sorted out.

Bindra indeed was influential. He had a sharp mind; he was a brilliant marketing man though he was a versatile bureaucrat. But, in the ever complicated affairs of the PCA, he had to heavily lean on Pandov, who was articulate and calculative. He was in constant touch with voters. Bindra could not part company with Pandov nor could he give over-riding powers to Bedi.

As a result of this vex situation, the problems between Bedi and Bindra became acute. Pandov even filed a suit against Bedi in the Patiala court. There was now no chance of Bedi returning to PCA. It suited both Pandov and Daljit Singh. In the heart of hearts, Bindra did want to embrace Bedi. But he was driven to such a corner that he could not risk losing his dominance on the PCA.

When Bedi was removed from the office of cricket

manager and chairman of selection committee, he went on record as saying: "It was a let down". Many in Punjab, including Bedi's ardent admirers, felt that he should have displayed "more maturity" in dealing with the situation. But he entered into a "fighting ring" knowing that it was a "losing battle".

The problems in the PCA apart, Bedi was reportedly unhappy with Bindra who, as a president of the Board, was taking decisions which were not much appreciated by the left-hand spinner. Bedi refused to see any virtue in Azharuddin after their fall out in England in 1991. Bedi soon realised that Bindra needed Pandov more than him. The misunderstanding became a rough rift.

# 35

# Ridiculous Action

A mountain was made out of a molehill during Delhi's third Test against Ted Dexter's England team after first two matches at Mumbai and Kanpur had been drawn in 1961-62.

A receptionist in the Imperial Hotel, where the Indian team were staying, lodged a complaint saying that she had been invited for drinks by one of the players. What was wrong in inviting a girl for drinks? What was wrong even dating a grown up girl? But this action was misconstrued by the Board and two players, Kripal Singh and Subhash Gupte, were penalised. It was a shocking decision. It was all the more shocking as an industrialist of the stature of MAC (M.A. Chidambaram) was then the president of the Board.

Life in Delhi, an over-grown village, in 1950s and 1960s, was concealed. There were no entertrainment outlets for players after sun had gone down. After day's rigorous work-out the players wanted to have some kind of relaxation. There was nothing wrong in this expectation. When a player of the calibre of Frank Worrell visited India with Commonwealth teams, he had a girl-companion at every centre. It was then said that a girl had even spent a night with him in CCI where the teams were lodged. No questions were asked from him and no eye-brows were raised! What was the need to destroy cricket career of two players, who had a lot of cricket still left in them?

Kripal and Gupte were room-mates in the Imperial hotel. Kripal reportedly phoned a receptionist inviting her for drinks after she was off from her duties. She should have taken as an honur for being invited by a Test star! But she mistook the call and lodged a complaint instead. The manager took the matter seriously.

When the Test was abandoned owing to rain, Gupte happened to meet Umrigar in his room. Umrigar then broke the news to him saying that complaint against inmates of room 7 had been lodged by a receptionist. He was taken aback as he was, in no way, involved in the incident.

Both Kripal and Gupte were suspended. The committee was formed. It was to meet at Kolkata but the meeting did not come off. It was held at Chennai where the team for the West Indies had to be finalised.

In the meeting, the Board Secretary A.N. Ghosh reprimanded Gupte for his failure to prevent his mate from phoning a receptionist. Gupte's reaction was: "How could I have"?

Gupte was however man enough to defend Kripal saying it was a mere phone call for drinks and thus far and no further.

Following inquiry, which was conducted in a haphazard manner with pre-conceived notions and observations, the verdict went against both Kripal and Gupte. The Board president Chidambaram directed selectors that Gupe should not be picked for the West Indies on disciplinary grounds. Actually, if Kripal had been more truthful than he was, Gupte could have been saved from undergoing needless humiliation.

Disappointed and dejected Gupte decided to marry a girl whom he had met many years ago at San Fernando and emigrated to the West Indies.

Gupte, an outstanding leg-spinner-and-googly bowler, had taken 149 wickets (average 29.55) in 36 Tests when he was done to death by the Board. It was a sad end of a bowler, who had faithfully served the country. To treat a bowler who had taken five or more wickets in an innings on 12 of the 36 Tests was unpardonable. Had he had better fielding side, his tally of wickets would have been much more.

Pataudi, who was making inroads in Indian cricket team felt: "What a shame India should lose two such good players, specially a great bolwer like Gupte, for what was, I was told, a rather trivial incident quite unconnected with cricket".

Quite a few resented against Board's action which, according to them, was very severe for the negligible offence, if it was an offence, at all.

Says Pataudi: "...I suppose, one must learn to be philosophical about these things. After all, one man's disappoitment is another man's opportunity, and pity the selectors, who can influence people but can never win any friends."

# 36

# Joke At VT Station

The four-member selection committee of Contractor (chairman), Ramaswamy, Datta Ray and Amarnath deliberated for more than two hours but could not decide who should be the captain to Pakistan in 1954. The decision was deferred as the appointment of the captain was linked with the appointment of the manager. There were rumours in the Cricket Club of India (CCI) that if X was the manager, Y might not go. Eventually, compromise was struck. Vinoo Mankad, an obvious choice, was made captain and Amarnath was chosen as manager.

There were several notable omissions, including that of Vijay Hazare who, despite his declining form, would have been a great asset to the team in Pakistan, where quite a few matches were played on matting wicket.

Eleven members of the Indian team left on December 23 for Kolkata en route to East Pakistan for the first leg of the Pakistan tour. When Merchant and many other cricket admirers and parents of players reached VT station, they found every one was laughing. The cause for such a big laughter was that the medical examination of the players was being carried out by some doctor in an adjoining compartment. The medical examination was indeed important but it should have been carried out in such a casual manner was cause enough for the laughter. The doctor, it was learnt, did not have apparatus that were necessary to carry out the examination. The examination, an eye-wash, placed Board in a very poor state of condition.There were some who were heard saying that it was not an examination but a huge joke perpetrated by the Board on the players before their departure! Had the doctor declared any one of the 11 players unfit, would the Board have been in a position to arrange a replacement on the spot? Vijay Manjrekar jumped into the train without even casual examination as he joined the party at Dadar. Who examined the remaining players who were already in Kolkata?

Bruised and battered in England in 1959, the Board suddenly woke up from its deep slumber to give some kind of attention to physical fitness of players before Australian team arrived. It was decided to organise a conditioning camp at Khadakvasla (Pune), away from distractions and hustle and bustle of Mumbai or any other metropolitan city. The wicket at Khadakvasla was a beauty, surroundings ideal and atmosphere conducive. The camp was progressing satisfactorily when it was decided that there should be a rigorous and scientific medical examination in the army hospital. All passed the examination except for India's most accomplished and technically soundest batsman, Vijay Manjrekar. He was suffering from diabetes. On the advice of doctors, he was sidelined from the series against Australia in the winter of 1959.

G.S. Ramchand was the new captain with Amarnath holding the reigns of the team. As India defeated Australia at Kanpur, complaint against Board resurfaced with intensity. The players felt—and rightly—that they were treated as second class citizens in their own country. They were provided inferior travel, lodging and board facilities to those provided visitors. In Kanpur, where they won the Test, their plight was pitiable. The organisers, led by Vizzy, did every thing for the Australians but neglected their own players.

For the Board, there were two sets of rules—one for foreigners and another for Indians. In the Ranji Trophy golden Jubilee function at Mumbai Indian officials and other invitees were accorded second class treatment while foreigners were given VIP attention. In the Board's golden Jubilee get-together, mediapersons who seldom covered cricket were invited while journalists, like, R. Sriman (Times of India) were ignored. This was because a section of journalists had revolted against DDCA management. If the DDCA erred, the Board should have intervened to do justice.

# 37

# Captain Today,
# Out Of Team Next Day

With Bishan Bedi dropped on 'disciplinary charges', Pataudi's India lost the first Test to the West Indies at Bangalore in November 1974.

As Pataudi had injured his finger, he was out of commission for the second Test at Delhi. Gavaskar was to take over. But he also could not as he had hurt himself while playing a Ranji match for Mumbai against Maharashtra. Usually, Board did not allow important players to take part in domestic matches when the foreign team was on tour to the country for Tests. No one could throw light as to why was Gavaskar allowed to play a Ranji match?

The second Test at Kotla was scheduled to start on December 11. No one knew who the captain was until evening of December 10. Frantic calls were being made and selectors were being contacted. The selection committee chairman C.D. Gopinath was held up in Chennai and was scheduled to arrive in the capital only on the morning of the match.

In the get-together on the eve of the Test, Ram Prakash Mehra, Vice-President of the Board, congratulated Farokh Engineer in presence of some friend-journalists. Some papers carried the news quoting Mehra as a source that Engineer was the captain.

This was, however, not to be. When Gopinath arrived, he was shocked to know that an announcement for Engineer to lead the side was made. His first reaction was who announced and what authority Mehra had to make such a declaration without consulting him. It was later learnt that Mehra had a talk with the Board President who had suggested him Engineer to lead the side in the absence of chairman Gopinath. Mehra had a point so that players could at least know who the captain was before the pre-Test meeting was held.

Gopinath threw the captaincy responsibility in the lap of Srinivas Venkataraghavan. The players were surprised at the last-minute change of captain. Engineer was visibly embarrassed at the sudden change. Mehra was equally hurt.

Confusion prevailed. India lost the Test again. The south lobby had won the first round. But Gopinath's arbitrary decision without proper concurrence of four other selectors led to needless acrimonies. The team, now trailing 0-2, was more divided than before.

Pataudi returned to captain for the remaining three Tests. He saw India win the next Two Tests at Kolkata and Chennai to make it 2-all. In the final Test, India were outplayed by the West Indies.

As Pataudi returned, Venkat was not only relegated from the post of captaincy, but he was altogether thrown out of the team. In his place, Prasanna was included. In the fourth and the fifth Tests, it was Prasanna who played while Venkat stayed indoors.

Captain in one Test, Venkat was dropped from the squad. The moot point that surfaced was that the only one, who was a certainty in the team, should be entrusted with the responsibilities of the captaincy.

# 38

# Appalling Facilities At Nagpur

The Board of Control for Cricket in India always practised two sets of rules—one for foreign visiting teams and another for the home team. The visiting teams travelled in comfort in special saloons and were lodged in decent hotels, palaces and with affluent families. The home team travelled by second or third class compartments; they were provided shabby accommodation and given pittance of allowance to fend for themselves. This scene continued for decades until India gained independence in 1947.

Then there was a marginal, only marginal, improvement in the attitude towards the home team. But the contrast in providing facilities to foreign teams and the home team was so vast that the Indians always seemed to lack in confidence.

India visited England under Iftikhar Ali Khan Pataudi in 1946 and India undertook a maiden tour to Australia under Amarnath in 1947. Then came the first West Indies team in 1948. The facilities provided to the home team were still much below the required standard for players to perform well.

Then it was time for the Commonwealth teams to be invited to play in the country. Kanpur (Green Park) rose as Test centre as Vizzy wanted to re-establish himself in the arena of Indian cricket. Green Park was a lovely green ground, but the facilities for the teams were appalling as there was not a solitary hotel of any standard in Kanpur. The result: the visiting teams stayed in Kamla Retreat where they were treated royally, while Indian team was neglected. It was shocking to see the accommodation provided to the Indian players. Toilets were dirty; players were given torn and good for nothing blankets in biting cold winter months of December and January. This was not all. But they were provided wretched food. More often than not the players had to solicit invitations to have food with local cricket loving families. In failing, they chose to have their food at some 'dhaba'. The protests lodged by captains, like, Vijay Merchant, went unheeded. During the course of the Test, Vizzy did organise one or two lavish get-togethers but the functions were more for him to gain mileage out of them than to cater to the needs of the home players. It was a pity that Indian players were orphans in their own country.

The things improved. There was improvement further when captains like Mansur Ali Khan Pataudi, Ajit Wadekar and Bishan Singh Bedi came on the scene.

As cricket flourished, new centres sprang up. One of them was Nagpur, where an unofficial Test was played against Sri Lanka in 1974-75. The Indian team was lodged in a dingy MLA hostel which lacked in the minimum facilities for the players. The manager (Bharat Khanna) and Bedi (captain) had been provided rooms, fitted with geyzers. The other players were given rooms which were tiny and dingy with no facilities at all. Their rooms did not have geyzers. The organisers perhaps thought that only manager and captain had to take bath, while others could reach the ground without bath. The arrangements for meals were also shocking.

Upset at the facilities which were not conducive to giving off their best, Bedi chose to have a word with the local organisers of the Vidharba Cricket Association (VCA). When Bedi pointed out to the VCA Secretary, the official had the temerity to say that it was not his concern. When Bedi told him that his boys were the main actors, the secretary said: "This is all that we can provide you and you are free to do whatever you wish to".

The matter did not rest here. The secretary complained to the Board saying that he had been insulted and humiliated by Bedi. A committee comprising the late M. Chidambaram, the late R.P. Mehra, then president of the Board, the late S.K. Wankhede, P.M. Rungta and NKP Salve was formed to inquire into the matter. The late Ghulam Ahmed (secretary) was the convener of the meeting. The meeting turned into a heated debate with Bedi standing by his convictions while members held the view that the controversy could have been avoided. Bedi's viewpoint was that nothing was more important than the interest of the country and, in view of it, the minimum facilities were essential for players to perform well on the field. Bedi reportedly asked one member: "Can a player feel fresh and relaxed if he has reached the ground without a bath?" The member agreed but he was quick to say: "It could have been handled more judiciously!"

Bharat Khanna (not alive) was not questioned but he reportedly told some committee members that they should have held the inquiry committee meeting in the MLA hostel instead of at the Mumbai's Oberoi hotel and then they would have got a true picture as to who was right— Bedi or the VCA Secretary.

This controversy took place in 1974. But as late as 1987, Nagpur lacked in facilities. Says Pakistan's leading writer, Omar Kureishi: "from the luxury of 5-star hotels in Kolkata and Bangalore, it was the no-star misery of lodgings in Nagpur".

On November 26, 1995 in a match between India and New Zealand one of the over-crowded stands at the VCA stadium caved in. Several people were killed and many hurt. The Board President I.S. Bindra sanctioned Rs. 50,000 to the family of each of the person who died owing to "the unfortunate accident". The New Zealand team also contributed a sizeable amount for the victims' families. The VCA, with shabby record, should have been barred from staging any international match. But who could bar VCA, which had a "glittering vote"? The vote was much more important than value of human lives. The VCA officials, always enjoyed "cover" of Salve.

There are several other centres, which lack in befitting facilities even now. In the two Test series between India and Pakistan (1999), Wasim Akram went on record as saying that it was a pity that his team could not have nets at Kotla. "How can I finalise my team without assessing the texture of the Kotla?" asked Wasim Akram. Imagine, Delhi is one of the oldest centres.

# 39

# Strange Doings Of BCA

When a batsman of the calibre of Vijay Merchant announced his retirement from first class cricket and he stuck to his word, the then Sports and Pastime (now Sportstar) (The Hindu publication) and Indian Cricket paid glowing tributes to a super star and super man in 1953-54. N.S. Ramaswami, doyen of Indian cricket, was the author of the articles published in two publications.

Shocking as it was, two august bodies—the Board of Control for Cricket in India and Mumbai Cricket Association—did not have even courtesy to make a passing reference on the retirement of Merchant who, according to critics worldwide, was unquestionably the most 'coveted an cultured' batsman.

Merchant, who played with 'straight bat' and also spoke 'straight', might have reservations about the doings of the Board. But it did not mean that the Board officials should fail to place on record his contribution and services to the cause of cricket and cricket team for more than 20 years. Merchant was more amused than shocked at the dubious doings of the Board officials. Merchant went on record as saying: "While on the one hand they think of benefit matches for cricketers whose services have not been outstanding, they do not extend the courtesy of even recording on paper the services of another contemporary sportsman".

If the BCCI's attitude was deplorable, the BCA officials should have hung their heads in shame for showing even apathy to India's greatest opening batsman. Not only the BCA did not display usual courtesy, but it even turned down the proposal of appreciating Merchant's services in some tangible form.

Vijay was a wealthy merchant. He expected nothing from the BCA for which he played dedicately for years and brought laurels to Mumbai and himself. What he expected was support, encouragement and sincere appreciation of his efforts. When the proposal for honouring or staging the benefit match for Merchant was made, some membrs argued that he was not a professional and hence there was no need for holding any such function. Merchant writes: "May I ask the BCA if Amarnath and Mushtaq Ali are professionals or amateurs and whether BCA opposed giving benefit matches to these two fine cricketers?"

It is believed that the president of the BCA told his members that the best way to appreciate an amateur's efforts on the retirement was to get up and give him a hand when he went out to play his last innings in first class cricket. Did not it display how ill-formed the president and his members in the committee were? Was not this observation silly and absurd?

Asked Merchant: "What happens if that player plays his last match outside the home town or for reasons beyond his control announces his retirement after he has played his last match?"

Adds Merchant: "I suppose the officials just get up, cheer in the committee room and show their appreciation of the amateur's efforts in this way!"

The BCA officialdom was reportedly against Merchant as he had allegedly criticised the functioning of the association while distributing prizes of the Purshottam Hindu Shield Tournament in 1952, a year before he retired. The chief guest at the function then was AFS (Bobby) Talyarkhan who, in fact, made some strong and constructive comments about the functioning of the association.

Merchant never made any remarks or observations about the BCA and it was sad that the officialdom should have accused him of comments that he never made. What surprised Merchant was that at least four BCA representatives were present at the function and yet president was briefed wrongly.

Surprising as it may seem, the only souvenir that Merchant got on his retirement was a fountain pen from the officials of the Police Invitation Shield Tournament.

L.P. Jai captained Mumbai from 1934 to 1936. Then the mantle of leading the side fell on Merchant. He captained successfully from 1939 to 1946. K.C. Ibrahim took over from Merchant. He captained for two years. Then the honour went to Dattu Padhkar, Madhav Mantri, Rusi Modi and Sohoni.

Mantri in 1951-52 was not only a successful captain but he kept wickets admirably and compiled runs meticulously. His performance saw him get into the Indian team for the England tour.

In 1953, Mantri was removed from captaincy. His crime was that he did not include Ramesh Divecha in the team. Some selectors reportedly made it clear that they would teach Mantri a lesson for excluding Divecha from the team.

Out went Mantri and Modi was made the captain. But he insisted on Mantri's inclusion in the side. The selectors did not appreciate it. On the plea of Mumbai losing to Maharashtra in the first round, Mantri was axed from the captaincy. Mumbai, in fact, had a very depleted side as five leading stars had been doing duty for India in the West Indies. In addition, the match was played on matting wicket at Sholapur.

When Sohoni was appointed captain, he made it clear that he would accept the responsibility provided Mantri was in the side. Sohoni also saw to it that Mantri was his deputy.

L.P. Jai was one of the selectors. But he could do little as other three selectors--M.S. Naik, R.J. Gharat and J.S.

Elavia combined together to over-rule him on many issues. There were many other better known players, like, Homi Contractor, Homi Vajifder, R.S. Godambe, available. But the BCA chose to appoint these persons to function in the selection committee. What was surprising was that Merchant was never chosen to be one of the selectors. The plea of the BCA was that Merchant did not make himself available as a selector. When Merchant did agree to be a selector, his candidature was thrown out in preference to those of Gharat, Naik and Elavia.

The year 1954 was BCA's silver jubilee year. Thanks to D.P. Thanawalla's untiring efforts, Pakistan Services and Bhawalpur Association Combined played two matches in Mumbai. Subhash Gupte claimed all 10 wickets in one innings. It was a great bowling feat. He should have been befittingly honoured. But the BCA did not even present him the ball with which he claimed all 10 wickets in an innings in one of the matches. Actually, the ball should have been mounted and presented to him at some suitably arranged function.

# 40

# A Surprising Declaration

A semi-politician leader was on fast unto death at Amritsar many years ago. As days trickled by, curiosity and anxiety increased. Many were surprised that the leader could be on fast even after 40-50 days.

A young and enthusiastic journalist thought it was a damn good copy. He rushed to Amritsar. His inquiries revealed that the leader was on fast.

Inquiries over, the journalist chose to have a look at the beauty and grandeur of the temple. The volunteers miscalculated. They thought that the journalist had left the temple. They served the leader with temple's "Parsad".

As the journalist was in the process of leaving, he saw from a distance that the leader was eating something. He took photos. Volunteers noticed it. He was manhandled and his camera was broken.

Returning without any concrete evidence, the journalist wrote: "Those who claim that the leader was eating were mistaken. He was not eating anyting". This gave rise to the controversy and his objective was fully achieved.

Reverting to cricket, in an unprecedented move, Sunil Gavaskar declared one run behind England's total in the sixth and the final Test against England at Kanpur on February 4, 1982. What was his philosophy to declare the innings closed when there was no chance of a decision and he had already won the series for India 1-0?

The details: England, batting first, declared at 378 for

nine wickets. Yashpal Sharma (55) and Madan Lal (1) were at the crease when Gavaskar declared 377 for seven wickets with three overs of the 20 mandatory overs remaining.

Mind you, the score-card officially stated that Gavaskar had declared the innings and the Test had not been closed by the umpires D.N. Dotiwala and M.V. Gothoskar. Would heavens have fallen if Gavaskar had declared after securing one run lead? Gavaskar's uncalled for declaration gave rise to many questions which, to date, remain unanswered.

Shrewd and calculative as Gavaskar has been, he has an answer or an explanation or a theory for every action that he takes. But it is surprising that he has not explained as to why did he declare a run behind England's total?

Could it be that Gavaskar declared because there was a heavy quantum of betting as to which side would take first innings lead? It might have sounded far-fetched in the beginning of 1982 but looking at the existing scenario anything can be possible.

The incident is enveloped with "possibility and improbability". An amusing story that runs parallel to the Test match incident is: A youngman was being taken for gallows. He was unusually happy; he was singing and dancing. He refused answering when a policeman asked him for his happiness. Perplexed at youngman's odd behaviour, a policeman rushed to the King. When the King, who came to see for himself, asked him for his happiness, the youngman reluctantly answered: "My horoscope says that I will be done to death by some condemned man". The King had no option except to grant him liberty.

In the toss imbroglised Test (Asif was accused of "rigging" the toss), Asif declared Pakistan's first innings closed at 272 for four in reply to India's 333 in the December-January) Sixth Test at Kolkata in 1979-80. Why did Asif Iqbal declare? He did not assign reasons for his declaration. Maybe, Gavaskar later thought there was no need to explain for his declaration!

# 41

# Unpardonable Behaviour

It was a run fiesta in the 1986-87 Duleep Trophy in which, except for Kapil Dev and Dilip Vengsarkar (because of injuries), all the Indian big guns were on view. While it was laudable to see stars in action, the incidents that unfolded in the South-West final at Wankhede Stadium (Mumbai) caused a lot of dismay and anguish. It was all the more disturbing because super stars were involved.

Gavaskar, batting at number five, could score seven in West's huge total of 516. Anshuman Gaekwad, Rajput and Shastri scored centuries. Then rude shocks followed as West resorted to tactics which proved conclusively that they were very poor and graceless losers.

South's opener, Srikkanth and Saldanha got entrenched and plundered 179 runs for the first wicket on the third day duplicating the Gaekward-Rajput effort. Both Srikkanth and Saldanha recorded centuries.

Now incidents occurred. They were unworthy of players of the likes of Gavaskar and Shastri. Srikkanth was hurt on the previous day. But he chose to stay on the field. When he came to bat again on the third day, he was seen limping owing to pain in his leg. Gavaskar then made attempts to aggravate his injury. He kept egging on his colleagues to take a shy at Srikkanth's end at the slightest of pretexts. This was a calculated gamesmanship that one sharp turn too many times might put the batsman out of action. The throw often was so directed that it could have hit the batsman who, despite an injury, was able to stay away from difficulties. Srikkanth, exuberent and extrovert, did tell Gavaskar that it was "not cricket".

This was bad enough. Worse followed when Azharuddin and Sadanand Vishwanath got settled down for the fifth wicket stand. They threatened to take the South total past 400 on the third day itself.

Azharuddin was batting superbly when Gavaskar appealed for a catch in the slips. The appeal was totally unworthy of the player of the calibre of Gavaskar as the ball had clearly rebounded off the ground. The fielders joined Gavaskar in chorus and gheroed the umpire. Azharuddin and Vishwanath were surprised at the attitude and behaviour of the West fielders.

As if these actions were not unworthy of the West fielder, Gavaskar walked up to Vishwanath, at non-striker end, and needlessly gave him a dressing down. Once a worshippr of Gavaskar, the non-striker was in tears as to why was he being verbally thrashed!. Gavaskar subesquently went on record as saying that he merely told Vishwanath that he had a right to appeal.

Both batsmen got rattled up and lost thier wickets. But Bharat Arun and W.V. Raman, both in the team for their bowling, put on a record seventh wicket stand of 221 and carried their team's total past 600. As if to rub salt in to the wounds, the previous record of 192 for the seventh wicket had been established by Gavaskar and Rajendra Jadeja in 1978-79.

The Duleep Trophy was a prestigious, official championship conducted by the Board. The officials should have swung into action and at least cautioned Gavaskar. If England authorities could take action against John Snow for running into the path of Gavaskar, why could not the Board take action against him? Is he greater than the game?

While writing about the 1986-87 Duleep Trophy, a fellow journalist says: ".....Gavaskar, who would like to give the impression that he can do no wrong, resorted to the type of gamesmanship and pressure tactics on umpires which have become the cause of concern for cricket administrators the world over".

Pataudi, in an article in Sunday entitled "The Decline of Indian Cricket", said: ".....Gavaskar was the greatest, and while no one doubted this, it is plain that only some Mumbai players paid him sycophantic homage. Perhaps the others were jealous but no matter how hard he tried, many cricketers from elsewhere were unable to give them their full trust. They felt that Gavaskar stood for Gavaskar though he had often clashed with the authorities for the benefit of the team".

# 42

# Stoop To Conquer

The 1948 final Test against West Indies at Mumbai—the second at Brabourne Stadium—Amarnath's Indian team was in elements. The visitors were contained for a modest total of 286 but India in reply was restricted to 193. Undaunted, the Indian bowlers again struck form dismissing West Indies for only 267. This was the first time when the visitors had been dismissed twice in the match. India were left with 361 to win in 395 minutes.

On paper, it looked difficult to make such a huge total in the fourth innings. But it was not beyond Indians who, if in proper frame of mind, could achieve any target. The wicket had surprisingly improved despite four days' play. There was little wear and tear on the pitch, so firm it stayed.

The openers, Mushtaq Ali and Ibrahim, were dismissed early. But Amarnath promoted himself in batting order. He went on to play a brief innings of 39. It exposed West Indies bowling might. Modi and Hazare were together on 90 for three at close of play on the fourth day. In fact, it could have been said that India were four down since Probir Sen was injured and Amarnath had kept wickets.

India had to make 271 with only seven wickets standing on the final day. The task of getting them was more difficult than it was on the previous day. But Modi and Hazare remained unbeaten at lunch after adding 85 runs. Now the target was 186 to get in two sessions.

The West Indies panicked. They resorted to negative tactics packing leg side with six fielders. There were no field restrictions in those days. In trying to force the pace Modi left. Mankad (14) also left soon. But Hazare duly completed his century. In Dattu Phadkar, he found a valiant partner.

Hazare moved on to 122 when he was hit by Prior Jone's ball. He now lost his rhythm and was bowled by Jones soon after. India now needed 72 runs with four wickets in hand and 90 minutes play left.

Adhikari belied expectations, while Shute Banerjee also departed. Only 40 runs remained for win with two wickets, including that of injured Sen, remaining. In came Ghulam Ahmed, a tall and lanky man with little reputation for his batting ability. But he seemed in resolute frame of mind. He stayed put while Phadkar did the bulk of scoring.

The stadium, packed with throng of spectators, was agog with an excitement. Fifteen minutes remained and 21 runs stood between India and victory with Phadkar and Ghulam in commad. The West Indies were now in tatters. Goddard asked for adjournment for drinks. They took longer time for their drinks than it should have been the case. The umpires A.R. Joshi and B.J. Mohini should have asserted as time wasting tactics at this juncture were highly improper. As if this violation of "spirit" was not enough, Walcott, the wicket-keeper, at least once ran to the boundary line and returned slowly to hand over the ball to the bowler. It was highly unethical but the Indian umpires stayed mute.

Only 11 runs remained for victory. Two overs still remained to be bowled. It was now possible to gain the cherished victory. Jones came on to bowl the penultimate over of the match. No stroke could be made on the first ball as it was well outside the leg stump. Phadkar hit the next short-pitched ball for a four through covers. The third ball yielded a single and another single could have been taken but both batsmen decided against it. The fifth ball was a bouncer, which was much beyond the reach of the batsman.

One ball and another over remained with India needing only six runs to win the Test. The umpire Joshi now seemed more nervous than excited. He erred in counting the balls and declared over when one ball still remained. He should have consulted scorers before declaring the over. There was more than a minute to go when Joshi nervously removed the bails and signalled that the time was up for the Test to end.

Incompetent umpiring and negative tactics deprived India of their victory. As Goddard, Walcott and their colleagues were returning, they were jeered and booed for what spectators thought was highly unfair. Gomes, who was the "brain" behind these negative tactics, did not think that he had done anything unsporting. "Test match is a serious business and I cannot hand it over on platter to my rivals to display my sporting spirit", said Gomes. Had Frank Worrell or George Headley or Learrie Constantine been there, they certainly would not have resorted to tactics that Gomes and Goddard resorted.

All stadia for all five Test matches were over-flowing with spectators. A lot of money was collected. But most of the centres showed losses. This was a practice then. Organisers made hay while sun shone. Then the terms with visiting teams were that they would be given a part of profit, if there was any. As losses were shown in most of the matches, the visitors hardly got any money out of India. The West Indies management was extremely unhappy with the Board.

Following these sordid deeds, the visiting teams had to insist on guarantee money and other perks and facilities. Much later, reciprocal terms were agreed to regardless of attendances of spectators.

With the passage of time, the facilities improved. Visiting teams declined to undertake long journeys by trains. They were provided air passages. They were also provided decent hotels wherever they played. While they received royal treatment, the Indian players were still treated like beggars in their own country. They had to travel by trains and made to stay in hotels which lacked in minimum facilities. What was most deplorable was that while players, main actors, were treated shabbily, the non-entity officials, who were essentially good for nothing, travelled in comfort and lived in style.

# 43

# Captaincy—A Musical Chair

Vizzy was not the president in 1958-59, but he was still a very powerful wheel in the corridors of the Board. He had befriended Amarnath and thereby he enlarged scope for intrigue. Amarnath was now a chairman of the selection committee. He was a law unto himself. He was keen that his friend Ghulam Ahmed should lead the side against West Indies in India and captain India on the tour to England in the summer of 1959. He was also planning that he could be the manager of the team to England.

Ghulam Ahmed could not attend the camp that was in progress for selecting probables. The selection of the captain was deferred until the match against Board Presidents XI against the West Indians at Ahmedabad. Ghulam Ahmed was injured while fielding. He withdrew from the match. But he was chosen captain of the team. Two selectors, L.P. Jai and Ramaswami voted against Ghulam saying that he was a poor fielder in addition to being over the hill. Amarnath exercised his casting vote to see Ghulam installed at the coveted position.

Like Vizzy, who never did his commentary for any match in Mumbai, Ghulam Ahmed also did not like to play there. He nurtured a feeling that the Mumbai officials as also spectators were hostile to him. He had a reason to feel so as he had often been mal-treated there. He withdrew from the first Test at Mumbai. Ghorpade also opted out.

In the two vacancies, Mumbai-based selector asked two reserves, Hardikar and Nadkarni, to report for the Test. When Amarnath arrived in Mumbai, he had a heated discussion with Jai. He told Jai that he had no business whatsoever to induct two reserves without obtaining permission from the chairman. In fact, Amarnath asked Jai as to who the chairman was! Jai felt insulted and chose to resign from the selection committee.

Umrigar captained the team in the first Test. The match ended in a draw. Ghulam Ahmed returned to lead India at Kanpur, where the Test was played on jute matting. It was a mystery as to why was the match played on jute matting when Green Park had a lovely turf strip. Had the match been played on turf wicket, India might have won the Test instead of losing it. Gupte was unplayable. He had a rich haul of nine wickets for 102. He should have taken all wickets but one wicket went to Ranjane. In fact, had Gibbs not been dropped by wicket-keeper Tamhane, Gupte would have had all ten—perfect 10. The visitors were dismissed for 222 and so were Indians on this identical total in their first innings. If there was a recovery for the West Indies, it was a collapse for India who, at one stage, were 182 for two wickets.

The West Indies openers, Holt and Hunte, were back with zero on board. Then Sobers had a lucky existence at the wicket. Fielders dropped catches while umpires negatived leg before appeals. Sobers, it was said, was mighty pleased at the generosity of the Indian umpires. The visitors went on to reach 443 for seven wickets declared. Sobers got 198 before he was run out. India made a promising start in chase of 443 runs. Then slumped and lost the Test by 203 runs.

India's overall doings had caused displeasure to ill-informed Kanpur spectators who resorted to hooting the players. The authorities feared trouble and the team members were provided police escort for hotel from stadium.

It was a massacre of innocents at Kolkata where

Indians were mauled beyond recognition. Ghulam Ahmed was so upset at these defeats and, with his own performance, that he decided to lay down his boots. The more Amarnath tried to persuade him to continue, the less he was willing to continue.

Now the vex problem surfaced as to who should be the new captain. Amarnath was inclined for Jasu Patel, while Ramaswami's horse was Kripal Singh. As the search was on, Vijay Manjrekar pulled out of the fourth Chennai Test.

Since Umrigar had led the team in the first Test, he was asked to undertake the responsibility again. Hardikar was to replace Manjrekar. But he got the information late and could not get onto the last flight from Mumbai to Chennai. The real drama now unfolded. Amarnath pressed for Jasu Patel. Umrigar's stand was a batsman should replace a batsman and not a bowler. Difference of opinion between selectors and Umrigar became so intense that Umrigar said that he would not captain the side if Jasu Patel was thrust upon him. Rattibhai Patel, president of the Board, was pressing for Jasu.

Amidst this uncertain situation, Umrigar resigned from captaincy on the eve of the match. He was asked to withdraw his resignation but he said that he had enough of it and he would not captain. Only about half-an-hour was left for the Test to commence when Vinoo Mankad was prevailed upon to lead the side. But Mankad had his say and young A.K. Sengupta played the Test and not Jasu Patel.

The West Indies players and officials were having a mighty laugh at the goings-on in the Indian camp. Eleven years into independence, India still remained as divided a house as it was in 1932 and in 1936.

India, broken in spirit, could offer no resistance to the West Indians and lost the Test by 295 runs.

As if three captains—Umrigar, Ghulam Ahmed and Vinoo Mankad in four Tests—were not enough, Amarnath and his august men chose Ramchand to lead the side in the fifth Test at Delhi. But somehow the decision could not be conveyed to Ramchand who had already left for Mumbai by train. It showed how ineffective was the functioning of the Board.

As the time passed by, the selectors had a change of mind. They chose Hemu Adhikari to lead the team at Delhi. This was laughable enough. But what caused great amusement was that Ramchand was not even chosen for the final Test. A captain today was sidelined from the team altogether. This kind of thing could happen only in this country!

# 44

# No Kit, No Play

Planning and programming have never been part of the system of Indian officials. They procrastinate until the last minute hoping against hope that providence will come to their rescue. Regardless of number of years they stay in an important office and regardless of number of set-backs and humiliation they suffer, their style of functioning remains the same.

In the chequered existence of 68 years in international cricket, India has had many firsts, including some dubious firsts. These are, however, moments to cherish. October 3, 1984 will go down in the annals of Indian cricket as one-day international match between India and Australia could not start on time for non-arrival of kit. Just as 15,000 strong spectators were getting restive for their wait, rain came down. This was a saving grace otherwise there might have been some casualties, including some fatal. Who says that God does not live in India!

Steel city (Jamshedpur) was, devoid of facilities for wide-bodied aircraft to land and take-off. Only tiny aircraft like, Fokker Friendship, could be pressed into service to operate. It was not big enough to accommodate baggage and kit of both teams. The organisers should have known this and should have made arrangements accordingly. But they did not. The result: total chaos.

The rival teams were scheduled to arrive at Jamshedpur

via Kolkata from Chennai. When the team landed at Kolkata's Dum Dum Airport, there was no one who had clear instructions as to how the baggage of the teams had to be transported to Jamshedpur. The rival teams checked in hotels, but the baggage remained unattended to. Some one from among Board officials eventually woke up from his slumber and organised a van to carry the baggage to Jamshedpur. It was about 4 a.m. and the time was not enough for the baggage to reach on time in view of erratic and heavy traffic en-route. Lo and behold! The interruptions surfaced and the baggage was delayed at border for hours.

The enthusiastic crowd was at the stadium well before the start of the match. The umpires walked in and had all formalities completed. The umpires then announced that the match could not start on the scheduled time because of "damp patches" on the wicket. This was understandable.

The umpires now came to know the exact situation. The start of the match was not possible because players, at least Australians, were without their kit. The baggage sent by the vehicle had got so far as the Bihar border which was jampacked with vehicles. The movement of cars, and buses was possible at snail's pace. There was no earthly chance of the baggage reaching on time for the match to begin on the scheduled time.

The visitors were in T-shirts and shorts. They were undergoing limbering up exercises. The home team did the same.

Amidst this confusion, there was an announcement that it would not be possible to play an international one-day match because of inordinate delay in retrieving the baggage. In view of it, the teams would be engaged in playing a festival match.

This announcement was enough for spectators to throw missiles on the ground. The organisers panicked. They now announced that it would be curtailed to a 24 overs a side international match. This pacified the spectators who had paid for the serious type of the match instead of a festival engagement.

Eventually the kit arrived and rival teams changed for the match.

The Indians were put in and Australian bowlers had bowled merely 5.1 overs when rain came down. It was more a downpour than rain. The match had to be halted and eventually it was abandoned because of rain. Rain was the saving grace for the organisers.

# 45

# Sin At Eden (1969-70)

Kolkata and Kolkatans remained unchanged even after Justice Sen's strictures. There was yet another riot and defeat after India had drawn second Test at Kanpur and had won third at Delhi by seven wickets against Lawry's Australia in 1969-70.

It was the penultimate day of the five-day Test. More than 15,000 people had been standing quietly all night to buy tickets for certain enclosures—most of them unreserved. A word from some one that there were no more seats available travelled like a wild fire. The queue was broken. From jostling it became free for all. Some people fell down and they were run over. Six of them died while about 100 were injured. Police again acted rough and tough. It was a sad state of affairs prevailing in Kolkata where riot could take place any moment and precious lives could be lost without any one bating an eyelid. It was yet again injudicious handling of the authorities that led to this unseemly trouble.

Trouble also erupted at Eden Garden. The cause for trouble was akin to one in 1967. The authorities had paid little heed to man-management. The match was held up because of unruly section of spectators who had spilled on to ground. Lawry and his men stood in the centre as if to guard the square. Utter confusion prevailed.

Amidst this confusion, a photographer walked in. He

wanted to capture Lawry and his men huddling together on the square. The photographer was merely doing his duty. Lawry should not have resented it. Lawry pushed him and he fell down. Lawry stooped to pick up his bat while many in galleries thought that the Australian skipper had attempted to hit the photographer with his bat. Photographer claimed that he had been hit. The incident should not have taken place, had Lawry stayed quiet at the wicket. There were different versions. Lawry said something and Stackpole another. Ray Robinson, one of the celebrated writers, in The Sun, Melbourne-said: "Bill said in trying to protect the wicket, he pushed the photographer with his open hand...."

Lawry wanted to act tough as did Douglas Jardine decades ago. Then the situation was different. People were meak and willing to undergo humiliations in silence. It was not the same situation now. Kolkatans always boistrous have invariably fought against any injustice.

This was not the first time a foreign captain or a player had acted boorishly. What would have happened if the photographer had retaliated and hit him back? Who would have been insulted—Lawry or photographer? If the fight between the two had ensued, the spectators would have dashed on the ground. They might have manhandled Lawry and his men. It would have been a very sad affair. Suffice it to say that all the goodwill generated by previous Australian teams had been nullified by Lawry.

Lawry hit winning runs, the spectators threw stones on the ground. It was difficult to visualise whether agitated spectators were showing their displeasure against Lawry's robust tactics or they were protesting against Pataudi (his indiscreet shot) and his team's dismal batting. When Pataudi had left the field, there were cries of "shame, shame". A night earlier, some unruly people had attacked the Indian players' hotel and had broken a few items of furniture. That was against India's collapse.

The incident, ugly as it was, made it clear that Kolkata was unwilling to accept India's defeat. This was a greater shame than Lawry's undiplomatic behaviour and Pataudi's rash shot.

Lawry, a strange man with lean and hungry looks, caused a lot of problems to himself and his team for no reason. He refused to laugh or smile at himself. As if what he did on the tour was not enough, he tried to give dramatic account of the tour incidents. The Indian Board was compelled to act. It wrote to Australian Board emphasisng that most of Lawry's observations were exaggerated, baseless and deserved condemnation. The Australian Board's reply was, in a way, diplomatic defending its captain as also agreeing with Indian Board's accusations.

"Not just for openers" was the book written by Stackpole in 1974 after his retirement. Here is a random sample of his outpourings:

"We noticed servants cleaning the dishes in dirt, not water. They sprinkled dirt on the dishes and then wiped it.

"The drive from the airport was about 30 miles in a truck that I am sure had square wheels. There were that many bumps. One of our constant trials was the long drives from the airports in clapped out vehicles.

"The train stopped at every station. We disembarked sleepless into the cold dawn, feeling as though someone had thrown sand into our eyes. The combination of poor accommodation, unpleasant travelling and unsuitable, unclear food was turning us into zombies".

The part of what Stackpole says may be true. But most white-skinned are "Bs". "B" is also for bluffers.

# 46

# Gavaskar Stoops

Sunil Gavaskar showed that he could stoop to any level if he thought that the things were not going in accordance to his wishes. Coming low down in order he batted left-handed in the second innings for Mumbai against Karnataka in the Ranji Trophy semi-final in 1981-82. Had similar kind of antics been indulged in by any other batsman, he would have summarily been mauled by the authorities. Gavaskar proved that when he was annoyed for whatever reason, he would take calculated measures to annoy any one regardless of consequences.

In reply to Mumbai's modest total of 271, Karnataka were 137 for four when Gundappa Vishwanath was declared caught at short fine-leg by Dilip Vengsarkar off Ashok Mankad. Vishwanath, of all persons, looked totally baffled. He stood disappointed for awhile with his hands on his hips before returning to the pavilion. Rajen Mehra was the umpire who upheld this appeal.

When Carlton Saldanha was walking in to replace Vishwanath, chairs were already being hurled from certain sections of the ground. Spectators dashed on the ground and angrily argued with him. Gavaskar was upset. The spectators, infuriated, manhandled J.D. Ghosh first before pouncing on Mehra. Policemen were present but shockingly they did not intervene. Sight screen on the BEML end was set on fire.

Karnataka rallied round to reach 470. The match was as good as lost for Mumbai as they had conceded 199-run lead. Gavaskar was off the field for most of the time when Karnataka were batting. He did not open at his usual number. But he came at number eight. He played 60 deliveries. He took guard left-handed and batted as such.

# 47

# Gavaskar's Painstaking Batting

Almost throughout the country, local league matches, nursery for youngsters, were of one-day duration. They were played on time divided basis. Invariably, one team batted for much more overs than the others. This was because one team, in the allotted time, bowled more overs than the other. In reality, it was not a fair competition but surprisingly it did not strike to any player or official to switch over from time-divided basis to overs pattern.

Regardless of the league system in Mumbai, Chennai, Kolkata and other centres, the fact of the matter was that the players had not applied their mind to one-day competition, which was born out of necessity in England where spectators were unwilling to watch three or five-day matches.

In dilemma, the Prudence World Cup was planned in England in 1975. In the inaugural competition, the Indians had a miserable experience. Their physical level was so pathetic that they were slovenly in fielding and running between the wicket. They could neither score runs through placements nor could they restrict opposition with their intelligent bowling. All in all, they seemed a bunch of novices in England.

England at Lord's scored 334 for four wickets in the allotted 60 overs. Gavaskar stayed at the wicket (he had three chances) for 60 overs reaching merely 36. He was unbeaten. His was mainly instrumental for the team reaching merely 132 for three wickets. It was a pathetic display of batsmanship. The more he was booed by a section of spectators for his dogged batsmanship, the more resolute Gavaskar became to stay put there.

Says Gavaskar: "As I waited for the bowler to run up and bowl, my mind used to be made up to have a shy at the ball, but as soon as the ball was delivered, my feet would move to a position for a defensive shot". He adds: "The awful noise made by the crowd did not help my thinking, but only confused me as hell. Right from the start, we knew that the chase was out of the question. Even my attempt to take a single and give the strike to the other batsman failed".

Gavaskar further said that he was never a batsman who could force the pace. He also said that England attack was too professional to have a wild slog.

The manager G.S. Ramchand, former India captain, censored him. In his report to the Board, Ramchand was critical of Gavaskar's style of batsmanship. Gavaskar was summoned to explain.

Ramchand's report, among other things, said that Gavaskar persisted in playing slowly that had a demoralising effect on other players. Board told Gavaskar that his explanation was not acceptable. But proceedings were dropped at the same time.

On instant cricket, Gavaskar reportedly had said: "It neither enthuses me nor embarrasses me".

# 48

# Rungtas "Dynasty" Continues

Purshottam Rungta, dark, tall, hefty and pan-chewing Marwari from Rajasthan, has been associated with the Board of Control for Cricket for about half century in one capacity or the other. He has been a treasurer; he has been a president and he has held various important positions. He is perhaps the only person-non-cricketing on top of it—who has "talked more eloquently" in the Board than performances of Sunil Gavaskar, Kapil Dev and Bishan Singh Bedi put together. While there are rules stipulated for change of selectors and other office-bearers, there seems to be no rule, which can prevent him from holding this or that office or staying as a chairman or a member of one or the other committee. It may not be incorrect to say that he is the "controller" of the Board.

When Purshottam was actively involved with the Board, his brother Kishan, a Ranji and Duleep Trophy player, rose from a member of the selection committee to the chairman of the committee. When grip of Purshottam and Kishan relaxed recently, in came Kishore, son of Purshottam, as treasurer of the Board. Who says dynasty in the Board does not exist?

Because of Rungtas' unprecedented control in the affairs of the Board, they have been virtual rulers of Rajasthan cricket, which continues to be in an awful mess. Even when most of the players, like, Hanumant Singh,

Kailash Gattani, Parthasarthy Sharma (all settled in Mumbai) combined to shake the might of the Rungtas in Rajasthan, they could not succeed because of vested interests obtaining in the Board.

All this might not be the cause for complaint or discontentment if the Rungta clan had contributed something concrete for the promotion of cricket in Rajasthan. Jaipur, a pink city of Rajasthan, has held Tests and one-day international matches. A lot of money has been earned through these matches. After all when other centres can make money through gate collections and sponsors, so can Rajasthan. Yet Rajasthan does not have its own stadium. Not only this. But it does not have its own ground and office where Ranji and other players can congregate. As someone from Rajasthan said that Rajasthan players did not even have the facility of a "toilet" and if they had to use it they were obliged to rush to MANN industries.!

When the India-Pakistan Test in 1986-87 was staged from February 21, Jaipur became the 51st centre and Sawai Mansingh Stadium 61 ground used for the purpose. (Sawai Mansingh is incidentally Government stadium, which is a kind of multi-purpose venue).

The wicket was rated as a "dead, clay monster". The stadium provided little facilities to players and spectators (not many) who had to rough it out in ill-equipped stands. Had not President of Pakistan, Gen Zia-ul-Haq chosen Jaipur as centre to meet rival teams, the arrangements would have been far worse than they actually were.

While Test looked drawn from the moment rival captains went out for the toss, because of dead nature of the wicket, the city was lashed with a high velocity of thunderstorm midway through the second day. The thunderstorm blew off the make-shift covers from the wicket and rendered the entire square puddled with water and mud. The Doordarshan box was blown away and hoardings lay scattered all over the ground.

Already inexperienced to handle the situation under

such abnormal circumstances, the ground-staff did not have implements to dry the square so that the match could resume after day's rest. The more they employed "improvised" methods, the less they succeeded in drying the square. In an anxiety to render it playable, some one suggested them to sprinkle saw-dust on the wicket. This naturally changed the texture of the wicket.

When Imran Khan came to the ground, he found the wicket had been "tampered" with and lodged an official complaint with the Board saying that laws forbade use of "external material" on the wicket.

Another controversy raged furiously. The umpires, V.K. Ramaswamy and P.D. Reporter, undertook three inspections before ruling out at 2. p.m. that no play could be possible on the day. With day's play forfeited in the "deserted" Rajasthan, manned by the Rungtas, there was nothing to enthuse over in the match. What however knowledgeable players and officials were talking about was that day's play would not have been lost had there been proper covers. Regardless of complaints and protests by players and negative publicity by media, the Rungtas thick-skinned, could not care less.

When there was a vertical split in the Board following rift between Bindra and Dalmiya, an attempt was made to establish a Trust in August 1997. The Board (special general meeting) agenda, among other items, said: "To consider and if thought fit to pass with or without modification, the proposed rules for creation of "Trust" in terms of rule 19 read with Clause 2 (h) of the Memorandum and incorporation to the rules and regulations of the Board".

The senior-most member of the trustees was to be chairman of the Trust. The senior-most living member of the Board was "PMR". He was the 15th President of the Board. The previous 14 were: R.E Grant-Goven, Sikandar Hyat Khan, The Nawab of Bhopal, The Jamsahib of Nawabnagar, Dr. P. Subbaroyan, A.S. deMello, J.C. Mukherjea, Vizzy, R.K. Patil, M.A. Chidambaram, S.S. Majithia, Fatehsingh Rao Gaekward, Irani and A.N. Ghosh.

# 49

# Australians Done To Death

Regardless of achievements or otherwise of the teams in the sub-continent, all Test stars of all countries are unanimous that there is nothing like the fervour and following that exists in India and Pakistan. Regardless of the state of the match, spectators throng stadia. Indeed there is a little bias where the home team is concerned, but visitors are applauded with all the intensity and that induces foreigners to undertake tours and accept unimaginative and zig-zag travelling. There was time when a player's cricketing career was considered incomplete if he had not played at Lord's. Now it is said that cricket player's life is not complete if he has failed to play at Eden Gardens, which has a seating capacity for more than one lakh spectators. Unlike Lord's which is cold, and unlike officaldom which is generally indiffeent to stars, present and past, Eden Gardens provides warmth and officials are generally caring and respectful. This is despite Kolkata's volatile record of resorting to rioting more often than it should be during the last three decades or more. Mohali is fast catching up with Eden Gardens.

When Richie Benaud's Australia undertook full tour to India, the visitors were plagued by stomach disorder before the first Test at Kotla (Delhi) in 1959-60. There was panic in the Australian management whether 11 fit players would be able to take the field. Despite untold problems,

Australia won the first Test on the pitch which took increasing spin over the four days' play. Benaud was the tormentor-in-chief of the Indian team with his "flippers" bowled with shortened run-in.

Kanpur's Green Park had now a newly prepared turf wicket for the second Test. Jasu Patel, who bowled his off-spinners with a typical, jerky action, had struggled to be chosen among 15. Some of the established Indian journalists had written in their pre-Test summary that Patel had no chance to play the match. But Amarnath, always known for his gambling instinct, felt that the wicket might suit a spinner from Ahmedabad. That was his "gambling" instinct. But he was equally keen on obliging Rattibhai Patel, the Board president. He conferred with skipper Ramchand and virtually insisted on the inclusion of Patel. Ramchand had his reservations, but Amarnath had made up his mind and he had his say.

To India's poor total of 152, Australia were 71 without loss. Patel had bowled a few overs without being effective. He then changed his end, which suited him. His off-spinners with low trajectory pitched on Allan Davidson's foot marks and turned sharply. He hustled batsmen. He took nine wickets for 69. This was the best analysis achieved by any Indian bowler in Test cricket. From 71 for no loss, Australians slumped to 219.

In deficit by 67 runs, India managed 291. Nari Contractor contributed 74. Left with a target of 225, the visitors found the going tough on the wicket which had been reduced to a virtual "wrestling pit". The ball did enormous kinds of tricks. It played pranks. Ramchand set an attacking field. Patel was again on the target. Polly Umrigar drew a leaf out of Patel's book. He also began bowling off-breaks. The move came off. The Patel-Umrigar firm destroyed Australians, who were shot out for 105 and India won the Test by 119 runs.

Benaud was man enough to say that India won the Test purely on merit instead of blaming wicket or umpiring. Amarnath, as expected, took the credit for India's win saying that it was he who had forced the inclusion of Patel in the team.

While doing a victory lap, Bapu Nadkarni fell down as he stepped on the unripe guava thrown in by an over-enthusiastic student-spectator.

Benaud had to face an amusing incident. The administrator-journalist wrote two articles. He praised Australians for their sporting spirit and displaying grace even in defeat in one and wrote entirely different piece in the next. While one article had been read by Australians, the other they had not read it as it appeared outside Kanpur. Some one, who knew Benaud, despatched a copy of the second article, which shocked Benaud and his men. When challenged, the administrator-journalist took the refute in the oft-repeated theory that he had been mis-quoted. This was far-fetched but Benaud had no option except to take it, as explained. Now it was the turn of the administrative-journalist to react. He demanded an apology from Benaud saying that he had doubted his integrity. Benaud and manager Sam Laxton refused point blank to say "sorry". This was not all. But both Benaud and Laxton saw to it that they did not have any dealing with the official who could indulge in any tomfoolery.

# 50

# Trouble At Delhi

The rise of Bishan Singh Bedi, who migrated from Amritsar to Delhi to better his cricket prospects, was the rise of Delhi's cricket. The rise of brilliant all-rounder Kapil Dev, at almost the same time, was the rise of the North Zone cricket.

Ram Prakash Mehra, "Lattoo", himself a fine player in Lahore (pre-Pakistan days), loved cricket intensely. He ate, drank and slept cricket. Kotla, Delhi's headquarters, was, in essentiality, his first home where he spent more time than in the Pataudi House (Daryaganj) where he stayed following partition.

Mehra nurtured a sanguine hope of Delhi becoming a Ranji champion. In Bedi, he found a player-captain, who could help translate his desire into reality. Bedi worked on his players rendering them physically fit and mentally alert.

Came 1978-79 season. Delhi became the new Ranji winners. Lattoo was happier than even Bedi and his players. Bedi did not rest contented on his maiden triumph. He continued to inspire and motivate his players. He saw to it that the players were not carried away about previous year's win. In came the 1979-80 season. Bedi and his men proved their last year's victory was no fluke. Trophy retained and Delhi, lowly-placed not long ago, rose as a big cricketing power in the country.

There were celebrations and more celebrations. Bedi thought that it was a right time to fire off a letter to Lattoo for undertaking much-needed improvements in the set-up of the Delhi and District Cricket Association (DDCA). In a charter of demands, Bedi had mentioned that the time had come when there should be an energetic and young secretary who could devote time to the welfare of players and health of cricket in the capital.

Most of the demands were routine. They did not upset Lattoo's powers in the DDCA where his word was a law. But to Lattoo's credit, it could be correct to say that he did not do anything that could undermine the interest of Delhi's cricket even at junior level.

The demand for the change of the secretary did not go well with Lattoo's thinking. Not that he was impressed or enamoured by the work of his secretary, Kewal Mehra, who happened to be his nephew. But he felt that the DDCA had gone from strength to strength and that there was yet no need to bring about change at this juncture.

Weston Electronics (Sunder Vachani), for once, organised a get together for the champion team at the farmhouse. It was a superb get-together. Most of the guests were "spirited". Lattoo, however, continued to be teetotaller. He broke the Gandhian silence. "Iss sardar key baarah baj gaye hai. Iss ko sabak sikhana ho gaa (This Sikh has gone amuck. He has got to be taught a lesson)". The more his two favourite journalist-friends tried to plead with Lattoo, the less he seemed inclined to see Bedi's point of view. The rift widened. Gulf increased. Now charges and counter-charges flew fast and thick. Unable to counter Bedi's immense popularity, the Mehra levelled several allegations against the captain. Among them were Bedi bringing in baggageman Balwant, with grey moustache, in plane with the team from Bangalore and his consuming more than two dozen bottles of Champagne by borrowing money from hosts.

There were wide cracks now. The players, with support of a few sports journalists, stood united. The Mehra dynasty was however shaking as many skeletons were allegedly stacked in the cupboard of the Mehra empire. As battle became a war of attrition, one thing became clear that Lattoo himself was an angel as far cricket in the capital was concerned. But he was a victim of circumstances. He apprehended that if Kewal was relieved of his responsibilities of secretary from the DDCA, he could be the next target from the office of the president next year.

The version of the Board in its publication of the 1980-81 season was:

"Delhi's second successive triumph in the championship of 1979-80 was followed by the formation of the Delhi State Cricket Association by the players, spearheaded by Bedi and backed by some important Delhi personage. At the function held to form the new body, one was told the purpose was to work in conjunction with the DDCA, the parent body, that had been running the game for nearly five decades, for the good of the game. However as it turned out in 1980-81, the season under review, there was bitter confrontation between the two which disrupted the programme in the North Zone....Matters reached a head when Delhi were to play Punjab in the last of their North Zone league match. With miscreants digging up the Kotla pitch, the match could not be played. After the personal intervention of S.K. Wankhede, president of the Board, an ad hoc committee was formed to choose the Delhi team to play Punjab in a rearranged fixture. However, this time there was utter confusion with two Delhi teams, captained respectively by Surinder Amarnath and Bedi, barging into the home dressing room and once again the match was not played. Ultimately Bedi's team—he was dropped from the captaincy for the earlier match for which the team was chosen by DDCA leading to a revolt by senior players—completed the engagement, with a court order restraining the DDCA from interfering with the conduct of the match or even selecting a team. The restraint was removed only after the final between Mumbai and Delhi had been completed".

There were many more dramas that unfolded before the season began. While two factions were fighting their own batttle—ruling clinque wanted to retain control over DDCA—the DSCA wantd to unseat them. Knives were sharpened; ammunition set at pivotal points. Armies were positioned to strike when the iron was hot.

There was different drama in progress on Ranji level. Mohinder was designated captain of Delhi. But he was in the process of considering an offer from Australia since he was unsure of getting justice at the Board level. He withdrew from the offer of Delhi captaincy. In came his brother Surinder. This did not secure approval of the senior players who thought that official vice-captain Vinay Lamba should be elevated instead of his being superseded. Five players, that is, Madan Lal, Rakesh Shukla, Sunil Valson, Arun Lal and Surinder Khanna, insisted on Vinay Lamba to lead the side.

In the meantime, the Mehra hatched a conspiracy. They thought the best way to silence Bedi was to make his disciple Madan Lal captain. They conferred with Madan Lal who made it categorically clear to Mehras that he would not do anything, even remotely, that could go against the interest of Bedi.

Lamba resigned after captaining the first match against Jammu and Kashmir at Srinagar. The responsibility did fall on Surinder Amarnath to wear Delhi's mantle. But he was so upset at the doings of the national selectors for not selecting him for the tour to Australia that he was in no mood to captain Delhi. He walked out of the responsibility. Bedi was penalised for the revolt that he had engineered against the authorities at Srinagar. Dissatisfied with the functioning of the DDCA officialdom and seeing harsh treatment meted out to seniors, all five remaining 'rebels' refused to play the second match against Haryana at Rohtak. The match started about 90 minutes behind the stipulated time. For this match Rakesh Shukla, one of the six rebels, was named captain. But he declined the honour, citing the "air of uncertainty" as reason. He and other four—Madan Lal, Sunil Valson, Arun Lal and Surinder Khanna were upset because Bedi had been dropped.

All five "rebels" were suspended. The efforts were made to bring about division. But they stayed together. The DDCA authorities now panicked. They reinstated all five back into the team. Bedi was however kept out. Not that they wanted to but they did not want to lose to Punjab as it would have further weakened their position. The match did not come off as, on the day of the match, about 100 marched on the ground saying that "No Bedi, No match". This was not all. But they dug up the pitch after uprooting stumps. The authorities requisitioned police protection but somehow it misfired.

The DDCA kept quiet for Delhi's match against Services. Five boycotters and Bedi chose to stay out. The match, however, came along. It was a high scoring match— Services 380, Delhi (for 9 wickets) 513. Delhi salvaged five points from this match. But Delhi (16) still trailed by a point from Services (17). At this point of time, Services had a chance, for the first time, to qualify for the knock-out stage.

The Delhi-Punjab match was rescheduled. Two teams, supported and chosen by different factions, were at the ground. Another controversy arose. The umpires said that it was not their concern as to which was the bona fide team to play the match. They said that their job was to supervise the match and thus far and no further. Eventually, it was left upon the Punjab captain to decide as to which side he would like to play against.

After a lot of cajoling, the Punjab skipper Umesh Kumar agreed. He however, said that he would choose the side only after he was given assurance that his decision would not be challenged. He chose Bedi's team. Now it was the turn of Surinder to feel upset. However, the umpires did not accept Bedi as Delhi's captain. They asked Umesh Kumar to toss with Surinder. Heated arguments followed. Umpires chose to walk out of the scene.

In the meantime, the authorities pressurised the umpires

not to accept Bedi's team. When Punjab captain was told to go out to toss with Surindeer, he refused point blank saying that he had already made it clear that his judgement could not be challenged.

The umpires, report went against Punjab. But no action was taken. A compromise was arrived at by which the Delhi-Punjab match was again re-scheduled. Two days before the match, DSCA secured an injunction from a "lower Court. The order restrained DDCA from interfering with the conduct of the match. The Ad hoc Committee, which was suthorised to organise the match, meant victory for DSCA. The Board, in the meantime, appointed an observer—Tulpule (Pune). Board's affiliated association—DDCA—could not do anything in the matter. Delhi got five points, moved into knock-out while Services had to stay out. The Delhi-Punjab match was played at the Railway ground.

In 1980 also, there was trouble between players and DDCA for every match. There was uncertainty about composition of the team.

Delhi was always an unpredictable centre. The doings of officials were more unpredictable in the matter of the selection of teams. Once, for a Ranji Trophy season, there were 18 players and as many as 24 stand boyes.

# 51

# Doshi Lashes Out

Dilip Doshi was no longer a blue eyed player of skipper Sunil Gavaskar on tour to Australia in 1980-81. Says Doshi in his book "Spin punch":....Sunil Gavaskar was going through a lean patch. Worried by this, he allowed things to drift and the morale of the whole team began to suffer as a result. He had little solace to offer at the team meetings. This was the situation as we approached our first Test in Sydney...."

In a state game against Victoria at Geelong, Doshi took medium-pacer Trevor Laughlin's ball on his left foot. He sustained a spiral fracture of the first metatarsal. He concealed this injury as he was keen on playing the third and final Test against Australia at Melbourne. He obtained permission from Durrani and Gavaskar to miss a practice session in the pre-Test match. His room-mate T.E. Srinivasan knew about the nature of his injury but he did not reveal it. In the meantime, he consulted a renowned physiotherapist Bill Giulliano, who advised him treatment to keep the swelling down.

Doshi was included in the team and claimed three wickets for 109 runs. He bowled as many as 52 overs. To bowl 52 overs with a fractured toe spoke highly of Doshi. India had not even a ghost of a chance to win the Test as Australia needed only 143 runs for victory. But sensational things happened. The drama unfolded through Karsan Ghavri who claimed two quick wickets. Doshi had one wicket as Australia stood at 24 for three wickets.

Kapil Dev, injured, joined the team as the game resumed on the fifth morning. He seemed motivated. He forgot about his injury. He bowled menacingly. Doshi took a leaf out of his book. They bowled with plan and purpose. They dismissed Australia for 83 to give India's morale-boosting 59-run victory. Kapil Dev had five wickets while Doshi took two wickets.

When Doshi told Gavaskar that he had a spinal fracture and he might be excused from playing first Test in New Zealand, skipper showed no sympathy. Says Doshi: "....He asked blatantly where is the X-ray? This, coming on top of the harsh remarks during the match, truly hurt me".

Doshi had no option except to get another X-ray to prove to his skipper that he was genuinely injured. When he presented him an X-ray, Gavaskar did not even glance at it. In the Press conference, Gavaskar had a word of praise for Kapil Dev and Shivlal Yadav. When a journalist asked him: "What about Doshi?" Gavaskar dismissed it with: "What about Doshi?" And that was that.

While in New Zealand, Doshi sought an opinion of Dr John Hislop, an expert. He observed that it would take about four weeks for Doshi to be alright. In other words he would be fit by the end of month (February) since he was hurt on February 1, 1981. He missed the first Test against New Zealand from February 21.

Doshi was to miss only one Test. But a cable had already been sent for Ravi Shastri to fly to New Zealand. According to Doshi, manager Durrani was for Rajinder Goel. But who was Durrani in comparison to Gavaskar? Shastri landed in New Zealand and played first Test at Basin Reserve (Wellington). He took six wickets in the match and scored 3 not out and 19. His performance was such that he had to be included in the next two Tests, in which Doshi also played.

Promising and talented Shastri indeed was. But should he have been rushed to New Zealand for merely one Test?

# 52

# Umpire Courageous

Vikram Raju possesses a large size photo which is neatly framed. It is meticulously hung on the wall of his home's drawing room. Cricket players in general and umpires in particular notice it as they settle down in the room. It reminds him loudly that he was a man among umpires who had the conviction, courage and, above all, sense of honesty to declare the last batsman, Maninder Singh, leg before off Greg Matthews with only one ball remaining. Vikram Raju's decision led to the India-Australia Test ending in a tie at Chennai on September 22, 1998. This was the second "tie" Test in the history of Test cricket. The first was between West Indies and Australia in Brisbane. If the first "tie" Test provided a tremendous boost to five-day version of cricket, the second "tie" Test cooled the tempers down to a great extent. It was, in a way, poetic justice that the match ended in a "tie" in which both sides were the winners.

In an anxiety to promote cricket and shower riches on players, the over-zealous Board officials act in a manner which betrays their sanity. A number of players, Indian and foreigners, have suffered and will continue to suffer because of playing in weather, which is not conducive to even stir out of the air-conditioned environment, leave alone playing.

To organise a five-day Test in Chennai in September was an act of sheer stupidity. If the Indian Board bungled, it was much more stupid for the Australian Board to have agreed to play there. Australia has a very well informed High commission which should have been consulted before agreeing to play in Chennai in September.

The Chepauk, where the Test was staged, was a full fledged oven. The locals, accustomed to living there, were burning within and outside despite being under covers. Dean Jones, now a golf addict, chose Chepauk and Chennai to display his skill and prowess. He went on to produce one of the finest innings of his cricket career. He scroed 210 in team's total of 574 for seven declared.

Jones was dehydrated because of excessive heat and humidity. Despite vomitting intermittantly, he executed strokes which spoke highly of his batsmanship. He often received first aid and consumed soft drinks during drinks intervals by gallons. His physical condition in the middle was pitiable, but he was unwilling to give away his wicket. He stayed mentally focussed. There were some who felt that had he stayed on there for another 30-45 minutes, he might have passed off : Had that happened, God alone knows what would have happened to Indian cricket and the Board!

When Jones was eventually dismissed, he was hardly in a position to walk. Actually, it would have been in fitness of things if stretcher had been rushed to bring him into the dressing room. When "installed" it was not he who had a bath but he was provided shower by his team-mates. Shower over, he was hardly in a position to "talk". He was rushed to hospital where he was straightaway put on "saline drip". That was the wisest decision.

Kapil Dev notched up a century, Srikkanth (53), and Ravi Shastri (62) as India managed 397. Comfortably placed with a lead of 177 Australia declared at 170 for five leaving India 348 to make in a day's play. India accepted the challenge. Gavaskar hammered 90 and Azhar 42. When Gavaskar and Azhar were together, there was more than a flickering of hope that India would make it. But when they left, the collapse initiated. Shastri was however in command. He did make some robust shots. In between, wickets kept falling. In came last batsman Maninder Singh with four runs to get for victory. Shastri had two. He should have retained the strike. But he did not. He took a single, which meant that India would not lose the Test. Many thought it was not a very wise strategy. Maninder Singh was now left to face Matthews. With fielders clustering around Maninder Singh's bat, Matthews bowled. The ball hit Maninder Singh's out stretched pads. A vociferous appeal rent the air. The appeal was so loud that it could have been heard in Melbourne. Up went Vikram Raju's finger. The match ended in a tie. Maninder Singh was bewildered, while some thought that Vikram Raju's sense of drama had encroached a bit on his sense of justice. Those who made such harsh observation were not doing justice to cricket. Were they? How did they conclude that Vikram Raju was enacting a drama!

# 53

## Bedi More Sinned Against Than Sinning

Irked at Supreme Court awarding "reprieve" to senior players for their alleged "disobedience and defiance" in stopping over in the United States to play a few "pyjama" matches to make quick bucks, the Board, in its wisdom, to bring about discipline among players chose Bishan Singh Bedi as a cricket manager. Bedi's initial terms were three series—one to New Zealand in 1990 another to Sharjah and third to England in 1991.

If commitment to cricket was the deciding factor, Bedi was unquestionably the best choice. But Bedi was not what Bedi used to be during his playing days. He was then totally players man. After retiring from competitive cricket, he underwent sea-change in his attitude and thinking about players and officialdom. May be, he was a wiser man now than what he was as a player.

Aware that Srikkanth was not getting any younger and also aware that he was not a certainty in the team although he had handled the side admirably in Pakistan (all four Test were drawn). the chairman of the selection committee Rajsingh Dungarpur did not think much of his captaincy.

Rajsingh may not have played Test cricket. But his knowledge and love for cricket is second to none. He reads cricket and there is a computer in his mind. His facts and figures are generally right. But he is highly self-opinionated monarch. If he makes up his mind on a particular aspect or about any player, he tries to translate it into reality. He was convinced that Srikkanth would not be an ideal choice for the tour to New Zealand. He was also convinced that religious-minded "Miya", minimum militant, would be the best player to captain the side. Governed by these instincts, he set the ball in motion. His collegues, who seldom did much home work, were over-powered by his logic. In addition, he was a person who could impress any one with his style of oratory.

Rajsingh flew to Bangalore where Duleep semi-final was in progress. While discussing with his colleagues, he dropped the name of Azhar. "Inexperienced (he had captained Hyderabad only twice and South zone by default), retiring, meak and shy", was the opinion of one or two selectors. To Rajsingh's proposal, no other name was proposed by any selector. While selectors were scratching their empty minds, he made further fool of them by saying. "Let us send the team without a captain and cricket manager (Bedi) to take charge of the side". The selectors were stumped. Rajsingh had won his point and the selectors nodded. When it was finalised, a phone call was made to the president B.N. Dutt whose consent was required, in accordance to the Board constitution. When he was told about Azhar's selection, he kept asking : "Was any other name proposed or considered?" When he was told that no other name was proposed or considered, he was visibly surprised.

Before the team took off, the feeling was that the tour would be a grand success. Azharuddin's friendliness, Bedi's experience and regard for mediapersons and Judge's (A.W. Kanmadikar) liveliness would render the team exceedingly popular in Kiwiland. Popular indeed the team was with New Zealand officials and players as also hosts of Indians settled in Kiwiland.

Azharuddin clicked with his men, senior and junior. There was harmony among them. There was no curfew on them. But Bedi was not as popular as he ought to have been. Not that he was unfair to any one. But his style of regimentation caused concern to many. His over-emphasis on work-out and physical fitness was not much appreciated by some senior players. Soon, there were murmurs. A few senior players were heard saying that they were so tired that they were unable to give off their best in matches. Obsessed as Bedi was with physical fitness, he was unwilling to understand the plight of players who were not used to carrying that much work-load. Bedi meant well for players, but his methods were hurting players. The result : there was an uncalled for drift between players and the cricket manager.

What should have been a comfortable draw became a nightmare for India in the first Test at Christchurch. Richard Hadlee indeed reached a magic figure of 400 wickets in Test cricket and Bedi spoke eloquently about his remarkable achievement in his home surroundings. He deserved the honour and he richly rose as Sir Richard.

On failure of Indian team, Bedi once said that the players were free to jump into the Pacific sea if they wanted to commit suicide. It was a remark made in a lighter vein. It was an observation that was made more out of disappointment than out of any anger. But it was completely twisted by some mediapersons. The stories painted Bedi as a villain.

Vengsarkar, who flew to New Zealand midway through the tour following injury to Navjot Singh Sidhu (he returned home), was not enjoying his cricket. Actually both Bedi and Azharuddin should have made it worthwhile for him with tact and friendliness. But no such measures were taken. That was unfortunate. The result : the Indians were beaten in Tests and one day competitions.

When Bedi was appointed cricket manager for three series, a section of people—a kind of a mafia in operation for years—was upset at Board's decision. They were secretly and actively at work to bring about Bedi's downfall. Their logic was that as long as he was at the helm of affairs, there would be hardly and scope for them to call the shots.

When Indian team failed in New Zealand and also in Sharjah, they planned that this was the time to strike.

On the eve of the Lord's Test, Bedi had a detailed discussion with his skipper Azhar impressing upon him why India should bat first if he won the toss. Bedi also impressed upon Azhar that he (Azhar) was the boss and that he should exercise his judgment instead of lending his ear to others. Azhar was receptive throughout and Bedi left the meeting under the impression that Azhar would bat first if it was his choice to decide. Madhav Mantri, the administrative manger, confirmed that India would bat first if it was left to Azhar to decide. When Azhar discussed the matter with his colleagues, some of them insisted that it would be better if India fielded first since the wicket was "fresh". Caught between Bedi and players, Azhar chose to go along with the players instead of acting, as discussed with Bedi.

There might not have been "much wrong" in Azhar going with his colleagues. But it was his duty to have informed the manager that he had second thoughts and he had decided to field first, if he won the toss. He would then have been unblemished.

When Bedi and Mantri came to know that England were batting first, they genuinely thought that Azhar had lost the toss. So far so good. Subsequently when Bedi came to know that Azhar had put England in, he was upset. He felt that he had been stabbed by his own skipper of all persons. He went on to tell players that it was a totally wrong decision of Azhar. Following Bedi's remarks against his skipper, Gavaskar seized the opportunity and criticised Bedi for "distancing himself with the decision". Gavaskar's piece added insult to injury. The pity was that two India's leading players had chosen Lord's a fitting venue to wash dirty linen.

Bedi was accused of playing to gallery. He was also blamed for putting his foot in his mouth. He got a stick from Indian media. But the fact was that he was not to blame. The captain should have told him that he was not abiding by the decision jointly taken by them.

India were mauled in the Test. It was more embarrassing for Azhar to suffer such a humiliation than Bedi.

Azhar has been much the wiser following that "blunder". But Bedi bears a grudge against Azhar. This is not a mature attitude. In criticising Azhar day in and day out for whatever Azhar does, it does not enhance Bedi's reputation. Despite Bedi's "stick", Azhar had survived as a skipper for most part of the decade.

# 54

# Evidence Destroyed

Amarnath's India were on maiden tour to Australia in 1947 when Vinoo Mankad twice warned Bill Brown, playing for Australian XI, for his backing up rather too soon. The batsman did not pay the needed heed to the warning.

Brown, an opening batsman, was 18 in the second Test at Sydney when he backed up too soon and Mankad, in his delivery stride, had the bails removed at the non-striker's end. The umpire had no hesitation in declaring the batsman out.

There were some, who felt that it was unethical for Mankad to have got the batsman run out in this manner. Many thought otherwise saying that Brown should not have been backing too soon when it was not permissible under rules. While skipper Don Bradman was supportive of Mankad, Brown was man enough to say that it was his fault.

Earlier, Brown, 30, was run out by Mankad in similar manner when he was playing for the Queensland XI. Here also Brown was warned.

Following this, the phrase "Mankading" originated. Bill Frindall in his book "The Wisden Book of Test Cricket" observed that : "Mankad created Test history".

If such a run out is considered "unfair", the bowler's reply is that it is equally unfair for the batsman to take advantage by backing up too soon. The law is straight-forward.

Don Bradman in his book "Farewell to Cricket", says: "For the life of me I cannot understand, the laws of cricket make it quite clear that the non-striker must keep within his ground until the ball has been delivered. If not why is the provision there which enables the bowler to run him out?"

There was commotion at St George's Park (Port Elizabeth) as Peter Kirsten was uncontrollable. His attitude, behaviour and abusive language would not have done credit to even a club class player. As if this unpardonable behaviour was not bad enough, Colleghen walked out of the dressing room and said quite loudly : "So this is what the Friendship Series is all about".

Why had all this hell descended at St George's Park"? Kirsten had been run out for backing too soon by Kapil Dev.

The fault was clearly of Kristen. He had been warned twice at Johannesburg for his repeated infringement of laws which prohibited a non-striker to back up too soon. Kapil Dev had adhered to the etiquette emphasising to the batsman that he would now be free to run him out if he violated that law. Kirsten ignored it and paid the penalty. He should have been man enough to have accepted his mistake. Just as a bowler was penalised for over-stepping on the crease, so was non-striker for leaving the crease too soon. It was certainly not ethical for a batsman to run a yard short for the stipulated run.

While incident was taking an ugly turn in the dressing room, it flared up as Kepler Wessels inflicted a blow on Kapil Dev's shin at non-striker's end. Kapil Dev did point it out to Wessels that it was "not cricket" that he was playing.

A series of protests followed. South Africans were in the dock for their crude and volatile behaviour. Heavy penalties and suspension on erring players should have been imposed. No player had a right to bring the game into disrepute. The United Cricket Board of South Africa (UCBSA) and its supremo Dr Ali Bacher had fully realised that the players had crossed all bounds of decency after erring in the middle. Caught in a very ticklish situation, UCBSA saw to it that the South African Broadcasting Corporation (SABC) did not have the required clippings of Wessels hitting Kapil Dev with his bat. The plea given by the SABC was that the cameras were following the ball. This was not all. But Clive Lloyd, the match referee, also hummed the same tune saying that he did not witness the incident. Who was he kidding?

The next evening, a Press conference was held and Kirsten was fined a mere 1000 rands, which amounted to 50 per cent of his match fee. It was a very mild punishment. There Lloyd went on saying that had he seen Wessels striking Kapil Dev with his bat, he would have awarded very stiff punishment to the defaulting player. Lloyd was trying to be more diplomatic than Indian management of Amrit Mathur and Ajit Wadekar.

If the South African players crred in the middle the management was guilty of destroying the evidence. Dr. Bacher and his men did not come clean in this controversy.

# 55

# Trouble Persists

"Come on, put your head down and get your game together". This was what skipper Kapil Dev told his senior colleague Sunil Gavaskar after India had not done too well in the first two matches of the 1983 World Cup in England.

Kapil Dev was in no way critical of Gavaskar. But he was just motivating him as he was relying upon his batsmanship. These words should have been taken in a proper perspective. But Gavaskar mistook Kapil Dev's observation. He rushed to P.R. Mansingh, manager of the team. "If Kapil thinks that I am not trying, he is welcome to drop me", said Gavaskar to Mansingh. Now it was Kapil who was hurt thinking that his well meaning words, without any malice, were being misconstrued by a batsman of the calibre of Gavaskar. Kapil Dev read much more than what Gavaskar had said. He felt that Gavaskar was doubting his integrity.

The vex matters did not get resolved. Gavaskar's dismissal at zero further ignited the situation. Now foolish allegations surfaced. Gavaskar was accused of throwing away his wicket. It was far from it. India slumped to nine runs for four wickets. The position further deteriorated as Yashpal Sharma was soon dismissed. The score-board made a pathetic reading of 17 for five wickets. The situation was alarming as defeat in this match would have meant India were out of the competition.

Kapil Dev did not indulge in his usual bang, bang batting. He managed a few runs through placements and deflections.

Kapil Dev was different batsman on resumption after lunch. He adopted a bold attitude saying it with his broad bat. He proved that "the attack was the best defence". He first took on Curren who was India's tormentor-in-chief until then.

He hammered sixes on a small Tunbridge Wells ground as also fours as India, with the help from Binny and Madan Lal, climbed to 140 for eight. This was some recovery.

Kapil Dev was now at his dazzling best. Kirmani offered him requisite help. The pair added 126 runs for the nine wicket and India totalled 266. Kapil Dev stayed unconquered at 175. His innings was until then the most devastating. But as luck would have it, there was no video coverage as the organisers had labelled this match as an "unimportant" one. Zimbabwe fought stoutly before losing the match by 31 runs.

The problem between Kapil Dev and Gavaskar did not reslove. They got compounded. Gavaskar did not play against Australia as he was not fit. He was sidelined against the West Indies. This was the only time in his career he had not been chosen when available.

# 56

# A Controversial Century

Sunil Gavaskar and Zaheer Abbas were good friends. They were prolific run getters. Indeed Gavaskar's record compiling runs was much better than that of Zaheer. Both had healthy respect for each other's skill, ability and also temperament. When Zaheer brought his Pakistan team to India in 1983-84 both were great friends. But when Pakistan's tour ended, they certainly were not as good friends as they should have been.

Zaheer had brought a very depleted side. There was no Imran Khan, there was no Sarfraz Nawaz and there were no Majid Khan and Asif Iqbal. Javed Minadad was the only trusted soldier from among established stars.

Bespectacled and tall with stately walk, Zaheer was a pleasant conversationist. He spoke precisely and to the point. Gavaskar, in comparison, was calculative. He had a gift of the gab and he was a person who could fit in any role off the field. In the middle his bat did talk in measured tone instead of with flashing strokes.

The first Test was billed for Bangalore, a city rich in cricket traditions. But as leading lights were missing from Pakistan side, the response from spectators was not as lively as it should have been. Yet there were about 20,000 spectators present when rival captains went out for the toss.

The Test did not provide lively cricket. Rain also played

a spoilsport. The proceedings were generally padestrian. But the match suddenly sparked into life as an avoidable controversy surfaced.

It was September 19, 1983 when Gavaskar, who was not 100 per cent fit, went out to bat in the second innings. As he to got going, his strokes began to burn the grass. When he got past his 50 he thought it was worthwhile trying for the century. Post-tea session saw Gavaskar at his usual best. Zaheer Abbas was unsure of the playing conditions. He kept asking umpires whether the game would finish immediately after 77 overs had been bowled or 20 mandatory overs had to be completed. The umpires kept telling him that the closure of the game midway through mandatory overs rested in the hands of rival captains.

Gavaskar, in his book "Runs'n Ruins, alleges that go-slow tactics were in progress before the first of the 20 mandatory over bagan". Writes Gavaskar : "If his intention was to waste time so that fewer overs were bowled before the mandatory overs count began, then he was partly successul. If his intention was to disturb the concentration of the batsmen, then he failed. He could have made these queries after the mandatory overs had started so that the loss of time would not have mattered greatly."

Gavaskar was on 87 and on a firm road to reaching his 28th century. The madatory overs were in process and Zaheer and his men walked off the field as there was no chance of a result. Gavaskar and umpires M.V. Gothoskar and Swarup Kishan stayed put. Arguments, which became quite heated frequently, ensued. It took 27 minutes for the authorities to persuade Zaheer to returrn to the field.

Unwilling Zaheer was, but he yielded under pressure, Gavaskar duly completed his century. He was now only one hehind great Don's 29. As he got his centrury, the teams walked indoors when there were still five balls remaining of the final mandatory over.

The details of the incident which led to drama, are :
Two different viewpoints surfaced. Zaheer's contention

was that the stipulated 77 overs had been bowled and there was no chance of a decision. It was, according to him, meaningless to continue with the game. Says Zaheer: "Cricket is a team game and rules governing the mandatory overs are operative only when a result is in sight". He thought both umpires were partisan. "Test matches are not played to make or unmake personal records", emphsised Zaheer.

Critical of umpires' anxiety for Gavaskar to get his 28th century, Zaheer asked : "Why did they close the match as soon as Gavaskar got his century without consulting me and without waiting for the over to finish". "Would the umpires have acted with similar enthusiasm if the Pakistan bowler had taken nine wickets and was in sight of claiming the remaining wicket to establish a record"? he asked.

Zaheer's point of view was that the umpires had not only to be honest but appear to be so.

The umpires' view was that "mandatory" word compelled them to continue with the game until 20 overs had been bowled. "We could have finished the game earlier only with the consent of both the captains", said Swarup Kishan. When asked how did they finish the game without seeking Zaheer's consent after Gavaskar reached his century, the umpires had no answer.

Needless to say that there was a controversy which could have been avoided. There are some dispassionate critics who said that the century was achieved by Gavaskar under "farcical" circumstances.

On the subject, Zaheer was candid. Friendship and captaining the team are altogether two different aspects. Can a bowler bowl full-tosses and half-volleys for a friend-rival to get a century?" he asked. "I have nothing against Gavaskar but spirit of the game must be respected, Zed had said soon after the series had concluded.

Accroding to Gavaskar "The walk-off by Zaheer had left a bad taste in the mouth and later in the evening on the flight to Delhi, some of his players were critical of his action, which they felt was unnecessary and unsporting.

# 57

# Sordid Incident

Communal disturbances at certain places and Bal Thackeray's Shiv Sainiks on rampage at their headquarters, Mumbai, were causes enough for Pakistan calling off their tour to country in 1990-91. No other team could undertake the tour as every one was engaged elsewhere.

How it happened? During a Dussehra rally, Bal Thackeray, in his usual routine speech to a crowded party loyalists threatened to have Wankhede stadium burnt down if the Pakistan team played in the city.

Pakistan intervention in Kashimr was Thackersy's call for Mumbai bandh on Oct 28, 1991, the day match was slated. This statement came five days (October 23) after 19 sainiks, led by Shishir Shinde, dug holes in the pitch with spades and shovels. They also poured grease and diesel on it. Outside the stadium, the banner said. "Pakistan cricketers, your entry into Hindustan stopped".

The Mumbai Chief Minister Sudhaker Rao had meetings with political bigwigs of Delhi and of Mumbai. While Shiv Sena was unwilling to withdraw bandh, the BCA president Madhav Mantri wanted to hold the match. In the complicated situation, the Board also scemed reluctant to take firm decision. There were apprehensions. Here was match that nobody wanted but nobody would dare to say as much.

Only four days ramined. BCA had not sold a single

ticket and hotel authorities were hesitant to lodge teams because of anticipated trouble.

Other political parties also jumped into the fray. They offered support to Shiv Sena in anti-match stand. There was now fear that matches in other centres (five one-dayers) would be disrupted. In Jalandhar, it was proclaimed : "To teach Pakistan a lesson for spreading terrorism in India". Reports from other centres, like, Gwalior and Chennai were also disturbing. Pakistan now took the plunge and called off the tour.

The cancellation of Pakistan's tour to the country was, in a way, a blessing in disguise because stars, human beings, needed rest to recover and recoup. It was also a fit occasion for domestic competitions, particularly Ranji and Duleep, to get a shot in the arm. It was a season for established stars to play and mix with budding players.

Mumbai cricket for decades throbbed because known cricket personalities were willing to play in the Kanga League. Apart from providing much-needed tips to budding players in batting, bowling and fileding, the presence of seniors automatically inculcated sense of discipline and spread cricket education.

Sadly, the Board of Control for Cricket in India (BCCI), now a mercenary body more than cricket promotional unit, did not utilise heaven-sent opportunity. The domestic competitions were conducted slovenly. There was utter lack of enthusiasm and discipline among outfits.

The West-North Duleep final, for example, became a football contest instead of a cricket match in which quite a few redoubtable stars were on view. The venue was Jamshedpur where spectators egged on players to indulge in acts which could not be termed as decent. There were needless appeals, protests and counter-protests and threatening gestures by some players who, it seemed, were out to settle their own personal issue.

The situation deteriorated to such an extent that Rashid Patel (West) and Raman Lamba (North) virtually came to blows on the ground. This was the first ugly instance of this magnitude in the competition played under the umbrella of the Board.

The situation reached a crescendo when Patel, armed with stump, following a no-ball call, chased Lamba, wearing pads and gloves, all the way to third man. When Patel reached within striking distance, Lamba waved his bat as if he was wielding a sword.

While Shastri was on the field when this sordid incident took place, Kapil Dev was watching it from the pavilion. Why these two stalwarts did not make these erring players to behave was difficult to understand. This was not all. But umpires were mute spectators. They should have given marching orders to both.

A picture of Patel trying to attack Lamba was carried by most of the newspapers in the country. Some foreign papers and magazines also published it. A cricket match had been reduced to a football mellee or wrestling bout. It was a condemnable incident.

Following umpires' report, the Board suspended both the players. Actully, a proper probe was essential and more punishment than mere suspension was in order. There were some who thought that teams also should have been penalised in one form or the other. The captains could not have been allowed to watch the situation to go out of hands. They were also, in a way, party to the shocking incident.

# 58

# Azhar's Three In A Row

In this country, usually every record, every achievement and every failure gives rise to an unseeming controversy. Sad though it is, it nevertheless is true.

When Azharuddin, find of the decade, got his third successive century in the first innings of the fifth Test against Gower's England, he rightly was accorded a standing ovation at Kanpur's Green Park in February 1985. At that historic moment when spectators and others were applauding lustily, Hyderabadi youngster was submerged in deep thoughts saying "thank you" spiritually to his grandpa Vajehuddin who had basically reared him up for this stardom.

Dilip Vengsarkar found his form. He scored a classic century as Gavaskar declared at 553 for eight wickets. England seemed unperturbed and replied with 417. Azhar was batting with 54 in the second innings and Srikkanth was batting on 41. The Test was dead as dodo. But Gavaskar chose to declare hoping that he might dismiss England in a short time to win the Test. To expect to dismiss England in 36 overs on a good wicket was nothing but a very wishful thinking. Some among many knowledgeable critics felt that this meaningless declaration was brought about to prevent a youngster from getting his fourth century.

The tension at Green Park had already been felt on the

second day when some journalists thought that Gavaskar had not come out to applaud Azhar's third century. Many newspapers carried the stories painting India's skipper Gavaskar "dark". Subsequently, Gavaskar went on record as saying that he was very much there but he could not be spotted as some taller players and officials were standing in front of him.

Whatever might have been the observations of mediamen, Azhar defended his skipper. Gavaskar had reportedly made it clear to his specialist batsman that he would declare and that they should go for runs. Says Azhar: "Yes, I might have got a century. But I might not have got it as I was going for pre-determined shots". He reportedly went on record as saying that there was nothing wrong in declaration as it was told to him before he was sent in to bat at number three.

Azhar rattled up 439 runs from five innings (average 109.75). Gavaskar on his batsmanship said: "He (Azhar) is a God's gift to Indian cricket". Azhar's batting display was all the more praiseworthy as he had got runs with a hair-line fracture on his right hand finger.

Those, who had studied Gavaskar's psychology as a player-captain, said that he was a person who would become spiteful if he was wrongly accused. He had reportely felt terribly upset when he was blamed for not according ovation to Azharuddin on his third successive century. This accusation led him to declare the innings closed to tease public and mediapersons.

# 59

# Prabhakar Painted As A Villain

The maiden series to South Africa in 1991 was more "egg", peg and leg" series than a historic or friendly tour. Aware that Indian Board as also Indian Government had played a key role in South Africa getting readmitted to the International Cricket Council (ICC) the cricket authorities were hospitable and generous to players and mediapersons. The facilities to mediapersons on stadia, including virtual complimentary faxes, transport and get-togethers, were provided with all the warmth. Once a local official, Chris Ray, who functioned as PRO (Public Relations Officer) organised a dinner at his residence with part of money contributed by Indian journalists as a gesture of goodwill. When a horde of mediapersons, numbering more than 20, disembarked from cars, the host announced: "Save my two daughters. All yours. Do what you want to". Two minutes later, he realised. He retured to say : "Also leave my wife alone".

Amidst happy-go-lucky doings, a difficult situation arose in Durban, main centre for Indians. A girl of Indian origin, said to be a journalist, carried a feature on Manoj Prabhakar who, in a way, was always a good copy if he was in a relaxed frame of mind. The girl-journalist, in her over-enthusiasm, put a lot of words in Prabhakar's mouth. She went on to say that "Prabhakar liked senior women and also those who he did not like". The feature article said: "He was called hunter because of his such interests".

When the feature article appeard in Durban daily, every one just laughed at it and forgot about it. But a team of English journalists, who were quite a few in Durban, sensationlised the story by adding "Mirch and Masala" for their tabloid. They projected Prabhakar virtually a villain.

The Board president Madhavrao Scindia read it in London. He was shocked. He made a call to Amrit Mathur (manager) insisting that Prabhakar should be sent back. Mathur suggested for grant of some time so that he could investigate the matter before his taking such a drastic action. Investigations showed that Prabhakar was not much at fault. In the meanime, PTI (Press Trust of India) also flashed a news item defending Prabhakar. While Prabhakar was totally non-plussed as his cricketing career stood on the verge of "termination", Azharuddin and others warned the young girl. She was told that she should stay away from the Indian players.

Following probe, Mathur explained to Scindia that there was not much truth in the tabloid story. "We have warned Prabhakar", said Mathur, adding. "Let him continue with the tour".

Even after the Prabhakar episode, some players continued to visit night-clubs. But it was with the knowledge of the management. The officials said that they were aware of players spending some time for relaxation in night clubs. "But all of them know their limits", the officials said adding: "They are grown up and they are aware of their reponsibilities".

# 60

# Gavaskar Has His Say

In a diplomatic gesture to say "thank you" to Sri Lanka, which had supported the joint India-Pakistan bid for staging the 1987 World Cup, India undertook the tour to Sri Lanka with Kapil Dev as captain in August-September of 1985. Neither players nor the Board had made adequate preparations for the tour which, they felt, would be a "picnic". It turned out to be a nightmare as India lost the Test series 0-1 and drew one-day 1-1 with one Test abandoned. India were beaten and, like all beaten sides, Indians accused umpires for the defeat.

When the side was being picked for the tour to Sri Lanka, Gavaskar made it known that he was in no position to open the innings. He gave the reason—not convincing though—that he was unable to concentrate in the 10 minute change over. He said that, after all these years, he deserved the right to bat lower down at the number he thought was suitable to him.

There were some who did not agree with Gavaskar's logic or reasoning. They asked: "If Kapil Dev had decided that he would now bowl spinners after all these years of service, should he have been allowed to switch over?" Or if Syed Kirmani, for example, had insisted that he would field instead of keeping wickets, would he have been chosen? An enduring service to team or country cannot certainly be a passport for "Dadagiri"!

Regardless of whether one accepts or not, Gavaskar's opting out of the opening slot did make a vital difference. He should have been man enough to have continued to open the innings. After all, during his long and cherished 14 year innings, he had scored 29 of the 30 centuries as an opener. He could have added one or two more on that slot. His presence in the middle as an opener would have had an added confidence provided to his partner and, more important, he would have prevented seamers from gaining a psychological advantage over Indian batsmanship.

When the combination of Srikkanth and Rajput failed in first two Tests, Gavaskar should have volunteered to open the innings. But he did not. As a result Ravi Shastri was pressed into service to open along with Srikkanth. This change also failed. Gavaskar's insistence to bat low in order had two depressing effects on the team. One was that the team had to look for two opening players and second was that it upset middle order batting which, before the start of the tour, looked settled.

Openers failed to give India a reasonably good start in all three Tests. Azharuddin could not get among runs. Gavaskar was not a failure but the team would have been better served had he opened the innings.

# 61

# Srikkanth Errs

A fierce controveray raged between two Boards, Pakistan and India, and between two captains, Imran Khan and Kapil Dev, before the first Test started in the 1987 series. It pertained to the playing conditions of bowling 82 overs in a day.

The Indian Board had sent a detailed draft of playing conditions to the Pakistan Board for approval. That was about a month before Pakistan crossed over to India. The Pakistan Board officialdom received the draft but they did not study it nor did they discuss it with the captain Imran Khan and manager Haseeb Ahsan. It was entirely the fault of the Pakistan Board. When no reply from the Pakistan Board came, the Indian Board presumed (this might have been far-fetched) that the playing conditions had been acceptable to Pakistan.

An argument ensued between officials of the two Boards. Imran Khan smelt rat in this playing condition. He thought it was Indian Board's calculated strategy to reduce effectiveness of Pakistan's fast bowlers. He thought the mandatory 82 overs could have been achieved only if spinners bowled more overs than fast or medium pace bolwers.

The Pakistan management, particularly Imran Khan, was emphatic that it was not possible to bowl 82 overs within stipulated day's playing hours. It was suggested that 20 minutes might be added in the playing time if the target was not achieved by the closing time (4.30 p.m.) It then dawned on officials that it would not be possible to play beyond 4.30 p.m. at certain centres because there would not be sufficient light.

The rule of bowling 82 overs in a day remained merely on paper as Pakistan averaged 71 or 72 overs in a day.

Javed Miandad was in his usual belligerent mood in the first Test at Chennai in February, 1987. He looked set for his century. He was 72 when there was a loud appeal for the bat-pad catch. The ball was held by Srikkanth off the bowling of off-spinner Shivlal Yadav. The umpire V.K. Ramaswamy rejected it. This infuriated Srikkanth who, in an unprecedented act, hurled the ball at the umpire giving vent to his feelings.

A genuine appeal or not, catch or otherwise, Srikkanth's behaviour was shocking. He had no justification whatsoever to react so violently and thereby marring his reputation and bringing disrepute to the country and the game.

Ramaswamy, an experienced umpire, did not mistake Srikkanth's reaction. "Players, even though grown up, occasionally behave like kids in a razor-sharp match", was the philosophy of the umpire. He held no grudge against the fielder. Srikkanth soon realised that he had made a fool of himself. He profusely apologised to the umpire. He also said "sorry" to Miandad, organisers and the Board for his intemperate behaviour.

Appreciable as it was, the Board should have clamped some kind of penalty or punishment on him. The action, if taken, would have had far-reaching effects.

The sequel to the "Srikkanth episode" gave a handle to Pakistan to raise controversy, which did not exist. Shoaib Mohammad (101) was given out leg before to Maninder Singh. To Pakistan authorities, ever ready to decry any and every decision went on record as saying that the umpire had "duly compensated" Indian team for refusing an apppeal against Minadad.

This accusation showed Imran Khan and his players in

a very poor light. Ramaswamy was too experienced an umpire to get brow-beaten like that.

With Javed Minadad out of the team owing to backache, Pakistan started their fourth Test at Ahmedabad in March 1987 disastrously losing two wickets for 33 runs. The visitors protested against both the decisions saying that both Yousuf and Rizwan were wrongly declared out by the umpires. Salim Yousuf reportedly told his team-mates that Kiran More had dislodged the bails much before he had collected the ball. Rizwan-ur-Zaman said that the ball had flown to Kapil Dev of silly mid-off off his pads and not off his bat and yet the umpire declared him caught. The visitors were now up in arms against the umpiring.

The ugly situation—totally unavoidable—followed. Younis Ahmed and Gavaskar were involved in heated arguement. The umpire had to intervene to prevent situation from deteriorating.

Actually this was the aftermath of the appeal for caught behind made against Younis. When the umpire negatived the appeal, Gavaskar reportedly asked Younis to stop grumbling about the umpiring now. This infuriated Younis who said something which did not do him any credit.

The game progressed but, by this time, there was needless tension. Younis, a veteran, aggravated the situation by showing his bat to Gavaskar. Gavaskar accepted the challenge. The umpire again intervened but Younis reportedly told Gavaskar that he would settle the issue in the pavilion. Younis painted a different story altogether saying that Gavaskar was needlessly abusive.

The confrontation between two mature players did not turn ugly although Gavaskar kept waiting for Younis outside the Pakistan dressing room. Younis of course did not come out. Regardless of who was to blame, both Gavaskar and Younis should have shown restraint.

# 62

# Players Yield

Even after Supreme Court verdict, the trouble between players and the Board persisted. The players were elated, while Board officials were behaving like wounded tigers. Their authority had been undermined.

The Board had prepared a new contract after consulting legal luminaries. The newly formed Players' Association had its own. It was prepared by Haresh Jagtiani, who was an advocate for Mohinder, now players' spokesman.

The players were not as united, as it was claimed. Each player suspected the other. There was too much at stake. No one was willing to sacrifice his place in the team. The Board officials knew about it. They thought it was right time to assert. The discipline, they argued, was much more important than individuals, no matter how good. They kept saying that none was indispensable as there was a lot of talent in this country.

The selection committee, in the meantime, was summoned to Delhi. They were given the mandate to select an alternative side, should the already chosen players show their solidarity or stubbornness in declining to go to Pakistan in the winter of 1989. While reconfirming the tour, the Indian Board apprised the Pakistan Cricket Board of the situation as it stood then.

Sandeep Patil, a professional with the Madhya Pradesh team, was contacted. He was asked whether he would be available to lead the side, if chosen. He confirmed his availability. Sandeep swung into action. He phoned his wife to retrieve the coffin (kit-bag). buried somewhere in the store room.

The news of Board selecting an alternative team was discrectly leaked out. It caused panic among players who were unsure of the players' Association's role in this vex trouble. Mohinder was in contact with the players but, by the time he arrived in Delhi, the players had already panicked and signed the contract handed over to them by the Board.

Mohinder was a very disillusioned man. He did not want to accept yet another defeat. But there was no option for him.

Mohinder, spokesman of Association of Indian Cricketers (AIC), rushed to Pakistan. He said at Lahore on December 6 that the written proposal for gradation of payment was being sent to the Board. "We allowed players to undertake this tour without accepting any payment and we also did not insist on the gradation of payment bacause time was short", said Mohinder, adding "We will not compromise on matters of principles".

According to Mohinder, the AIC was writing to the Board that they would not let Rajsingh Dungarpur represent the Board when the discussion on players' demand was held. "We want anybody except Rajsingh", he added.

Mohinder said that the AIC expected decision before the Board's special general body meeting was held at Hyderabad on December 16, 1989.

Two days later Mohinder contradicted from Sialkot. He said that he never said that Indian players would boycott the tour to New Zealand if gradation of payment was not made. While insisting that he had been misquoted, he said : "It is never the intension of players to hold the Board to ransom". All I said was we would like to negotiate with the Board before the meeting on December 16, he added.

Mohinder had a detailed discussion with senior players

while being in Pakistan. He also met other players. He found that players were, by and large, against any confrontation. On return to India Mohinder did not continue with his favourite subject of gradation of payment. Actually players were not as united as he had thought. He felt it was pointless to continue this battle when there was not much possibility of victory.

# 63

# Twists Of Destity

Raman Lamba, a flamboyant Delhi batsman played himself in for the first Test at Karachi in 1989 as he slammed a hurricane knock aginst the BCCP Patron's XI. Azharuddin, still in indifferent form, could not get among runs. The team management, with Chandu Borde as manager, did not want to risk inclusion of any one who was not in form. When Azhar readied himself to leave the hotel to meet his relations, he was told that he would not be among 11. He was out of the team after playing 30 continuous Tests.

Lamba, in the team, had suddenly developed a sore ankle. Some felt that he had chickened out as he thought Karachi was not a right centre to make a beginning. He went to Borde and showed him his sore ankle. This was on the morning of the start of the Test. Borde was upset with him for not informing him about his injury a day or two earlier. Lamba's answer was that he was hoping that swelling would subside with rest and treatment but unfortunately it did not.

Out went Lamba and in came Azharuddin. Luck now befriended Azhar who took five catches in an innings to equal the world record. Some of the catches that he plucked were simply marvellous.

Batting with a changed grip, as recommended by Zaheer Abbas, Azharuddin made 35 beautiful runs before he attempted an unorthodox cross batted shot and was dismissed by Imran Khan. But his delightful knock had pleased both skipper Srikkanth and Borde. It raised hopes that he was returning to form that he had displayed against Gower's England a few years ago. He again made 35 when he was declared caught at wicket off Abdul Qadir. His two knocks were not substantive enough, but they were good enough for him to stay in the team. He had already proved his worth as a top-class fielder.

When Lamba had opted out of the Test, some journalists felt that it was a diplomatic pulling out of the team. A senior journalist R. Sriman wrote a copy on these lines in a Gulf paper. Lamba had read it and he felt terribly upset. Sriman, in his usual exuberance, took some Pakistani friends into the Indian dressing room the following afternoon. Lamba showed his rudeness to him within the hearing of Borde who, instead of reprimanding Lamba, asked the journalist that he might have avoided coming to the dressing room.

Sriman, one of the most seasoned journalists, was disappointed at Lamba's behaviour and Borde's attitude. He realised that it was not very judicious on his part to have gone to team's dressing room. Sriman was not the first nor would he be the last to be insulted if journalists and others took the liberty of rushing to dressing room which was players' private room.

Azharuddin was dismissed for zero in the first innings of the second Test at Faislabad, But he played a grand knock in the second innings. He scored a classic century, which was his first outside India. In jitters in nineties, he had also the mortification to see Sachin Tendulkar getting run out because of gross misunderstanding between the two. There were some who felt that Tendulkar had sacrificed his wicket to let the settled batman continue his innings. It was indeed a great doing by a youngster, who was not yet 17.

Azharuddin continued to display his form in the next two Tests at Labore and Sialkot. The tide had now fully turned. His mother's prayers had done him world of good to his cricketing life. From the brink of being sidelined in the first Test, he rose to become a formidable batsman. He rose to become India's captain on return from Pakistan. His elevation also saw his friend Srikkanth being sidelined from the team altogether. This caused him a great anguish as Azharuddin thought Srikkanth had a lot to offer to the Indian team. Such are the twists of destiny!

The sudden and untimely permanent termination of Lamba through a blow of the ball at Dhaka spread a widespread gloom in the cricketing world.

No sooner Lamba's last remains were consigned to flames at Nigambodh Ghat than the evil and vicious head of money surfaced. Differences between his wife kim (Ireland) and his brothers surfaced with all the intensity.

When Lamba was hit by the ball, he lay in comma. An emergent operation was performed. Doctor from Apollo Hospital subsequently flew to Dhaka at the behest of Sonia Gandhi. But it was too late. His battling in hospital became his eternal sleep.

Lamba was essentially a very fine human being.

# 64

# Scindia Succumbs To Pressure

The Punjab Cricket Association (PCA) bosses were strange officials. One moment they could be generous and magnanimous and next moment they could be petty and mean.

For the Delhi-Punjab league match in North zone contest in 1990-91, one of the official umpires did not turn up because of lack of adequate communication between the umpire and the Umpires Sub-committee. B. Nagarala Rao (Karnataka), a last minute replacement for A.V. Jaya Prakash (Karnataka), could not reach.

Venkataraghavan, one of the celebrated umpires in the world, was at Kotla. The more pleadings were made to the manager Bishan Bedi and PCA management, the less they were willing to oblige. Urgent telephone calls were made to the powers-that-be but no worthwhile result could be had. Eventually a former Ranji player and a recognised umpire Pritam Sood was drafted into standing in the match. This was not accepted by Bedi and the Punjab team and the match was played under protest. This was first time Ranji match was being played under protest. PCA had made a mockery of Indian cricket and national championship. Ranji must have turned upside down in heaven.

Bedi luckily did not doubt Sood's integrity but suspected

his "capability". As no DDCA official was present, Sood was replaced with Anil Choudhary at the insistence of Bedi. It was a shocking decision as Chaudhary was not a Ranji panel umpire. Sood replaced Choudhary. This led to protest by PCA.

Punjab lost the match conclusively at Kotla by nine wickets. But PCA went to court challenging the qualification of Delhi and Haryana from the North Zone for the knock-out stage. The protest was not as much against poor umpiring but to malign the Board president Madhavrao Scindia. The court case led to suspension of the knock-out round for two months. The competition resumed on April 16 and the final was played in the first week of May, which was hardly conducive for competitive five-day match.

Bedi, world class spinner in his days, should have shown magnanimity and carried on with the game instead of playing "under protest". The Delhi-Punjab match was not local engagement. Bedi was upset at DDCA's handling emphasising that "DDCA officials acted as if they were a law into themselves".

Whatever might be Bedi's pronouncements, he did not endear himself. The match could not have been postponed or cancelled on account of non-arrival of one umpire. When one umpire could not reach, the Delhi-Haryana match went on without any problem. Instead of reaching Gurgaon (Haryana), the umpire in question reached Goregaon (Mumbai)! Amusing is not it!

During this period, another stiff controversy surfaced. Dissatisfied with the Rungtas, almost all players had formed an independent state body to help promote and popularise cricket in Rajasthan. Two teams were now being chosen, one sponsored by former stars, and another by the Rungtas. The players were right and the Rungtas were wrong.

Venues were changed overnight and district administration informed. Police bandobast was made at venues, should there be any violence. The players' cause was genuine and they were almost set to steal a march over the sitting unit of Rajasthan.

Driven to desperation, Purshottam Rungta sought support and patronage of the rival faction, dominated by Jagmohan Dalmiya and Inderjit Singh Bindra. The Board's meetings were held at Oberoi's hotel and not Taj Palace. When Scindia relinquished his office after completing his term, the Board's hoteliers were again changed from Oberoi to Taj Palace.

In the lobby of Oberoi hotel, Dalmiya and his men said that they had sent an SOS to Scindia that if Rungta's team did not play Ranji matches, no matches would be played in East Zone. Scindia succumbed under pressure. He thought that he would get a bad name if Ranji Trophy could not be finished. He let Rungta team play instead of the side supported by former stars of Rajasthan. Scindia sadly did tremendous disservice to Rajasthan cricket which continues to suffer because of indifferent organisation.

# 65

# Rumour Mill At Work

The three-nation tournament comprising India, Pakistan and West Indies in Sharjah in October 1991 raised bitter controversies. India had to play one match when street lights had been on and baseless allegation was levelled against skipper Azharuddin for not giving off his best against Pakistan as he was a Muslim. Never had desert smelt so bad !

The Indians, seldom comfortable in Sharjah, began well beating Pakistan and West Indias in style. The expatriate Indians, for once, nurtured a sanguine hope that India might do the trick this time. They flocked in larger number at stadium than before. But five Indian expatriates could not be equal to one Pakistani expatriate in shoutings and drum-beating.

When India met Pakistan in the last group match, the approach to the wicket and outfield were extremely soggy following previous night's heavy downpour. The start of the game had to be delayed. The reduction of overs should have been enforced. But the rival teams and umpires decided to play full quot of 100 overs (50 overs each side). It was a very injudicious decision.

When India's reply started, the light was failing rapidly. When the 43rd over began, the light was very dim. No one, none at least in the Indian team, was aware what the playing conditions were. Each was consulting the other.

When the 45th over started, with fast bowlers in operation, the street lights had been switched on. Sanjay Manjrekar, who was keeping India's challenge alive, was batting from his memory as assessing pace of Wasim Akram and Waqar Younis in that light was impossible. Luckily bat met the ball beautifully in virtual darkness. The light was so poor that even spectators did not know what was happening in the centre.

Now there was total confusion in the players' pavilion. Asif Iqbal was seen pacing up and down. He was seen discussing with the Board president Madhavrao Scindia to sort out the matter. What was happening at the stadium caused a lot of anguish to both cricket manager Ashok Mankad and skipper Azharuddin. But they could not be considered unblemished as it was their blunder not to have studied playing conditions. The Sri Lanka umpires were as perplexed as the batsmen at the crease were. The Sri Lanka umpires should have called off the game as there was a great danger of any batsman getting seriously injured.

Pakistan tactices of employing fast bowlers was extremely deplorable. It was all the more shocking because India had allowed them to substitute as many as three players. According to rules they were not permitted to do so. Pakistan play their cricket against India as if they are on war front. They do not believe in "grace" and "ethics" they practice in winning by hook or crook.

The victory gave Pakistan added confidence and that helped them run over India in the final. As Azharuddin was dismissed for yet another zero–second in succession expatriate Indians started making foolish and absurd allegations. Heavily losers in their gambling, they started alleging that Azharuddin had deliberately thrown away his wicket as he was a Muslim. What was most obnoxious was that it was rumoured that Azhar had been a beneficiary and had received a lot of money for "gifting" away his wicket. Nothing could have been more disturbing than this allegation which had no substance whatsoever.

Iftikhar Ali Khan Pataudi, Ghulam Ahmed, Mansur

Ali Khan Pataudi and Azharudding all have led the country faithfully and dedicately. Host of others, like, Abbas Ali Baig, Abid Ali and Syed Kirmani have played with utmost care and enthusiasm for the country. It is foolish to doubt their sincerity. What is most shocking is that it is the officials and petty-minded office bearers who indulge in such tomfoolery.

A former Indian cricket manager once said that cricket in Sharjah is for the Pakistanis, by the Pakistanis and of the Pakistanis. The majority of the people looking after CBFS are Pakistanis with Asif Iqbal and Asif Noorani at the helm of affairs. The CBFS officials do harness support from one or two "super star Indians for certain consideration". This is the most unfortunate aspect of Sharjah.

The Indian Board president N.K.P. Salve's car had a minor accident. He was waiting for a taxi or some car which could transport him to the hotel. Says Salve: "In the meantime, a jeep full of enthusiastic young supporters of Pakistan stopped in front of us. They were delirious with joy and were shouting, dancing and chanting slogans "Pakistan Zindabad, Hindustan Murdabad. The jeep stopped right in front of us and perhaps seeing the car with Indian flag, they were provoked. In a frenzy, they started shouting. Hindustan Murdabad with renewed vigour. They obstructed the traffic and would not move. They commanded us to join them. We stood absolutely dumbfounded and extremely confused at the situation. On our non-compliance with their orders, indignation of the occupants of the jeep kept constantly rising, making them dangerously oppressive and they lavished choicest abuses and invectives on us in chaste Urdu".

In April 1986, Javed Miandad hit a six off Chetan Sharma's last ball to give Pakistan one of the most sensational victories over India. A ball earlier, the last batsman Tauseef survived an easy run out chance as Azaruddin could not hit the stumps from a close range. This single brought Miandad to striker's end.

Let there be no mistake. Sharjah is a miniature Patistan.

There everything is permissable as long as it benefits Pakistan. Take, for example, umpiring. It was blatantly in favour of Pakistan. Leg before wicket decisions apart, there was no consistency in calling "wide ball". Had umpires called wide, Pakistan might not have won their match against West Indies. What was shocking was that the umpires erred in counting "balls". These mistakes took place at crucial stages.

The consensus among Indians, settled in UAE (United Arab Emirates) is that Indians, unconcerned about their self respect, play in Sharjah to "shop" and then play. It should be other way around. They should first play and then shop.

Organisers in Sharjah are totally partisan. Yet foolish Indians play there because both players and officals are beneficiaries. For an Indian, money is a deciding factor. If it is black money, it is all the better.

In the name of "Cricketers Benefit Fund Series (CBFS) commercial benefits are being achieved. To Abdul Rehman Bukhatir, it is one of the lucrative business avenues. To Asif Iqbal, it is one of the sources of "livelihood". To Indians, money is all pervading even if reputation is marred and dignity deflated. To Board officials, free travel, sumptuous meals and "black-lebel" are refreshing enough even if the team suffers humilating defeats. "So what" says an official, adding : "one team has to lose".

# 66

# Vilification Campaign
# Against Azhar

Azharuddin's batting had fallen apart as he had scored
only 50 runs in five innings on the tour to Australia in
1991-92. Caught amidst his own batting failures, an
essentially reserved man became a loner. He had however
a complete support from his players, particularly jurniors,
but there were many who considered his captaincy a
suspect.

Disturbed at his personal failures and sub-standard
doings of the team, an influential lobby initiated a move in
India calling for a change of the captain for the World
Cup. Newspapers and magazines painted him as a villaim.
The newspapers were full of stories highlighting
Azharuddin's failures during the pendency of the tour.
Opinion polls were organised. Criticism, malicious
occasionally, projected only one thing and that was an
anti-Azharuddin lobby which was at work. In the
vilification compaign against Azharuddin, many senior
journalists failed to realise that there were still two Tests
left and it was unfair to condemn the man at this point of
time. Upset Azharuddin was but he was shocked as to
why change in leadership for the World Cup was being
demanded by people when he had already been announced
skipper for the prestigious event.

The tide turned in the second innings of the fourth Test

at Sydney, where Azharuddin silenced his detractors with a masterly century. His valuable knock of great authority came to naught as two umpires, Peter McConnel and Darrel Hair, were at work. Their supervision left much to be desired. They seemed more incompetent than the umpiring in sub-continent. Sunil Gavaskar wrote that India were up against 13 players. What was published in Indian papers was carried back to Australia through news agencies. One Australian paper further sensationalised the issue by headlining it "Cheats". The Australian umpires were reportedly contemplating a legal action but good sense prevented them from doing so. The consensus in Australia was that the umpires had erred and the criticism against them was not wholly unjustified.

During Melbourne's second Test, Australians appealed for a catch in slips against Azharuddin. The umpire negatived it. Allan Border thought Azharuddin was caught and the umpire had erred. "Why don't you walk", Border reportedly told Azharuddin. The Indian skipper said that he had not seen the catch being taken and therefore he would go by the decision of the umpire. This was one of the rarest of rare incidents that an Indian batsman had got a benefit of doubt, if there was an element of doubt. Actually, the series witnessed such controversial umpiring that Border should have been man enough to have asked his men to "walk" instead of asking Azharuddin. Had umpiring been as impartial, as it ought to have been, India's overall performance in Tests would not have been so depressing.

The team did not perform to its potential in the World Cup also. But Azharuddin batted superbly scoring four half centuries. The storm pertaining to captaincy, however, continued when the team returned. All out efforts were made to dislodge Azharuddin from the office of the captaincy. Wilful criticism was launched against him. Some retired players went on record as saying that it was imperative to bring about change in the interest of the Indian cricket. The louder was the criticism, the more restraint Azhar became. He replied his detractors with silence and dignity.

On Azharuddin's silence, this amusing anecdote is worth narrating. A British journalist was attending a Press conference called by a Japanese. The Britisher stayed there for 5-10 minutes, but the chairman did not say a word. After another five minutes, the Britisher thumped his feet and stamped the table saying why was no one speaking. The chairman quietly rose from his chair and said. "Silence is golden, if you can improve upon it, you are welcome".

In private discussion with his intimate friends, Azharuddin is reported to have said. "If I tell the truth about a few persons and their doings, there would be far greater uproar in the country than what people have been hearing".

Azharuddin's reaction is the same as that of Kapil Dev who had gone on record as saying that he also wanted to withdraw from playing at Kolkata. "But if I had done that I will have hell to pay for it", he had said.

Azhar's innings of captainy continued uninterrupted, thanks to support from the "invisible finger of Indian God". But his "blues" surfaced when he tried to project that he had come of age and he also had his opinion. This was not likened by the "Indian God".

# 67

# Opposition Silenced

Purshottam Rungta used to call Amrit Mathur as a "Junior Maharajah". Ajit Wadekar, a former India captain and a cricket manager, confirmed it in South Africa in 1992-93 saying that he was helpless as he (Mathur) was 'Maharajah's man. He was candid in saying all this as decisions pertaining to strictly cricket matters were taken more by Mathur than by him. Mathur had gone on tour as administrative manager.

When the team returned from South Africa, Wadekar was retained as a cricket manager. He formulated his own "code of conduct". Among them was "no personal engagement during a Test match". Before putting his "code of conduct" to practice, he had a friendly chat with all the chosen players. "Be frank and let me know whether you approve of them"? he asked. The players surprisingly went whole hog with him. The first hurdle crossed, he now thought of developing togetherness among 11-14 players.

When the question cropped up about captaincy, Wadekar reportedly made it clear that it would be easier for him to get along with Azhar than with any other player. He argued that the continuity was essential and he whole-heartedly supported Azhar's candidature. There was still a strong lobby at work against Azhar. The lobby's slogan was that he was too withdrawing a player to get the best out of his players. Wadekar stood by his conviction that Azhar should be persisted with against England (1992-93) in the home series. The selection committee was divided but it respected Wadekar's decision partially by appointing Azhar for two one-dayers and a Test.

Azhar dazzled in the first Test at Kolkata, his favourite Eden Gardens, where he played an innings of his life. His 182 ranked one of the best of his career, took the series away from England. This knock and India's 3-0 verdict against England forced his detractors to lie low.

Supported by Wadekar, Azhar continued at the helm of affairs for another three years. Another round of controversy began as India failed to perform in the Wills World Cup followed by indifferent showing in the Singer Cup at Singapore and the Pepsi Cup at Sharjah. As if cricket controversies were not enough, he was involved in "personal problems" which were sadly highlighted by Press. His manhandling of a photographer at Bangalore was held against him. His affair with the film actress Sangeeta Bijlani and his divorce with his wife Naureen were published with a lot of "mirch and masala". Amidst this vex scenario, Azhar failed in batting often. He was accused of lacking in motivation. All kinds of allegations were levelled against him. That was most unfortunate. His manager in England in 1996, Sandip Patil, also failed to "guide" him. He did not adhere to rules of the team discipline. In addition, he occasionally got out trying to execute atrocious shots.

Azharuddin was relieved of captaincy as the team returned from England. Sachin Tendulkar, 23, was given charge of the team. He attended selection committee meetings but, being a voteless member, he often did not get the team he wanted. He was heard but his views were not respected. Over-burdened with responsibilities of captaincy, which he was not enjoying, his batting did not flourish. He soon got disillusioned. He was caught between devil and deep sea. He did not know how to handle the situation. The selectors were dominating. They gave him even 11 for the match. He felt indignant. He was at the helm of affairs for only about a year when he suddenly made up his mind. He relinquished from the office. His supporters (at least two former stars), who were also detractors of Azhar, felt upset. But nothing could be done.

The selectors were left with no option. They brought Azhar back. They gave him the reigns of the team. This happened after the secretary Jaywant Lele had issued a statement saying that "Azhar should be taught a lesson and he should have been dropped from one-day home series against Sri Lanka". Sunil Gavaskar, while commenting on Azhar's run out during the Champions Trophy in Sharjah, had said on television : "He is running as if there is no tomorrow for him".

Azharuddin's "perfect past" came to his rescue for the dissent against umpire S.K. Bansal's verdict in the India-Australia Test match at Bangalore in 1996. The match referee John Reid took a lenient view and let Azhar go with a warning. His dissent led to spectators throwing bottles on the ground. He had to undertake "peace march" around the ground to pacify agitated spectators.

Azhar was again out and Tendulkar was back in the saddle as captain. For a short while he was even out of the team. But he submitted his fitness certificate (shoulder trouble) and regained his berth in the team.

# 68

# Rungta's High Handedness

Kishan Rungta, like his elder brother Purshottam, did not use his powers discreetly. He caused an uproar when he took an unprecedented action in sacking Madhya Pradesh professional and captain Chandra Kant Pandit on the futile plea of "not trying enough". It was a too serious charge and a wild allegation against the professional captain, who had done a lot in promoting MP cricket. It was also said that Kishan Rungta had not concurred with his colleagues before dismissing Pandit from the captaincy of the Central Zone.

Rungta was singing songs of praise of Pandit when Central Zone was sitting pretty. Suddenly, Central Zone went down in dump with three run-outs and the Deodhar Trophy match against West Zone ended in a tie.

Following criticism, the meeting was held at the Railway sports control Board (RSCB) office. The meeting lasted for 100 minutes. UP's representative Anand Shukla supported Rungta. The Railway coach Venkat Sunderam wore the garb of neutrality. So did Chandu Sarvate (M.P.) If Rungta's decision was "dictatorial". The committee verdict was "laughable".

Rungta should have been censored by the Board, particularly by the Central Zone authorities. But no action was taken as he was a "chum" of the Board president Rajsingh Dungarpur. Friendship was one aspect but administration was entirely another. There should have been a healthy mix of both but sadly Rajsingh had different views.

The Board's former president Madhavrao Scindia, president of the Madhya Pradesh Cricket Association (MPCA) had made public utterances that he would see to it that justice was done to Pandit.

Holding that sacking of Pandit from the captaincy and team (Central Zone) was nothing short of highhandedness by the national selector and zone chairman Rungta, Scindia said: "It was unheard of that a professional should have been dismissed on the plea that he had not been trying hard enough for the team". "The action by Rungta smacked of bad taste and victimisation as Pandit had done a great deal for the upliftment of the MP team", added Scindia.

In reply to Board's letter of February 27, 1997, says Pandit in his letter of April 22, 1997. In brief, "I have to submit that after the match (Central-West in Deodhar Trophy), which ended in a tie, the chairman of the Central Zone selection committee approached me and informed me that I have been dropped from the team as I had not done my best for the team. He, however, added that if I desired I could declare myself unfit. I was shocked at the action taken by the chairman. He did not give me even a chance to explain what he meant by saying 'I had not done my best for the team'. To add insult to injury, he advised me to declare myself unfit when, in reality, I was not at all unfit. The extreme action on the part of the chairman, to say the least, was unfair, arbitrary and amounts to victimization, particularly when other selectors of the zone were not consulted.

"In my view, this was a very bad precedent as by this method any one could be removed from the team or the captaincy by one single individual selector, and it will have far reaching effects on the players, not only Central but all over India. Later, I was informed by the MPCA secretary that the CZSC was told I was dropped on cricketing grounds, but if I tender apology to the satisfaction of the chairman, I will be included in the team. I cannot understand that if the action against me was taken on cricketing gound, why I was not informed earlier and secondly how an action taken on cricketing ground could be compounded with my tendering apology. This was the worst humiliation".

The matter was scheduled for discussion at Mumbai's working comittee meeting on April 22. The matter was not discussed. Subsequently, the case was closed.

Who says friendship in the country is not more important than Justice and fairplay.

# 69

# Stubborn Behaviour Of Gavaskar

Hardly had the first Chennai Test between India and Pakistan ended on February 8, 1987 than Sunil Gavaskar issued a statement emphasising that he would not be available for the second Test and one-dayer at Kolkata because of "personal ressons".

Soon "personal reasons" were pushed into background as it came to surface that Gavaskar had withdrawn from playing at Kolkata to stick to his "vow" in 1984-85 when, while playing against England, he and his wife Pammi had been allegedly insulted by infuriated section of spectators. Already upset at the exclusion of Kapil Dev for one "rash" shot at Delhi, the spectators booed and jeered Gavaskar throughout the match for his "unimaginative" captaincy. This was the cause of Gavaskar's annoyance and he had publicly announced there and then that he would "never again play in Kolkata".

Almost entire country, including Gavaskar's ardent admirers, felt that his decision to withdraw from the Kolkata Test was hasty, impulsive and over-emotionalised reaction. The dispassionate critics held the view that cricket players as also matinee stars, were public heroes and they should learn to live above mundane level of mass hysteria. When they do not mind an exaggerated quantum of praise, they should also suffer criticism and cat-calling occasionally. The consensus was that "little master" should have been magnanimous enough to have forgotten the episode and fogiven Kolkatans for their boorish behaviour. Had he done it, he would have endeared himself more throughout the country, particularly in Kolkata. The more appeals were made to him and more persuasive letters and messages were sent to him, the more stubborn he became. Instead of seeing reason that he had made his point of view loudly enough, he kept on harping that he was not available for the Kolkata match.

When all persuasion by honourable citizens of Kolkata and Government failed, Kolkatans now wore a very strong posture. They lashed out at Gavaskar. Among many accusations, they said. "We give a damn to personal reasons. Wanted information, age 37, height 5'4" not a sportsman". The Kolkata Press carried all kinds of caricatures and sketches condemning him for his stubborn attitude. So upset were Kolkatans that they even burnt his effigy.

Following unprecedented appeals, Gavaskar now turned polite and diplomatic. He said: "Thank you for your message. The sentiments expressed are much appreciated. Even in the circumstances of my availability were to change, it would be unfair of me to deprive a player of his place since the side is already selected. Thanks once again and with sincere best wishes to you and the people of Kolkata". This telegram was sent by Gavaskar in response to the Minister Subash Chakroborty's message.

Pakistan "coloured" this Gavaskar episode differently. Bashir Khan, a radio commentator, in his book "Pakistan in India 1987" (the para has been reproduced without his permission) says: "Gavaskar, though greater than any of the sporting greats India has produced, should have been sensible enough to learn from some of his predecessors who had become the target of public fury in the past. For instance, when Bill Lawry's Australians defeated India at the Eden Gardens in 1969-70, the then Indian captain, Mansur Ali Khan Pataudi, was meted out a most discourteous behaviour by the Kolkata crowd. So much so that when one spectator threw a chair at Pataudi, it was not him who lost his cool, rather the Australian captain, Bill Lawry, reacted so violently that he in fact gave a thorough beating to the offender. But unlike Gavaskar, the Nawab kept his cool; did not vow never to play at the Eden Gardens or issued unsporting statements about the Kolkatans. Not that the Nawab was an ordinary player. In the category of Manjrekar, Lala Amarnath and Vinoo Mankad, he was, at that juncture in the history of Indian cricket, a cricketer par excellence, a celebrity. Despite being a Muslim, insulted and abused by a predominantly Hindu crowd, the perfect gentleman not only obliged the selectors when he was recalled in 1974-75 to lead India against Clive Lloyd's West Indians, but played at Kolkata without any reservations. This "forgive and forget attitude" rehabilitated his image in the eyes of Kolkatans in particular and the Indian public in general".

The Para speaks for itself. Where is the question of giving the Gavaskar episode a communal touch. Only Pakistani fanatic can indulge in such propaganda.

# 70

# Decline In Mumbai Cricket

What Lord's stands for English cricket and MCG (Melbourne Cricket Ground) for Australian cricket, Brabourne Stadium in Mumbai stood for Indian cricket for about half-a-century. It was a stadium, which was solid in structure and impresive in design. It had cricket imbedded in bricks, walls and ground. A precious gift from Anthony (Tony) de Mello, Maharajah Bhupindra Singh Patiala and Lord Brabourne, the stadium was unique in many ways. It retains its glamour, grandeur and warmth even after 65 years. It was a nursery for budding players, home for established stars and mecca of Indian cricket. Lindsay Hassett, Australia's vice-captain at one time, observed: "It is the only Test centre in the world where one can swim in the morning, play cricket in the afternoon, then dance in the evening all without leaving the enclosure". Similar sentiments were expressed by several other foreign cricket personalities. Sir Frank Worrell was in love with the stadium, including Cricket Club of India (CCI), where he felt as much at home as at his own home.

The idea for CCI and stadium was conceived in 1933 when 15 persons, all cricket lovers, affixed their signatures. In May 1936 Lord Brabourne, the Governor of Mumbai, laid the foundation stone in a solemn and impressive ceremony. December 7, 1937 was the auspicious day, when magnificent stadium was opened for an inaugural match against Lord Tennyson's team. CCI went from strength to strength, thanks to Sir Homi Mody, many years its president.

Host of several national, international and charity games, every cricket player, young and renowned, longed to play at the Brabourne Stadium. The matches were played without any problem. Both Mumbai Cricket Association (BCA) and CCI were the beneficiaries. The BCA was the rightful allottee of the fixture while CCI hosted it. A simmering problem over quantum of tickets and allotment of an important enclosure led to a serious row between BCA and CCI. It was an issue which should have been sorted out amicably in the interest of Mumbai cricket in particular and Indian cricket in general. But sadly it could not be.

It was a battle between CCI's Vijay Merchant, who had generally played cricket with straight bat, and Maharashtra's influential politician, S.K. Wankhede, who was soft-spoken, pleasant and ever smiling, but he was highly egoistic. Dissatisfied with CCI's functioning and Merchant's utterances through Press (here one national daily went all out to support CCI), Wankhede became all the more resolute to break away from the CCI.

The CCI's strength lay in Brabourne Stadium. Merchant and his supporters felt that the BCA could not "survive" without the "patronage" of CCI as there was no other stadium, which was good enough to stage an international match, particularly a Test match. Wankhede had faith in himself. He was aware that he had requisite influence with the Mumbai Government to get a suitable land allotted and a stadium constructed.

Merchant had erred in his Judgement. Bulk of profit went to Brabourne Stadium, while BCA got only about 20 per cent of profit. As if this was not enough, CCI refused to grant additional seats for its member clubs. Instead of avoidable confrontation equal partnership between CCI and BCA would have been in order because BCA was, after all, real alltottee for staging the match.

When Wankhede expressed his desire and also made known his plans, there were some who felt that the politician was talking rather too loudly. But Wankhede had done his home work before he went public. In no time he got the land allotted near Churchgate station and got plans prepared. He experienced no problem in conceiving as also in execution. Major part of funds were raised through industrialists, business tycoons and also Government agencies. What seemed a far-fetched dream, it soon became a reality. The work was undertaken on a war-footing. While engineers and architects were busy getting work done round-the clock, Wankhede and his team of officials undertook periodical vistits at odd hours to see for themselves that there was no laxity whatsoever. This was because Wankhede himself was the president of the BCA, while fifth Test between India and the West Indies was scheduled three months later from January 23, 1975.

When Clive Cloyd's West Indies team arrived in India and stayed in Mumbai, they undertook a visit at the stadium under construction after their nets. There were bamboo scaffolding lying scattered all over and there were coconut palms for lining. The material was lying strewn and the stadium-in-making looked more a jungle than a cricket playing field. They were unwilling to accept that this mess could be translated into a stadium for the Test.

When they arrived on January 21 for their scheduled Test, they found that the miracle had been achieved and there stood a brand new stadium with a brand new wicket.

The visitors had nets at the adjoining wicket. But they began to feel that the wicket was under-prepared and could break midway through the match. One of the officials took many photos of the pitch.

Contrary to West Indian players fears and apprehensions, the wicket "behaved". Lloyd struck his golden patch in the match. Dropped at 8, 70 and 154, he went on to hammer an unbeaten 242. His hurricane innings saw visitors run away with a comfortable win by 201 runs.

Following this defeat at the new stadium, constructed by a hard-core politician for his ego, glory and name, the BCA has been involved in several problems. There was time when Mumbai's second string could win Ranji Trophy untroubled. Now Mumbai's full side does not always qualify from its zone (West) for the knock-out contest.

# 71

# Who Paid Kapil's Expenses

There was no love lost between two of India's greatest Test players, Kapil Dev and Sunil Gavaskar. There was a constant under-current of friction between them even when they were members of the same national side. Gavaskar was an accomplished opening batsman of proven ability and skill, Kapil Dev was an excellent all-rounder with swing bowing being his forte. There was no justification whatsoever for two greats not seeing eye to eye. Sadly two could not bury the hatchet despite efforts by seniors, like N.K.P. Salve.

When Gavaskar retired from international cricket after amassing 10,000 plus runs and establishing world record of 34 centuries in Test cricket, many felt that the controversy between the two renowned personalities would die for the good of country's cricket. But sadly it did not happen.

Haryana were to take on mighty Mumbai in the Ranji final in Haryana. But Mumbai Cricket Association (BCA) made a fervent appeal to the Haryana Cricket Association for the change of the venus from Haryana to Mumbai.

The HCA consulted its senior players and, after detailed deliberations, HCA acceded to the BCA's request. It was an act of magnanimity on the part of the HCA players who, instead of playing amdist local environment, decided to challenge Mumbai tigers in their den.

Following this unprecedented arrangement between two state bodies, Gavaskar in his syndicated column entitled

"Who paid Kapil's expenses?" says: "Keeping part of the profits for the benevolent fund for former players started by the BCA is really a laudable one and in fact it should have been announced before the game for it may have attracted more people to the stadium. In any case profits of the game are known only after deducting the expenses and ensuring that these expenses are kept to the minimum.

"Will the BCA then tell us who paid for the expenses of Kapil Dev who stayed at a five star hotel while the rest of the Haryana team stayed at the BCA Garware rooms. Was Kapil's stay in a five-star hotel also a pre-condition to Haryana agreeing to play the final in Mumbai? There is no point saying that even during the semi-final at Kolkata Kapil stayed in a five star hotel while the rest of the Haryana team stayed elsewhere.

"This is not anybody's concern excepting Kapil and Haryana Cricket Association; but if the BCA profits are reduced because of having to pay Kapil's expenses, then they owe an explanation to the cricketing public of Mumbai and specially to the former cricketers for whom the benevolent fund is set up".

Kapil Dev was reportedly more amused than anguished at this highly exclusive news, called "scoop" in newspaper language.

# 72

# Spectators Trouble At Karachi

Ever since Pakistan has been born, there have been controversies in matches against India. When complaints against sub-standard umpiring subside, there is students or spectators trouble which has led to interruption of matches. Measures are undertaken but fanatics cause surprise to orgnisers and bring disrepute to their country. Hooligans however could not care less.

On February 3, 1983 at National Stadium (Karachi), a handful of spectators calling themselves as members of Islami-Jamait-u-Tulabe broke all barricades and rushed on to the pitch. Some of them uprooted stumps and started digging the pitch. While Indian players ran indorrs, Imran Khan and Sarfraz Nawaz thought of having a word with the hooligans before they could retrieve.

There was nothing much to enthuse over in the match. India had already lost the series 0-3 and this Test was heading for a draw when political activists were in action. Only handful of spectators were present on the ground.

The trouble erupted soon after lunch break. The agitated mob even attacked Press enclosure after asking visiting journalists to clear off from the enclosure. A team of journalists and officials of the Indian High Commission took shelter in the Indian dressing room until rioters cleared. The Indian ambassador K.D. Sharma and his deputy Consul General G. Parthasarathy were eye witnesses to this ugly incident.

The umpires made an attempt to restart the match, but it was not possible as the wicket had been tampered with.

Another incident took place when India were playing in Karachi in 1989. A spectator identified as Ziauddin, a calligraphist from an Urdu paper and a member of fundamental religious group, scaled the barbed enclosure on to the field. Shouting slogans, he tore Srikkanth's shirt and also had a confrontation with Kapil Dev.

Bearded Ziauddin in Awami suit, reportedly slipped through the security cordon before "gheroeing" Manoj Prabhakar. Abusive, he made some anti-India remarks and shouted about Babri Masjid. Srikkanth was visibly shaken. He was heard saying that anybody could have been injured had the offender been carrying a weapon or a knife. "The security arrangements are very poor", said Srikkanth. When he was told that the security bandobast had been reinforced and he should resume the match, he declined. At that juncture Pakistan was precariously placed. The Indians were shaken badly and were in no mood to resume the match.

A match in one-day series between India and Pakistan in 1991-92 had to be cancelled as vandals dug up the Wankhede Stadium wicket. The hoodlums had tampered with the wicket following a fiery speech by Shiv Sena chief Bal Thackeray who had gone on record as saying that the stadium would be burnt if Pakistanis were brought there to play.

The Mumbai Cricket Association joint secretary Bal Mahaddlkar was present at the stadium when activists dug up the pitch with sickles. He shouted for police but, by that time, the miscreants had fled. Not content with this, Thackeray gave a call for a bandh on October 28, the day of the scheduled match.

The Mumbai match was cancelled. The venue was shifted to Gwalior. But more threats were issued by Shiv Sena. The two Boards conferred and they decided that "discretion was better part of valour" under these existing circumstances. They chose to call off the series. Following this cancellation, India undertook a historic tour to South Africa.

It is a total misnomer that the series between India and Pakistan brings players and peoples of the two countries together. Cricket between the two countries is no longer a sport to enjoy and recreate but it is a war game, which promotes violence, accusations of cheating through umpires.

In inaugural series in India in 1952-53, India managed to win 2-1, but forced a draw in Pakistan in 1954. Another drawn series in 1958 in India when no exchange of visits between two countries could be possible as armies were in action. It was at Kanpur (1958), Pakistan skipper Fazal Mahmood pencil-marked pitch after day's play as he suspected that organisers would "tamper" with the wicket. Many eye-brows were raised at Fazal's action. Two wars were fought in 1965 and 1971 when yet another new country, Bangladesh, came into being.

When exchange of visits was resumed, many unforeseen controversies surfaced.

1978 : India lost the series to Pakistan. Bishan Singh Bedi, dismissed from captaincy, was bitter about umpiring and complained about bugging of telephones.

1979-80 : The series was marred by incidents. The Indian umpiring was questioned and Sikandar Bakht kicked the stumps down in sheer disgust. Pakistan skipper Asif Iqbal accused of "selling series to India".

1982-83 : India "Imraned out" by Pakistan

Indians, bothered by pace and swing, accused umpiring for their defeat.

1983-84 : Rift between two friends, Sunil Gavaskar and Zaheer Abbas, surfaced. The bone of contention was different interruption pertaining to bowling of 20 mandatory overs. Gavaskar, on way to his century, 28th, was of the view that the continuation of the game was in order, while Zaheer felt that it was pointless to continue with motions since there was no hope of a decision. He thought it was the team game and there was no room to continue with a view to establishing records.

1984 : Gavaskar lashed out at umpires emphasising that it was a sheer miracle that India could force a draw at Lahore, thanks to Mohinder's lusty century.

1986-87 : "Cricket diplomacy" brought Gen Zia-ul-Haq to Jaipur, But the series was marred as Pakistan fielders were stoned by a hostile crowd.

1989-90 : Spectator violence persisted. One fanatic scaled the wall and tried to manhandle Indian senior players, like, skipper Srikkanth, Kapil Dev and Manoj Prabhakar.

When someone asked when is cricket not cricket, out came reply: "When it is played between India and Pakistan". There is needless tension between the two teams, officials of two Boards and people at stadium and on TV net-work.

1999 : spectators at Chennai showed how cricket should be watched. The behaviour of spectators was exemplary. Delhi crowd did not display the spirit shown by Chennai spectators. Kolkata destroyed the atmosphere altogether.

# 73

# Umpires Err At Hyderabad
# Against NZ

What should have been an easy series against New Zealand in 1969-70 became rather-tough as Indians played casually instead of displaying keenness and enthusiasm. Unlike Kiwis who were inspired and motivated, the Indians wore complacency. This made all the difference in out-cricket of two teams.

India began their campaign well winning the first Test at Mumbai by 60 runs. They should have capitalised on this victory. Instead they plunged head-long in to trouble at Nagpur where they lost by a huge margin of 167 runs.

During the Test some players, who were "spirited", had a brawl on the main road (Nagpur). They were lucky that they were not arrested.

As if this deplorable performance was not bad enough, the Indians went on to give a pathetic display at Hyderabad. To New Zealand team's modest total of 156, Indians surrendered nine wickets for 49. Then Bedi lent some support to Venkataraghavan putting on 40 runs for the last wicket to help India manage 89.

The Test was wrapped up in controversies now. The umpires S. Bhattacharya and M.V. Nagendra erred in failing to cut the grass on the pitch on the rest day (third day) as it was agreed upon by teams in playing conditions. The umpires wanted to take law into their hands and cut the grass on the fourth day (Third playing day). Dowling made it clear to the umpires that it was not permissible now. The umpires had the temerity to say that they forgot to do so. Dowling's answer was simple. "Do two wrongs make one right"? To this, the umpires had no answer.

Law said : "In a match of three or more days duration, the pitch shall be mown under supervision of the umpires before play begins on alternate days after the start of a match but should the pitch not be so mown on any day on account of play not taking palace, it shall be mown on the first day on which the match is resumed and thereafter on alternate days (for the purpose of this law a rest day counts as a day)".

The Law was slightly ambiguous, but the New Zealand captain and manager Gardon Burgess were right when they said that the pitch should have been mown on the rest day.

Dowling reportedly told umpires that he would not resume play if the pitch was mown. The pitch was, however, not mown. But the umpires complained to the Board against New Zealand team's interference in their duties.

A thick blade of grass saw Hadlee in particular secure a lot of purchase. He moved and cut the ball skilfully. He tormented Indian batsmen who looked a bunch of novices at the crease.

As if deplorable batting of India's top batsmen was not enough, a youngster got past the security cordon and rushed to the middle to congratulate Venkat and Bedi for their stubborn 10th wicket stand. Security guards, caught unawares, dashed in and thrashed the youth instead of just escorting him out, as it ought to have been done. The result : unrest and the spectators became agitated. They broke gates, burnt chairs and lit fire. The Central Reserve Police Force (CRPF) unit retaliated and started attacking innocent spectators. Play had to be abandoned on the day.

With a lead of 92, New Zealand rattled up 175 for eight declared. Left to get 268 for win, Indians were in tatters losing seven wickets for 76. Judging from their display, they should have lost the Test. The series ended 1-1 but, in fairness, Kiwis should here won it 2-1. They were definitely much better side in the last two Tests after losing the first.

The Indians were booed and jeered. Skipper Pataudi got so upset that he left the field for the dressing room. The match showed that Indians were not only vulnerable to speed but they were also unable to tackle moving deliveries. Hadlee, for example, was not very quick. His forte was movement of the ball through air. The Indian batsmen were often tentative and hung their bat out only to run into trouble.

New Zealanders, on paper, were a very average side. They were more so on Indian wickets. If Indians could not dominate Kiwis on their home wickets, who and where could they have?

The arrangements on ground were not adequate. Paying spectators were not provided the minimum facilities. They were naturally restive. When the riot broke, the situation should have been handled with calm and tact. Instead soldiers started acting tough and rough. This aggravated the situation.

# 74

# Bucknor Buckles

The two-member Indian team of officials, Ajit Wadekar and Amrit Mathur, were more soft and pliable than the occasion demanded on the tour to South Africa in 1992. In comparison, Dr Ali Bacher was highly calculative and shrewd. He was articulate and persuasive. His timing for serious discussion was as uncanny as his batting during his best years of cricketing life. Whatever he wanted to achieve, he did it. He wanted Coocabra balls for use in matches and he saw to it that the Wadekar-Mathur team agreed. Then he secured consent for TV umpire (third eye) for run out decisions.

Sachin Tendulkar was the first victim of the TV camera. He was given run out by the third umpire in the first Test of Durber. It was a very close decision and only slow-motion camera could have picked up the decision. Since Tendulkar was run out, there could be no protest from Indians while the home team were extremely happy on bagging the most important wicket.

Came the second Test at Johannesburg. South Africa had run into trouble gainst Prabhakar and were precariously placed at 26 for four wickets. Rhodes and McMillan, a defiant batsman, were engaged to rescue the side. They had managed some recovery when there was a run out appeal against Rhodes. Umpires Steve Bucknor negatived it. The fielders appealed again. They then pleaded for a reference to TV umpire. Bucknor, stubborn as he was, refused to refer to "third eye". The TV replays showed that Rhodes was at least one foot outside the crease. He went on to score 91. This decision was instrumental for South Africa saving the match.

On the insistence of the match referee Clive Lloyd, Bucknor addressed a press conference. He was candid in saying that Rhodes was run out, as projected by the TV camera. "Seeing that as I did, I now will not hesitate to refer the appeal to third umpire", said Bucknor. It was a significant departure from his pre-series statement in which he was forthright in saying that he would not depend upon the TV camera.

# 75

# Shocking Attitude

India's maiden, historic and friendship tour to South Africa in 1992-93 was enjoyable but it was not free from controversies. The Indians could not play to their potential as they had to attend several official get-togethers in addition to money-spinning private functions. No wonder India lost the Test series 0-1 and one-dayers 2-5 causing a great deal of embarrassment to a huge Indian population settled in South Africa for decades.

The Indian team, among other paid get-togethers, attended a function organised by Investe Bank in Cape Town on the evening of December 5, 1992. The function was arranged by Ebrahim Keskar, managing director of Orient Promotions at the behest of Amrit Mathur, administrative manager.

The management had demanded 1000 rands as appearnce money for each player. The bank authorities expressed their inability to pay cash. Then it was settled that each player would be presented a gold coin (Kruger)

The bank management had made it clear to the team officials that only those players/officials who were able to attend the function would be presented a Kruger, valued at Rs 10,000. But when the team arrived at the venue, Old Mutual Mission Hall, the management demanded Kruger for even those players who had not been able to make it.

Three senior players could not attend as they had prior

commitment elsewhere. The management insisted for a Kruger for them. Ken Joubert, director of the Bank, said that he was acceding to Indian team management's request as he did not want to disappoint them nor did he wish to spoil the function.

Surprisingly, the Indian management had advised the bank authorities that no Indian mediaperson might be invited for the function. Sunil Gavaskar was however present. He was there not because he was a mediaperson but because he was a celebrated cricket player.

Another controversy surfaced when Indians demanded appearance money from even Air India which, as co-sponors of the Test series, wanted to organise a get-together to market their airline.

Air India function got cancelled twice. Once on account of political reasons and the second time when the one-day international match at Johannesburg had to be postponed to the next day because of rain.

Eventually, Air India held a breakfast get together for teams and guests at Johannesburg Holiday Inn as the teams had a brief halt there from Bloenfentein to Durban.

Air India official V.K. Verma, in his brief observation, said that his airline had managed to force land in South Africa after two misses. To this, Mathur said: "Air India's force-landing has been a crash for the Indian team".

When the team was on way home, another controversy surfaced. It now pertained to players extra heavy baggage. The commander said that the flight could not be air-borne for Nairobi with so much baggage. He had a consultation with his bosses who advised him to carry all the baggage by defuelling the aircraft (flight SA-182). For doing this, he had to make a technical halt midway to uplift fuel. Because of this unscheduled stop mid-way, the flight arrived Nairobi Airport three hours behind schedule.

When the flight was nearing Nairobi, the cock-pit crew had a "dig" at the Indian team. The commander said: "Best of luck. You beat England so that we feel that we are better than Englishmen". The co-pilot went one better. He said: "Please do come again with a note-book and with a few other players so that we may be able to provide you one or two more lessons".

In sharp contrast to the attitude of players on the historic tour to South Africa in 1992, Don Bradman played cricket for recreation and pride and not for money. Sample this.

Sir Don eventually broke his "Gandhian" silence as he spoke his mind. When he gave a television interview to the ABC prior to the Ashes series, it came as a shock. He was then 82.

In those hory days of pre-World War II and thereabout, when Bradman was dismissed for a score inside of three figures like 99 or 90 or 85, the headline used to be, "Don Dismissed Cheaply". Those were the days when, attired in flannels with a flat cap, he was smitting the world's menacing bowlers to all corners.

It was indeed a touching farewell to Don who, in his final innings at Oval in 1948, was dismised for zero and four more runs stood between him and his achieving an average of 100. Such is cruel luck.

There is hardly an instance in the history when a son has expressed his desire to change his surname. That was in the case of Bradman's son who found it difficult to withstand the pressure of his father's high reputation.

Unquestionably Australia's most famous and enduring man, much ahead of Barry Humries and Paul Hogan, he was candid in saying that he was still spending three-four hours a day in answering fan mail.

When on a tour to England in 1948, Bradman was engrossed in handling "fan mail" aid official letters whcih were more than a "century" of letters in a day. He disposed of mail the same day. Maybe, Vijay Merchant followed in his foot-steps. He also used to acknowledge all the letters the day he received them.

When Bradman made 452 runs, it was said that he got his runs from 400 minutes. It was a totally wrong or inaccurate observation. He might have stayed at the crease for 400 minutes but he did not get 452 from 400 minutes. This has been cricket's biggest fallacy prevailing even now. A batsman can get runs only of balls bowled at him and not of minutes.

When Bradman was reconfirmed as world's greatest batsman in 1930, he went on record as saying that he wanted sport to be a recreation, adding: "I played it for pleasure". What a difference between him and modern players who demand money for even displaying their faces or taking food!

# 76

# Gardens Becomes Hell

It was March 13, 1996 when India lost every thing in the world of cricket. Reputation was marred, image was sullied, and Eden Gardens became hell as, on a night of shame, a section of unruly and uncivilised spectators brought yet again another round of disrepute to Kolkata and Kolkatans. This act of vulgarism was enacted when India were about to be done to death by inspired and motivated bunch of Sri Lankans in the 1996 World Cup semi-final.

Jagmohan Dalmiya's unintentional mistake of relaying the damaged strip following ill-fated opening ceremony was compounded into a blunder by skipper Azharuddin who allowed first use of the pitch to Sri Lanka. This was a very unwise decision.

The Eden Gardens was jam-packed. It was said that at least 10,000 tickets more than the capacity of the stadium were sold by the authorities. In the absence of turnstiles, it could not be ascertained but about 1.30 lakh spectators were present at the stadium about an hour before the start of the semi-final. Percy Abeysekara, one-man Sri Lanka army, and his friends were also at the stadium.

To Sri Lanka's 251 for eight in the stipulated 50 overs, India slid from 98 for two to 111 for five wickets. The situation worsened as India lost three more wickets while score moved to 120. There was no ghost of a chance for India staging a come-back in the match. The crowd now turned hostile. The words that they used were simply shocking. The venue became an unruly cauldron. A section of spectators resorted to throwing bottles and missiles. Effigies were burnt.

It was hot. There was hardly a drink to be had anywhere. But plastic bottles that rained down indicated as if entire Kolkata had been quenching its thirst.

There was total chaos at the stadium. The authorities did not know how to pacify unruly spectators, who were indulging in behaviour which could not have done credit to even urchins. The authorities, particularly Jagmohan Dalmiya, should have made an announcement that the match would be awarded to Sri Lanka, if the spectators failed to "behave". No such thing was done.

Amidst these chaotic conditions prevailing at the stadium, Upal Chandana, 12th man, fielding for the dehydrated Mohanama, was hit by a glass bottle. The umpires said that they were genuinely frightened to stay in the middle for any longer.

Several bonefires were lit in the stands. Clive Lloyd was witness to all the hooliganism that was let loose. He scurried to the middle and interrupted the game to ensure security of players.

Lloyd now swung into action. He had debris cleared from the ground. He then asked police to act in controlling the crowd. The game stayed suspended for awhile. All felt that sanity would descend on the sporting crowd. Lloyd came out in the middle to see whether it would be in fitness of things to resume play. He found it was a futile exercise to risk resumption in an environment, which was not conducive for play. He then reluctantly awarded the match to Sri Lanka.

It was a disgusting behaviour. It was watched by people world over. It provided an awful poor reflection on all Indians. It was more so to Kolkatans who were never tired of boasting about their stadium and their sporting links. Every sane Indian present at the stadium had to hang his head in shame. When Indian players came out for presentation, they were hooted, booed and jeered.

Who was responsible for this sordid behaviour? Indeed a section of spectators. They were indeed knave. But the fault was of some influential people who, after selling tickets in black and involved in heavy betting, were responsible for causing all this vulgarism at stadium. A fellow Journalist said : The mob spoilt this day. Some one instigated the mob".

Subsequent placards of "regret" and "we are sorry" carried no meaning whatsoever. The damage had been done and Kolkata had been burnt alive and all Kolkatans had to drown themselves in Hoogli, flowing nearby.

# 77

# An Injudicious Decision

The Board's committee, in an unanimous verdict under the chairmanship of Rajsingh Dungarpur at Mumbai in early 1998, took an unprecedented decision. It awarded equal punishment to both Tamil Nadu (tampering wicket at M.A. Chidambaram Stadium) and Delhi (refusal to resume play) from further participation in the National Championship (Super League Group B) on the accusation of "bringing the game into disrepute".

The judgment defied logic and common sense. How could both teams be guilty? Tamil Nadu were the hosts. The upkeep and maintenance of the wicket was their responsibility. Also what were three officials doing? Did they not notice or observe any violation of playing conditions? Did they not observe the wicket being tampered with by bowlers through spikes? Was the pitch in the same condition on the fourth morning as it was at close of play on the third day? Was the character of the pitch changed on the fourth day? If, according to umpires, the pitch had been tampered with, why should Delhi resume on a "dangerous" pitch.?

The question that arose was who was bringing the game into disrepute—the players or the Board officials? By this senseless decision—the Board had virtually committed "rape" in Indian cricket and, in the process, throttled many young and keen players from further participation.

If the Board action was correct, then the ICC should

have awarded life term to the entire Indore groundstaff and should have barred India and Sri Lanka from playing international cricket for at least one year for their refusal to play on the "dangerous" pitch.

If the match referee Pamanmal Punjabi, a former Test player, and umpires D.K. Kar and P.S. Godbole, observed that the Tamil Nadu bowlers and fielders were guilty of trampling upon the virginity of the pitch, then Tamil Nadu alone deserved to be punished. But if the three officials thought that the wicket had not been tampered with, wilfully, then Delhi should have been summarily dismissed.

Another question that should have been addressed to by the committee was who was guilty for causing this ugly situation? Was it on account of Ajay Sharma, scorer of 28 centuries in the National Championship? Had he gone crazy to act so irresponsibly at the ripe age?

The Board president should have examined the report of the umpires and the match-referee. If they had failed to discharge their duties faithfully and competently, they should have been dealt with instead of debarring the two teams and players.

The Board's judgment has set a very dangerous precedence.

# 78

# Gavaskar Assaulted

There was a lot of enthusiasm at Lord's as many Indians, settled in the United Kingdom, had turned up to watch Sunil Gavaskar and others after India's stupendous doings in the West Indies. The weather was warm on July 27, 1971 but it was no deterrant to players and spectators.

The Test throbbed into life as India seemed on high road to achieving a victory. India needed only 183 to win on the wicket which was playing easy. The visitors did lose two wickets, those of Ashok Mankad and Ajit Wadekar, early but Farokh Engineer and Gavaskar got firmly entrenched displaying variety of strokes. No one looked disturbed by the English attack which was not difficult to handle.

The pair had raised the total to eighties when an unfortunate incident occurred. John Snow, England's paceman, deliberately ran into Gavaskar. The master India batsman lost his balance and fell down. It was a horror of horrors. It was an incident, which had never taken place in the annals of international cricket. The officials of the Test and Country Cricket Board, MCC members and others were eye witnesses to the deliberate assault by Snow on a relatively tiny Indian batsman. It was a slur on the name of Englishmen. Once known for their exemplary conduct and behaviour even under exacting circumstances, the Englishmen seemed to have fallen on bad days. The wheel of cycle seemed to have turned full circle. Known for their good manners and behaviour, Englishmen seemed to have turned "villains" while Indians, once known for their bad conduct, appeared to have progressed.

Serenely moving to win, Engineer pushed the ball and called for a single. Gavaskar accepted the call and was in the process of running when Snow suddenly shoulder-charged him. Gavaskar lost his balance and fell down despite his effort to continue to run. He lost his bat, which was lying quite a distance away from him. Engineer reportedly shouted: "Hey Snow you should pick on someone of your size and height".

It was an ugly sight for a bowler charging a batsman without any reason or provocation. It was all the more horrifying as it happened in the Test match at Lord's, mecca of cricket. Snow apologised as he regained his composure. He apologised again. Gavaskar forgave him. But the incident was too serious for the authorities to take it lying down. He had already marred England's reputation as the incident was watched by thousands of peoples on TV worldwide.

Basil D'Oliveira, fielding in slips, says: "Engineer tapped the ball and went for a single. I remember Snowy running from the bowler's end and looking for Gavaskar out of the corner of his eye when he came level with the bowler. Snowy leaned on him and sent him flying. Snowy then threw his bat and the game went on. There was a big uproar about the incident and I remember telling Snowy in the dressing room. "What the hell did you do that for?" He said that Gavaskar had got in his way, but then Ray Illingworth told us both to shut up. Just then the action replay of the incident was shown on the dressing room TV. They stopped the action just as Snowy drew level with Gavaskar and it was clear that he was waiting for the little Indian".

D. Compton labelled Snow's behaviour "disgraceful". He pointed out that Snow's omission from the team for the second Test at Old Trafford was tantamount to a fine of

£50 that an English player used to get as match fee at that time.

According to Gavaskar, the whole affair had been blown-up out of all proportions to the actual happening on the field.

The Test ended in a draw. Any side could have won it. Rain played spoilsport.

# 79

# No Indian Was Invited

As money grew fast and true in cricket in 1970s through sponsor and TV networks, rumblings between players and managements surfaced. The managements, miser in their concept and thinking, wanted to continue to have lion's share, while players, essentially main actors, wanted to make dent into the profits made by the authorities through organisation of matches, Tests, one-dayers and others. The players' viewpoint was simple and straight-forward. "We rough it out in middle to earn a penny, while organisers sitting in cosy, air-conditioned rooms, bag bagful of pounds". The war of attrition began and awakening dawned on players. Each country threw up one or two "rebels" to improve the lot of players.

Amidst this vex scenario, the war between Australian Cricket Board (ACB) and Kerry Packer, a high profile boss of Channel Nine, erupted. From initial eruption, it raged furiously as Packer assumed tough posture saying that enough was after all enough. The trouble arose on television rights. The ACB was granting rights of telecasting international matches to only Australian Broadcasting Corporation. This was resented by Packer who said that his bids were better and the ACB could no longer be partial to ABC.

Packer's pleas fell on deaf ears. The ACB was unwilling to see reason. He said that he would organise his own series. The ACB laughed it off. Packer now said: "Now or never". He planned a series under the name World Series of Cricket (WSC). He made fabulous offers and sent advance money to players through his emissaries. Stars fell for money and signed up for his series. Coloured clothes and night cricket were born. The ACB panicked. It sought support of the ICC. All out efforts were made to prevent Packer Series from making a successful start. But it could not be schieved.

Players were barred by thair respective authorities but they could not care less as they were reaping harvest of riches through Packer WSC. Players from England, West Indies, Pakistan, Australia and also from South Africa were on view. When India undertook tour to Australia in 1977-78, only glamour fast bowler Jeff Thomson was in official side. All other renowned players had crossed over to the Packer Circus. Bobby Simpson (42) was dug out of his retirement to lead the Australian side. Litigations followed. But the Packer Series stayed unbothered and unconquered. He was adequetely helped by his two loyal and faithful officials, Andrew Caro and Lynton Taylor. They toured and recruited the players.

It is learnt—even now it is vehemently said so—no Indian, not even Gavaskar, was officially invited by the WSC officials though some kind of negotiations were made on phone. The players did not have faith in themselves to walk out of the Indian team though they whispered that they were joining the Packer faction to gain, regain or retain their berths in the team.

When India were on tour to Pakistan in 1978-79, Lynton Taylor was there. He was seen discussing with some Indian stars. Bedi happened to get in the same room by sheer chance. No one knew what actually transpired. But the fact of the matter remained—and it still remains— that no Indian player was ever officially invited.

Gavaskar went on record as saying that he and Kirmani were offered contracts. The Board acted. Kirmani, it was said, was sidelined from the team to England and Gavaskar lost his captaincy. How far this was true, no one could confirm.

Packer, Australian business tycoon, merely changed white flannels into coloured clothings but players have altered a noble discipline into money minting game. Players now attend dinners/lunches only when they are paid in cash or kind. The game has been prostituted from nobility.

# 80

# Shocking Decision

A team comprising youth and experience was sent to Sri Lanka in January 1974 to help them mature before they undertook tour to England a few months later. Pakistan was already supportive of Sri Lanka and India was playing its role so that Sri Lanka could be sanctioned full membership of the ICC.

In the match against Sri Lanka Board President's XI at initial stage, a minor accident took place within an hour of the game. Gundappa Vishwanth dashed for a ball racing to boundary. In doing so, he tripped over the boundary rope. Being short, he plunged and twisted his right knee which had sustained an injury some time ago. Swelling on his knee reappeared. He sat down and was carried off the field by a few players, including Madan Lal and Salgaonkar. He was provided first aid in the dressing room. Swelling subsided. It was not a serious injury in any case. Orthopaedic doctors and physiotherapists were optimistic that he would be fully fit in a day or two. Vishwanath was also certain that there was no cause for alarm as he found that the pain was reducing. Within two hours of the injury, he restarted limbering up exercises.

Without any justifiable reason, the management phoned the Board president Purshottam Rungta informing him about the minor injury sustained by Vishwanath. Without ascertaining facts properly, Rungta directed the manager to send Vishwanath back as Parthasarthy Sharma, of Rajasthan, was being flown as a replacement. Vishwanath was at nets when the news of his returning and Sharma's arrival was announced.

As Sharma landed at Colombo, Sri Lankan Board made a fine gesture saying that Vishwanath could continue to stay here and expenses incurred on him would be borne by them. But the Indian Board, for reasons unknown, rejected the offer.

Vishwanath, a gentleman of the highest order, was considerably shaken at the decision of the Board president. Almost all players were unanimous that there was no reason whatsover for his return and replacement coming. But that was Rungta who, in a heat of moment, could take any decision. There might, however, be no truth in the observation that he was keen on sending a player from his state and therefore he insisted on sending back Vishwanath.

Vishwanath, good-humoured and ever friendly, hardly spoke when he was being driven to the airport from his hotel. He picked up his baggage, walked normally and even moved about vigorously to prove that he was absolutely fit. His colleagues, who were with him at the airport, were sympathetic but they could do no more than that.

It was a pity that a player of his ability and skill as also of his temperament should have been meted out such harsh treatment by the Board president Rungta whose only role seemed to be to prove that he was the boss.

A few months after the return from Sri Lanka, the Indian team for the first Prudential World Cup was picked. A mere five-day conditioning camp was organised at Mumbai before the departure of the team to London on May 25, 1975. Venkataraghavan was the captain and Sunil Gavaskar was vice-captain.

Venkataraghavan could not attend the eyewash conditioning camp as he was already in England assisting Derbyshire in the County Championship. The responsibility of conducting the camp fell on Gavaskar.

For some unknown reasons three players Vishwanath, Kirmani and Mohinder played truant for four days before arriving in Mumbai on the eve of the departure of the team. Some other selected players went through the motions in the farcical camp which, needless to say, served no purpose.

Six players, who were attending the nets, were to stay at Wankhede Stadium where arrangements for their lodging and board had been made by the Board. The manager G.S. Ramchand allowed 'local players' to stay at their respective homes, if they desired.

When Rungta had come one morning to have breakfast with the six players having nets, he asked Gavaskar whether he was staying at Wankhede Stadium or at his home. When Gavaskar told him that he was spending nights at home, Rungta fired him impressing upon him that he should set example by spending all the reserve time with other players with a view to developing team spirit. Rungta ignored Gavaskar's reply that he was returning home with manager's permission. Rungta switched over to Solkar who seeing president's mood, stated that he was staying at the stadium although he too was returning home. Gavaskar was reportedly upset that the manager did not undertake the responsibility of telling Rungta that he had granted permission to Gavaskar to return home. Was this the reason that Gavaskar occupied his crease for 60 overs (36 runs) to teach manager Ramchand a lesson?

What team-spirit by only six players in five days could have been developed? Only Rungta could answer.

# 81

# Pride Of Punjab

"Pride of Punjab", and "Symbol of rejuvenated, vibrant and zestful of Punjab" are some of the many adjectives attributed to Punjab Cricket Association (PCA) Stadium at SAS Nagar (Mohali) which not long ago was a hide-out for militants.

The stadium, with ultra modern facilities and amenities, is considered equal to some of the best in the world. All players and all mediapersons have been singing songs of praise for the stadium, including out-field on which players do not feel scared to dive.

The stadium, virtually single-handedly constructed by Inderjit Singh Bindra, president of the PCA and important wheel in Board then, raised controversies. Some Board officials got upset at Bindra's unqualified success in raising the stadium, which became a talk of the cricket world. Jealousies surfaced. The dissatisfied and disgruntled element succeeded in initiating a probe against the PCA and Bindra for the methods employed in raising the Rs. 23-crore stadium

On February 27, 1997, Bindra, in a Press briefing, himself demanded a probe by a High Court Judge into allegations that "undue favours" were shown to the association while allotting the land and giving a sum of Rs. 8.5 crore by the Punjab Urban Development Authority (PUDA) for building the stadium.

Bindra also criticised the CBI (Central Bureau of Investigation) for registering a mala fide, malicious and motivated FIR (First Information Report) for "undue favours" shown to the PCA.

Bindra said "it was a misfortune that all this has happened at the instance of one of my service officers (former Chief Secretary V.K. Khanna). Today I am feeling ashamed that I belong to that service (IAS). "We will expose the baselessness of the charges of the former Chief Secretary and the then Chief Minister Rajinder Kaur Bhattal", added Bindra. "If PCA had done wrong so had Pandit Jawaharlal Nehru, then Prime Minister, in allocating land to the Delhi Golf Club (DGC)", he reiterated, adding: "Similarly Defence Ministry should also be prosecuted for allotting part of the Fort William complex to the Cricket Association of Bengal (CAB). Bindra cited some other examples of allotment of land at throw away prices to other associations, like, Hyderabad and Mumbai.

The view of many seasoned bureaucrats was that the controversy would have died a natural death, had Bindra not made needless references and claims.

The investigations revealed that the entire case was put together by the then Punjab Government and finalised between February 5 and 7 (Punjab went to polls on February 6, 1997. Bhattal's note said:"Huge funds and assets handed over to the PCA have been misutilised and that there is a clear connivance of senior officers. It is not a matter of procedures but gross abuse of authority. The PCA has taken 20 acres of land and money was collected under pressure. The lessor had given a free hand to the lessee with the Government having no role to play. The lessee has also been given the right to mortage the land".

Bindra denied Bhattal's observations. He said that the funds were not collected forcibly. "As PCA president I had written to about 500 companies and corporations all over India giving an offer for the sale of corporate boxes. The commercial proposition proved good". The contributions followed a decision of the Governor-in-Council (S.S.Ray) that private and public sector undetakings should contribute to sports promotion", said Bindra. The critics said that companies responded favourably because Bindra was the Industries Secretary. One firm, according to them, paid a whopping sum of Rs 50 lakh to PCA. Bindra's contention was totally different. He said his dapartment did not promote cricket but cricket was a vehicle to promote industry in Punjab. Charges and counter charges continued to fly thick and fast.

Following these allegations and counter allegations that were highlighted in Indian Express (Chandigarh) in March 1997, a case was filed in the court. The Chief Judicial Magistrate Darshan Singh on March 14 directed the Chief Secretary of Punjab R.S. Mann to produce all relevant documents in the court pertaining to the allotment of the land to PCA.

The stadium was raised at the area which was once "Kumbra Village". As it was uneven and as it was ravine terrain, it was treated as "wasteland". When stadium was raised, it soon became "prime land".

Amidst this raging controversy, Bindra wrote letters to the Prime Minister H.D. Deve Gowda and CBI director Joginder Singh, alleging that Bhattal and Khanna had sought "undue favours", from the PCA. In the rigmarole, the Punjab Government rescinded the case and asked the CBI to drop investigations. The CBI refused on the plea that once the state Government had issued a notification for handing over a case to CBI, it had no authority to pull out.

More cases were filed in court. Public Interest Litigation (PIL) was also registered. As heat was on, the former Chief Secretary V.K. Khanna was charge-sheeted by the Punjab Government under Rule 8 of the All-India Services (Discipline and Appeals) Rules, 1969.

The Punjab Finance Minister Kanwaljit Singh termed CBI probe as "ridiculous". He said that it was Government land, sanctioned to PCA for sports promotion. "PCA was not a commercial organisation", he said adding : "The stadium has put Punjab on the world cricket map". Soon after, the CBI probe was dropped.

The CCI, for example, was allotted 83,526 square yards of land for the Brabourne Stadium for 99 years on May 23, 1937 on payment of Re 1 (if demanded). Of this land at least 40,000 square yards were to be utilised for play field.

When Wankhede stadium came up, the BCA was sanctioned 43, 977 93 metres of land for Re 1 per square yard for the built-up area and 10 paise per square-yard for the unbuild area. (deed for 50 years)

The CAB was allotted 14.99 acres of land by the President of India through the Defence Estate officer on June 15, 1987 against payment of Rs. 22,500 a year (half yearly instalment)

The Chennai Cricket Association (MCA) was allotted (Chepauk) by the Tamil Nadu Government on lease for first 10 years at the rate of Rs. 859.16 per annum. The deed was signed on February 9, 1996. For the next 10 years the payment to Government will be Rs. 12,88.74 per year.

The Chandigarh U.T. Administration leased out 132 acres of land for 20 years at the rate of 3.25 per cent of the cost of original building, six per cent of the cost of additions made and six per cent on additions to be made. In addition the Chandigarh Golf Club pays Rs. 30 per acre for 132 acres of golf course at the annual lease money. This deed with CGC was signed on March 16, 1998.

With so many examples, it was surprising that the administration should have acted tough with the PCA

# 82

# A Total Flop

The much-talked about and the much-publicised 1996 World Cup opening ceremony was a failure. Many well known sports personalities among more than 1 lakh spectators were heard as saying that the Durga Puja celebration in Kolkata had far greater pomp, show, dignity and solemnity than Jagmohan Dalmiya's two-hour presentation at Eden Gardens on February 11, 1996.

The Rs 11-crore demonstration failed to stir the imagination and emotions of paying public which could not make out as to what was happening in the centre of the stadium. The Indian mediapersons were equally disappointed and disillusioned as there was hardly any thing to rave about. The foreign mediapersons could not care less as to what was being enacted in the centre. The plight of officials was pitiable. They failed to get befitting cover to hide themselves. Mismangement of ceremony apart, it was nothing but a comedy of errors.

The organisers showed thoughtlessness in erecting a huge and heavy stage on the square meant for the pitch. The Cricket Association of Bengal (CAB) surprised all by relaying the wicket instead of undertaking repairs of it. The time for one month or about was not enough to prepare a good wicket. There was outcry by some for instituting a probe as to who exactly was responsible for holding the function on the "square" and as to what necessitated in relaying the wicket.?

There was no quarrel in Bengal Chief Minister Jyoti Basu inaugurating the mega event. But had he been accompanied by sub-continent's two outstanding all-rounders, Kapil Dev and Imran Khan, the event would have got an additional aura of stature and dignity.

It was beyond comprehension as to why was "Half Moon", a foreign firm, entrusted with the responsibility of organising the function. The theme should have been the events displaying rise of cricket in sub-continent instead of providing a platform to Half Moon to reduce the entire ceremany into a mockery.

Dalmiya's reaction was totally different. He thought and said in as many words that show was a success. To this, many Bengalis possessing aesthetic values said: "He was merely trying to defend the indefensible".

When Italian firm's chief Lunette said that Sushmita Sen would "undress" during the ceremony, there was a virtual trouble in Kolkata. Controversies gripped the city. Lunetta had said this in lighter vein but he was misunderstood in the city.

India and Pakistan teams, in their respective national colours, were accorded vociferous appreciation by enthusiastic spectators as teams marched in. Sadly, the top models, who led the teams, were not wearing sarees, as it was planned. Only Miss India, Sandhya Chib, was able to wear saree, dazzling light blue, to lead Azharuddin's team. Other 11 models were wearing apparels picked up by them from the streets of Kolkata. For this unexpected "mix-up", the blame was levelled on Kolkata traffic. Did not this show lack of planning? Why could not all models be given their saress days in advance of the ceremony?

The wind blew off the laser show as the image wriggled and danced disobediently. The fireworks also failed to impress the spectators, who had bought tickets at the exhorbitant price.

As Basu declared the World Cup open, Sushmita emerged amidst background music and blinding lights. Here again, there was a mix-up. It was announced that she would descend from sky. Instead she rose from the ground. She presented Board flags to 12 participating teams. It was indeed a touching occasion.

Asha Bhosle's rendition of Sanskrit hymns, Tanushree Shankar and her troupe's ballet as also dance by a mass of children were likened by spectators. But Saeed Jaffery's introductory remarks made nonsense of the entire show. He bungled often. He could not differentiate South Africa from Zimbabwe. What was the grand idea of choosing Jaffery for this solemn function?

All in all, it was not a show worth Rs. 11 crores. Had the responsibility been entrusted to any Indian producer, the show would have been far more captivating than it had been. But the organisers had money to squander! No questions were asked!

# 83

# Much Ado About Nothing

Clash of dates between two events—Commonwealth Cricket in Kuala Lumpur and Sahara Cup in Toronto in 1998—gave rise to trouble between two bodies and two officials, Rajsingh Dungarpur and Suresh Kalmadi. Each threw blame on the other for the needless fiasco. Each tried to shout down the other. Statements and counter-statements were issued in written and electronic media. Both also showed that power had sunk so deep in their minds that they had forfeited sense of sanity despite their ripe age. Suffice it to say that both succeeded in making a laughing stock of themselves.

Toronto series was a "tamasha", a kind of money-making five-game ritual between India and Pakistan. The inaugural meet in Kuala Lumpur had nothing to boast of in this mercenary world except a medal, prestigious indeed for only those who cared for values more than glitter of money.

There was plenty of time for both Board and Indian Olympic Association (IOA) to arrive at a mutually rewarding decision for the prestige and honour of the country. But both chose to procrastinate, as is the wont of all Indians and Indian sports bodies. Deadlines for submitting names, etc. were flouted, as again is the wont of Indians.

Eventually, Board gave precedence to money while Kalmadi, for a change, talked about the importance of the medal. The bearded IOA chief, who has always believed "style is the man", was displaying keenness for the medal not for the sake of the country's honour, but to impress upon the Government the role he and his IOA was playing in the arena of international competitions.

Kalmadi's role was dubious. It was Kalmadi, who threw away heaps of money on foreign athletes for their mere "apperance" on Indian soil when his own athletes lived in penury. It was he who was displaying glitter of money through ITC while trying to change the face of Indian athletics without any success. It was he who put up an ultra-modern stadium at his home town Pune. Sadly, Pune's stadium is even more "white elephant", than Delhi's Nehru Stadium.

Whatever might have been IOA's demands and many other compulsions, if any, Rajsingh should have shown his cricketing wisdom and announced well in time as to who would constitute what competition. He knew it that England, floater of the Commonwealth Games, was not taking part in the contest at Kuala Lumpur. Sri Lanka and South Africa sent their second strings and so did Pakistan, which sent its full side to Toronto. Only Australia decided to send its full strength at Kuala Lumpur because players were free from their otherwise arduous schedule.

Instead of playing with "straight bat", the Board needlessly indulged in playing "dirty tricks" trying to prove the organisers to disqualify India from taking part in the event.

After a lot of bad blood that polluted the columns of newspapers, the Board chose to select two equally balanced sides. This was what Kishan Rungta, chairman of selection committe asserted in an interview. The two-team theory however flopped. The collapse of the theory was decisive as India failed to achieve any fruitful outcome either at Kuala Lumpur or at Toronto. In the aftermath of debacle in both events, there was a heap of broken images and wounded national pride.

Failure to perform at Kuala Lumpur and Toronto was

bad enough. What was most shocking was that the Board, in its wisdom, had made arrangements for four players to fly to Toronto when Kuala Lumpur meet was still in progress. The four players were Sachin Tendulkar, Ajay Jadeja, Anil Kumble and Robin singh. They were reportedly booked on the flight before semi-final berths were finalised. If this was indeed so, it was an act as disgraceful as that of alleged match-fixing allegation.

Both Tendulkar and Jadeja had a long and tiring flight although cabin crew made all that they could to make their flight comfortable. Luckily flight was not late. They had only about 12 hours to rest and relax. Acclimatisation was difficult. Naturally, not much could be expected from players under such circumatances.

Money appears to have placed a layer of crocodile skin on both Board and stars. They have reached a stage when they could not care less about their image and reputation.

# 84

# Hazare In Controversy

A gentleman-cricketer like Vijay Hazare was involved in a controversy against England in the second Test at Lord's in 1952. Laws stood between Godfrey Evans and his getting century before lunch but Hazare was accused of "slowness". There were three opinions : of umpire Frank Chester, of Evans and of Hazare. They were.

Says Chester : "Vinoo Mankad had just finished an over and my colleague Frank Lee, thinking that there might be time to start another over, walked away to the square-leg position. V.S. Hazare, the Indian captain, walked up to the bowler's end, where I was already standing, and handed me his cap. He ordered for change of one or two field placings but by then the clock showed exactly half past one. I looked at Lee, he nodded, and I had to take off the bails. A gasp went around the ground followed by some mild booing. I went to Evans and said : "I'm sorry, Godfrey, but its half past". As great a sportsman as he is a player, Godfrey was less worried than anyone and said : "I'm perfectly satisfied, Frank, you are quite right'.

Evans needed only two runs to complete his century before lunch. Had he got he would have then become fourth batsman to have achieved this distinction.

Chester went on to say: The laws must be respected and this is one that is perfectly clear : an over must be started before the hands of the clock point to the agreed time of an interval or drawing of stumps.

According to Chester : "The suggestion was made that the Indians had made a deliberately slow change-over, but this was unfair and far from the truth. I know that all Indians were deeply disappointed that Godfrey could not establish the record. Hazare would be the last person to delay intentionally".

Evans in his book "The Gloves are off", says : "I think I would have got the 100 had it not been for the slowness of Hazare in resetting the field. I don't know for certain whether Hazare was deliberate in his slowness. Perhaps he was—perhaps he was not. If he was, a reason could be that he had no taste for being the captain of a side that might have a record of this devastating kind made against them".

Says Hazare : "As the last ball of the over was about to be bowled, Evans was 98 and there was clearly only a minute to go for the lunch interval. We all realised, therefore, that if Evans had to get his hundred before lunch, this was his only chance. As he failed to connect and the umpire called over. Graveney, who was a non-striker, started walking towards the pavilion thinking that there was hardly any time to commence another over. I was standing at mid-off then, and was surprised to see Chester standing at the wicket, all ready, instead of calling time for the lunch interval. The moment I realised this, I hurried up to his end to start bowling. . . and fielders automatically took their positions. I was ready to bowl to Graveney. Evans was the non-stricker, when dramatically Chester removed the bails and started walking towards the pavilion. . ."

Hazare adds : "We all liked Evans, for he was a grand sportsman and we were as much disappointed as he was for not getting his hundred before lunch. We all would have been greatly pleased had Evans, the lovable charactor that he is, got this unique honour".

In October 1978 at Faislabad, in the first India-Pakistan Test, there was no "clock" at the stadium. The watches of umpire were not synchronised. There was a difference of 20 minutes between watches of two umpires. Gavaskar called for his captain to set the matter right. The mediapersons thought Bedi had been called to lodge protest against "intimidatory" bowling. The news was filed. But it was far from correct.

# 85

# Fictitious Cable

"Selection of such a team is a disgusting insult to India. Recommend add stars or cancel tour altogether". This was the urgent cable purported to have been sent by the Board of Control for Cricket in India (BCCI) to MCC at Lord's.

The MCC bigwigs immeditely held an emergency meeting. After datailed deliberations and scrutiny of players, the MCC came to conclusion that Douglas Jardine's team to tour India in 1933 was strong enough to take on any side despite non-availability of famous players, like, Walter Hammond, Bert Sutcliffe, Harold Larwood, Eddie Paynter, Leyland, Wyatt, Voce and Allen. Ames had originally agreed to tour but the Kent Committee prevailed upon him to withdraw suggesting him rest instead of undergoing rigours of the Indian tour. There was not much cricket in those days but counties and MCC cared for their players.

MCC shot back a cable emphasising that the team of Jardine, E.W. Clark, Verity, Bakewell, Walters, Barnett, Nichols, Marriott, and James Langridge was extremely well balanced in all departments of the game and there was absolutely no need for any change.

The Board officials were in a quandary now as to how and who had sent this cable to MCC. Investigations were undertaken. It was subsequently found out that some one had felt extremely hurt on the composition of the England (MCC) side and fired that "mischivious" cable. Exactly who the culprit was could not be ascertained. There were suspicion on two persons—one belonged to the Board and another belonged to Indian Telegraph Office. The Board did not consider it prudent to continue with the probe after peace had descended on both MCC and the Board.

Earlier, there were untold problems to finalise the centres to stage Test matches. In those days, money was hard to raise. The Board had stipulated guarantee money of Rs. 20,000. Mumbai was the only certainty because there were several wealthy businessmen to provide money for the Test. Neither Kolkata nor Chennai had people readily available to offer their share of money for the Test match. Amidst this situation. Nawab of Moin-ud-Dowlah, a great promoter of the game, readily agreed to pay the entire guarantee money if the match was allotted to Secunderabad.

Following this offer, the Kolkata and Chennai authorities went on a virtual, "borrow and steal mission" to raise the required amount for the Test. In Kolkata, European clubs, which were quite a few then, chipped in with a sizable amount.

The tour was a grand success with Jardine showing his ability and skill as a skipper and also a tremendous judge of men and matters off the field. He did not let any one, not even Viceroy, interfere with his decisions. He made it clear to the authorities, stationed in India, that he was the boss of cricket and he would brook no interference whatsoever from any one, no matter how important he was. Once Viceroy "ordered" him to dance with a particular lady. He chose his own partner!

Jardine's MCC lost only one first class game on a bumpy, matting wicket by 14 runs at Banaras (Varanasi). Apart from arduous journey (Punjab Mail) the visitors were weary as they chose "dance, whisky and women" until wee hours of morning. Following this defeat, Jardine did not allow his key players to "dance" beyond certain time.

# 86

# Bedi Not A Good Team Man, Ousted

The Mehras empire on Vizzy's flimsy Willingdon Pavilion started shaking as Bishan Singh Bedi's vicious left-hand spinners started pitching on the dangerous spot. The more Mehras tried to smother them or wriggle out of them, the less they were successful. The players, young and veterans, utterly dissatisfied with the Mehras, turned against them. Most of the 2,000 plus voters joined the Bedi camp and even some office-bearers of the Delhi and Districts Cricket Association (DDCA) sommersaulted. The Press, at least two national dailies, campaigned against the mis-rule of the Mehras. The Members of Parliament and the concerned departments in Government were now convinced that it was time to get rid off the Mehras as they had outlived their utility. They all thought that they had retained their "Gaddi" far too long. The pressure on Board mounted. The Board officials thought that they could no longer be mere mute spectators. Threats were issued to the DDCA that the India-England Test in December 1981 would be shifted in view of stiff bickerings in the corridors of the association.

The Mehras assessed the situation and reluctantly agreed that they might not be able to stage the Test. The players and the promoters pleaded for allowing the rival faction, Delhi State Cricketers' Association (DSCA) to organise the Test. The meetings were held and it was decided that the Test might be conducted by the Special Committee, appointed by the Board. This was first time that the Board's affiliated unit had been directed to stay away for the Board to conduct the Test. Some of the members of the committee were not exactly "desirable". The exhorbitant over-head expenses were made on needless travelling, lodging in five star hotel and lavish hospitality. Despite extravagance, the committee showed much more profit than the DDCA had ever shown durnig the last two decades or more.

The Test over, the Mehras found maintaining their stranglehold on the DDCA was difficult. There were now heaps of complaints against their functioning. Many loop-holes were discovered. Aware that there were many skeletons in their cup, they tried to bury the hatchet. But they failed.

The date for election, under court supervision, was announced. The proxies were collected, as was the practice. L.N.Tandon, then a powerful wheel in the DDCA, was the one entrusted with the responsibility of collecting proxies for the ruling group. But in the election, the sitting faction conceded defeat. As Mehras were defeated, CBI (Central Bureau of Investigation) probe was intensified against some members of the Mehra group.

The Bedi group gained a complete control of the DDCA in September 1982. There was widespread jubilation that Delhi cricket, for once, would be controlled and managed by cricketers, for cricketers and of cricketers. Post and Telegraph bureaucrat Kamlesh Sharma, a good university level left-hand spinner, became the president, while Bedi was installed as sports secretary. Kamal Nath, a high flown Congress MP, was the patron. He held most of the meetings and retained many strings of the DDCA.

The mandate from voters was massive. The players were all supportive of the new faction. Clubs were beholden to Bedi. But, alas inside of three months, the happiness turned into despair as secretary and president drifted away from each other. The drift in current led to breaches and breaches became cracks. Players, including Ranji stars, got disillusioned with the functioning of the new group, while clubs, participating in league, were utterly disappointed. It soon became clear that Bedi and Sharma were pulling in different direction. Office-bearers and two Govrnment nominees, Ravi Kathpalia and Inder Mohan Sahai, were as much disappointed as players were dejected.

In this unsteady scenario, the Manmohan Sood group, led by Hari Shastri, son of former Prime Minister Lal Bahadur Shastri, jumped into fray. A known cricket enthusiast and a Congress MP, Shastri obtained clearance from the Prime Minister Rajiv Gandhi for seeking election in the DDCA. As Shastri got PM's nod, Kamal Nath backed out of the contest asking Sharma to oppose Shastri for the election in September 1983. Sharma agreed to seek re-election if Bedi was dropped from the post of the sports secretary. It was then said that Bedi was unable to devote time to the DDCA duties as he was out of Delhi often on national selectorical assignment. The conspiracy to sideline Bedi from the DDCA was hatched when he was in Pakistan as a selector.

Shastri was upset that Sharma had gone back on his word and was contesting against him. Shastri then made a futile attempt to prevent a Government official from opposing the ruling party Congress (I) MP.

In a straight contest, Sharma prevailed upon Shastri through the weight of proxies already collected by him. Sunil Dev, a disciple of Kamal Nath, became the new secretary in place of Bedi.

Since then, the DDCA has never been the same although several acrimonious elections have been held. It is agreed by all that Ram Parkash Mehra (lattoo) was an angel as compared to all the office-bearers that have been polluting the corridors of the DDCA. Currently, C.K. Khanna is the boss. All the strings are with him. He decides who would be placed where. Once in awhile, Bedi raises his head to unseat the ruling faction without any planning or preparations.

# 87

# A Very Difficult Decision

Mohammad Azharuddin was a natural ball player. He possessed an extra-ordinary batting skill which was noticed when he was in the Amarnath camp at the age of 16. Every knowledgeable person thought that here was a "ladka" who would surely don national colours.

While fielding, Azharuddin sustained a fracture on his finger at Ahmedabad's newly constructed Motera Stadium where under-25 verses David Gower's English team were playing in 1984-85. The next morning, the telegram addressed to Azharuddin, who had padded up, was received by the skipper Ravi Shastri. He read it and was about to "pocket" it when Azharuddin pleaded to him that he should have a look at it since it was addressed to him.

The telegram said : "Grandfather serious. Start immediately". Azhar was rattled. He had loved his grandpa Vajehuddin intensely. Grandpa was yougster's life and soul. "I'm going, I have to go, please", pleaded Azhar to Shastri. "How old is he?" asked Shastri. When Azhar mumbled he was about 90, Shastri in his typical tone said: "If he is 90, he has to go some day". This further upset Azhar, who stopped talking to Shastri. When P.R. Man Singh was contacted on trunk, he revealed that the grandpa had already died but the family did not think it judicious to put it in the telegram.

Azhar was persuaded not to jeopardise his cricketing career since the calamity had already come upon him. He stayed back . He went on to score a century which played a pivotal role for him to gain a national recognition. Azharuddin was elated at his elevation but his grandpa's oft repeated words that he would wear national colours kept ringing in his ears.

Azhar returned to Hyderabad as soon as the game was over. His father was at the airport. "Sab kutch ho gaya na Abba", he asked as he broke down in his father's arms. Not a word was spoken but Azhar now knew that he stood alone without the precious and valuable guidance of his grandpa.

Similar was the state of mind of Sachin Tendulkar when he came to know of the premature death of this father Ramesh Tendulkar. Sachin's love and respect for his father, a noble man, was as intense as that of Azhar's for his grand-pa. It was a very difficult decision for Sachin whether to stay to continue to assist India in the on-going World Cup (1999) or return to Mumbai to attend to his father's funeral. As a fine yougman with an impeccable character, he contemplated. The Board and cricket management left upon him to decide. He chose to return to Mumbai. It was purely a personal decision. There were some who felt that he should have stayed back since the tragedy had already struck. It was easier saying than doing. Had he played against Zimbabwe, who knows, India might have moved into semi-final.

# 88

# Strange Doings Of DDCA

The Delhi and Districts Cricket Association (DDCA) is one of the strangest bodies in the country. Its constitution, an amusing document, allows "paanwallahas and sabziwallahs" to secure membership and cast their votes. For the last two decades or about, the elections—whenvever held—are conducted under the supervision of the retired judge and proxy forms to over 3,000 members are sent by courier service or through resgistered letter. Bulk of the members are "dummy" voters aligned with this or that faction with no interest whatsoever in cricket. Regardless of the fact whether a member makes use of the club or not, he gets a pass for every national or international match staged at Kotla. While majority of members play truant, guests, fond of cards and bar, utilise the club frequently. As if all this in itself is not bad enough, officials of clubs form their own groups. These officials are usually vociferous. They are promoted by this or that disgruntled office-bearer. There is virtual jungle raj. In DDCA non-entities in every walk of life, ride over men of merit. Delhi is one of the oldest Test centres but it lacks in atmosphere for cricket. If the players have risen, it is not because of the DDCA but despite DDCA. Of late a few players have occupied national scene for considerations other than their ability and merit. Indeed quite a few other centres in various parts of the country are as bad as Delhi but it is not a healthy argument as Delhi is the capital of the country.

In the sharply divided Board elections in 1997, DDCA's sports secretary Sunil Dev got aligned with the Bindra faction. He had acted more on his personal whims and fancies than in the interest of the DDCA. The Bindra faction had projected victory in the Board elections and offered an important office to Sunil Dev. This was good enough for Dev to issue statements. He alleged that Jagmohan Dalmiya was involved in business transaction with Doordarshan and World Tel for the Independence Cup. His argument was that the Board should have shown more transparency in awarding huge commercial contracts. Sunil Dev also accused Dalmiya of dabbling in the Board politics while occupying the office of the president of the ICC. (There seems to be some truth in what Sunil Dev alleged in his statement.)

To Dalmiya's legal notice of defamation suit of Rs. 15 crores, Sunil Dev sent a notice for 24 crores. The DDCA prasident K.K. Mehra reacted and sent a letter to Dalmiya's advocate. It reads :

"I deny each and every allegation made against this association. The allegations are not only incorrect but distorted as well. In the first place we vehemently deny that the DDCA has anything to do with any alleged letter allegedly written by Sunil Dev to either Rajsingh Dungarpur or to your client or that these letters contained and alleged defamatory allegations against your client. A bare persual of these letters which you have attached with your notice under reply clearly show that these have been written by Sunil Dev in his personal capacity and not as sports secretary and on behalf of the DDCA.

"I also mention as a fact that this association has not authorised Sunil Dev to enter into any correspondence with Dalmiya or Rajsingh, much less to make alleged false, malicious and defamatory aspersions and innudendoes against your client.

"It is also false to suggest that Sunil Dev wrote any such alleged letter on behalf of the DDCA as its sports secretary or that all officials of the DDCA connived with Sunil Dev with a motive of defaming and maligning your client. It is also further false to suggest that Sunil Dev does have any independent locus dehore DDCA in respect of and/or related to the subject matters of BCCI. The officials of the BCCI are elected as individuals.

"An attempt of your client to involve the association apart from being incorrect, is also highly illegal. If your client has any grouse against Sunil Dev, he is fully entitled to take any action he so desires. However if he falsely implicates this association or its officials in any manner whatsover, he shall have only himself to blame for all the consequences".

The legal battle did not continue, but Sunil Dev was barred from attending Board meetings. Instead C.K. Khanna was deputed to attend the Board meetings. He shrewdly joined the Dalmiya-Rajsingh faction and became Board's vice-president. Khanna is now the king maker in DDCA where all other officials are virtually pigmies. His success lays in his persuasive methods. He does what ruling faction in the Board directs him to do and the Board, in turn, obliges him.

Khanna now enjoys full support of Arun Jaitley, a powerful minister.

# 89

# Wadekar Cooks His Own Goose

There was undeniably a goof up of the worst kind la affaire Delhi's Mithun Minhas in September 1999. The Board of Control for Cricket in India (BCCI), rated efficient and wealthy, made a laughing stock of itself in the eyes of cricket players, young and not so young, throughout the country.

It was a blunder which seemed to have cost Ajit Wadekar his job in the Board. The high flying Wadekar fully deserved the wrath of the Board for not keeping abreast as to who was who in Indian cricket. It was a sheer carelessness which did not portray him in good light. But in his unceremonious exit was a silver lining as, in his place, re-entered Chandu Borde who would perhaps maintain better media relations than Wadekar had been able to manage.

In the unaccountable blunder was Wadekar's hidden dictatorial attitude. He took approval of four other selectors for granted. He named Minhas in India 'A' team for the farcical Los Angeles tour presuming that he was an all-rounder, a medium-pacer and a batsman. Had he taken the trouble of phoning or consulting Madan Lal, a north zone nominee, he would have saved himself from the ignominy that he was called upon to endure.

Haste and over-confident were the causes that saw Wadekar slip into trouble. So many meaningless tours and matches were on the anvil that mistake could creep up. Add to Wadekar's flippant functioning was presence of the Board secretary Lele who could be equally indifferent and could succumb under pressure.

Lele was however a man enough to express regret on behalf of himself and the Board in Press conference on September 25, 1999. When told that the Board had caused damage to the confidence of the youngster, Lele said "I'm sorry, Board also expresses its regret and nothing more than this can be done", emphasised Lele.

While facing journalists' beamer manfully, Lele revealed "Inside of 10 minutes after mistake took place, I phoned Delhi informing the concerned person that Minhas had inadvertently been shown in the team. The person concerned did not act in the matter swiftly enough" adding "But I am here to own my lapse".

How goof up came about. Minhas, who was not in Delhi's Ranji team last season, was shown as picked for India 'A' team, which was scheduled to play against Australia 'A' at Los Angeles. His selection came after two India 'A' players, Jacob Martin and Amit Bhandari, had been promoted to India team as replacements for Sachin Tendulkar and Ajay Jadeja for the team's participation in Toronto against the West Indies.

The selection of Minhas looked dicey because he was merely a batsman. What India 'A' team needed was a bowler in place of Bhandari, a medium pacer. When some mediapersons pointed out, Wadekar backtracked instead of owning up his mistake. He said that he had named Ashish Nehra and not Minhas. He started accusing mediapersons for the "mix-up". It was a case of "ekk chori" doosra seena zori (highhandedness). Had Wadekar owned his mistake, the controversy would not have taken such an ugly turn.

Whatever might be Wadekar's assertions, Minhas had "inadvertently" been chosen in India 'A' team. Lele did inform DDCA's C.K.Khanna from Singapore communicating both decisions : elevation of Bhandari and selection of Minhas in India 'A' team. Delhi quietly took the credit for it. This was not all. But Khanna contacted Minhas, who was holidaying in Mumbai. He duly rushed back to capital. He reported to the manager Srikkanth, stayed a night in hotel and even attended nets.

If Wadekar could be accused of making a mess of an easy job, four selectors were guilty of functioning as dummies. It was said that they should have resigned en block. But they chose not to do so. They however gave their mind to the president Rajsingh.

In the end, Wadekar was not ousted by Board. He wrote his own exit warrant.

In 1995, Wadekar had problem in BCA when he was a vice-president. He was accused of being a mercenary. He was labelled as working against rules laid down in the constitution. The charge was that he held personal interest more important than BCA's. Then allegations were made by a faction opposed to Manohar Joshi, president of BCA. The main issue pertained to the contract between BCA and Selvel advertising company. Wadekar, it is said, played a "dubious" role and BCA had to lose sizable amount as Selvel backed out.

# 90

# Damn Shame, Shouts Wankhede

"Damn shame" shouted the former president of the Board of Control for Cricket in India (BCCI) (late) S.K. Wankhede on the resting of Sunil Gavaskar in one-day international against Australia in the winter of 1986. Wankhede mustered enough support from other members and they all shook the Board and his team of selectors. All hell broke in the Board's working committee meeting at Mumbai in September 1986. What was cause for concern was that agenda was set aside to discuss Gavaskar's "resting" in one of the one-dayers.

It was not the fault of Borde and his men. They "rested" at the behest of the Board's spokesman who directed them that, in view of the forthcoming World Cup in the sub-continent, young players could be tried.

Borde told his colleagues what had been communicated to him by the Board spokesman. The members discussed at length before deciding to "rest" Gavaskar. Three selectors were in favour of Gavaskar "resting" and two were opposed to it.

Many analysts felt that it was not a very injudicious decision since Gavaskar was already 37 and one-day contest was not, in essentiality, his cup of tea. This was what he had been shouting from house-top.

There were protests from certain quarters on Gavaskar being "rested". Borde received even threatening calls at

Pune home. But being a seasoned batsman he negotiated the rising deliveries with his usual skill of calmness.

Wankhede, supported by the Board president S. Sriraman, was critical of selectors for "resting" Gavaskar. On the comment of Wankhede, Borde said "I am pained that Wankhede, of all officials, should have rushed to Press using harsh words against me and my colleagues without verifying facts".

Borde was also disappointed that he was not invited to attend working committee meeting to provide members correct information as to how and why was Gavaskar "rested". Following hue and cry, Borde and his team succumbed under the weight of the working committee and Gavaskar was included in the side. Opinions on this subject were divided. Some were vocal that the selection committee should not have reversed its decision. "They should have resigned in protest against working committee's interference in matters pertaining to selection", said one senior official, adding "Selection committee is autonomous and it should brook no interference". "Three years ago in the World Cup in England in 1983, Gavaskar was dropped from the team in the return match against West Indies", asserted Kapil Dev, skipper, in an interview, in Chandigarh Indian Express on July 5, 1983. He said: "The tour selection committee felt that Dilip Vengsarkar should not be given only one chance" said Kapil Dev, adding "Gavaskar was not dropped because he was unfit".

According to Kapil Dev, it is not right to change and chop the team. "If a player gets into the team, he should be given proper chance before he is discarded", he added.

# 91

# Princes Refuse To Help

To say that K.S.Ranjitsinhji was wizard would be emphasising the obvious. But he refused to play for India. Not only that. But he did not let even his nephew, K.S. Duleepsinhji play for the country of his birth. "Duleep and I are English cricketers", Ranji told to Anthony de Mello and others when approached for help and advice. Had he taken some interest in Indian cricket and had Duleep played for India, Indian cricket would not have been mired in such unseeming controversies in 1932 and 1936 when Maharaja of Porbander and Vizzy were captains. What a team it would have been with Iftikhar Ali Khan Pataudi, C.K. Nayudu and others assisting Duleep!

Ranji was the first Indian who shone brightly outside the borders of his own country. Yet, shockingly, he refused to wear dual roles of being an Indian prince and Indian cricketer. No one knew and no one yet knows what his compulsions were in refusing to assist his country.

As a president of the Chamber of Princes, Ranji could have done a lot for Indian cricket. But he was never even seen at a game of cricket in India. He spent every summer in England where his flashing bat had done a lot of "talking" and had left an everlasting impression on English people. Despite his aversion to play for India, it would be wrong to say that he was not loyal to his own country. He did a lot for Nawanagar people.

de Mello, in his book, "Portrait of Indian Sport", says : "There was talk too of an unhappy love affair and certainly as an Indian Prince, Ranji, could not have married an English girl (the daughter of the Reverend Louis Borrisow, the Chaplain of Trinity College, Cambridge). All this, let me hasten to say, is no more than gossip and rumour but, if true, it will take us a step nearer to the explanation why Ranji left his heart somewhere among the green fields of England."

Apart from this English woman, Ranji was in deep love with a "parrot". It was said that he and "parrot" were virtually inseparable.

Like Ranji, Munsur Ali Pataudi was also fond of a "parrot" which used to greet visitors with : "Ulu Ka Patha".

There was another similarity between Ranji and Mansur. Ranji lost his eye in "Shikar", Mansur in a road accident in England. Mansur played most of his international cricket with one eye.

In England, there were cricket personalities who considered Prince greater batsman than Dr. W. G. Grace because he had more strokes than doctor. A.C.M. Croome, perhaps the most famous of the cricket correspondents of the Times also reportedly rated Ranji greater than Grace. He started as a player of violence and then translated his violence into sublimity and grace of the highest order with constant practice.

Duleep did not play for India, but he did write about Indian cricket. He was covering for the Reuters the India-Australia series in Australia in 1947 when he had several unseemly controversies with skipper Amarnath. He was critical of Amarnath's captaincy, while many cricketer-turned-journalists, like, J.H. Fingleton, were supportive of Amarnath's handling. Occasionally the controversies between the two greats became very personal which became quite embarrassing to others around.

# 92

# A Fictitious Toss

When Sunil Gavaskar's India defeated Pakistan by 10 wickets in the fifth Test at Chennai in January 1980, he announced that he would not captain the sixth and the last Test against Pakistan as he was not going to West Indies soon after because of "personal reasons". No one knew what his "personal reasons" were. But there was a controversial twist to it. It was alleged that he was withdrawing because he had used harsh words against West Indian people tantamounting that they were uncivlised people. It was further alleged that Gavaskar was not the same batsman that he was and he was not prepared to face fast bolwers in their country. As the tour fell through, one Mumbaiwallah, in a lighter vein, said : No Gavaskar. no West Indies tour. It was also said that Gavaskar had withdrawn from the tour because the schedule (16 Tests in 29 weeks plus five in West Indies) according to him, had become too 'tough'.

While announcing that he was quitting the Indian captaincy from the final Test, Gavaskar also hinted at his deputy Vishwanath to take over although this was strictly for selectors to determine.

Vishwanath was duly appointed captain in place of Gavaskar for the Kolkata Test. There was a huge controversy. It was alleged that Pakistan skipper Asif Iqbal had rigged the toss. Both Vishwanath and Iqbal duly went out for the toss. Asif threw the coin up and Vishwanath called. Asif Iqbal stooped, picked up the coin and said that Vishwanath had called it correctly. The day was December 29, 1979 and there were many, including Pakistan's cricket supremo Imran Khan, who had alleged that Asif Iqbal had rigged the toss meaning he had predeterminedly decided as such. Surprising as it might be, Imran Khan, in his autobiography did not touch upon this vital incident.

The rigging of the toss was second allegation levelled against Asif Iqbal. The first was that he had 'sold' the series to India, which won the six Tests series 2-0. The Kolkata Test, however. ended in a draw. Imran Khan had bowled devastatingly in the match.

Apart from these allegations against Asif Iqbal, it was alleged that he and the manager had not exercised enough control on players, who were busy in extra-curricular activities of "egg, peg and leg". The team members dreaded returning to Pakistan though Asif Iqbal had gone on record as saying that his team had been beaten fairly and squarely.

Vishwanath continued to be captain in the one-off Test (Golden Jubilee) against England at Mumbai in February 1980. England were precariously placed at 143 for five wickets when wicket-keeper Bob Taylor was given caught at the wicket by Hanumatha Rao. Taylor looked baffled at the decision. Vishwanath, always a gentleman, consulted close-in fielders, including Gavaskar. In his usual characteristic way, Gavaskar reportedly told Vishwanath. "You are the captain now, and you should decide". But judging from the gestures of other fielders, Vishwanath seemed convinced that Taylor had not snicked the ball.

Gentleman as he was, Vishwanath again asked umpire Rao whether he was entitled to withdraw his appeal. Rao agreed. The appeal was withdrawn and the decision was reversed.

Taylor helped himself with 43 as Ian Botham helped England rally to 229.

In England's second innings, Geoff Boycott was given out caught at the wicket. Boycott stayed put. He completely ignored Rao's raised finger as if nothing had happened. Kapil Dev was the sufferer and Kirmani was the "keeper. Neither Vishwanath nor other fielders insisted and the game continued without any acrimony or controversy.

Another amusing incident took place at Delhi where India were playing against Pakistan in 1979-80. Without obtaining umpire's permission and when the ball was not dead, Dilip Doshi walked up to the umpire to protest against the shadow. When Doshi explained as to why he had left his crease, Majid Khan withdrew his appeal.

In the 1989-90 series, at Lahore, Srikkanth was given out leg before by Shakoor Rana but Imran Khan withdrew his appeal. Srikkanth failed to take advantage of this noble gesture and was caught at the wicket by Salim Yousuf. The snick was so loud that Srikkanth did not even look back.

The captains world over are magnanimous only when there is nothing much at stake.

# 93

# Sood Ditched, Pat Captain

Mansur Ali Khan Pataudi in "Tiger's Tale" concludes : "In the country of the blind, it had been said, the one eyed man is king. But in the keen-eyed world of cricket a fellow with just one good eye and-a-bit has to settle for something less than the perfection he once sought. Lucky me, despite this, to have been able to play the game all over the world in the company of the giants, I look forward to passing on the experience I have gained to those young Indian players who could prove to be the giants of tomorrow".

Pataudi, just 21 plus, captained India against the West Indies in 1962 when Nari Contractor was maimed. He captained Delhi in 1963 Ranji Trophy. He, however, spent his summers in England where he played County cricket.

Manmohan Sood was appointed captain against Jammu and Kashmir 1964 match by the DDCA boss Ram Prakash Mehra. When Sood asked him whether he was captain for the entire season, Mehra confirmed it saying that he would not be unseated. The match at Srinagar was on October 16-18, 1964. Soon after, Pataudi put in his appearance at Kotla. Without batting an eye-lid, Mehra deprived Sood of captaincy and gave it back to Pataudi.

Sood resented it. He and his supporters made a representation to Mehra who, while agreeing for the wrong done by him to Sood, said : "Bear with me, I am helpless". The players were unwilling to see his viewpoint. They argued that no pressure was insurmountable.

Controversy raged for a few days. When Mehra refused to "see reason", Sood and his supporters revolted.

"We will not play if Sood is not reinstated as captain", threatened players. Mehra stayed unmoved by these threats. Pataudi captained Delhi against Southern Punjab on November 12-14, 1964 while some stalwarts stayed out. One by one, the agitators returned while Sood continued to stay out.

Mid-way through sesson, it became clear that Pataudi was not enjoying playing for Delhi. He mixed with players less than he used to do. He did attend nets without taking much interest. He found the atmosphere "suffocating". He had a reason to feel so because there were quite a few who disapproved his leading the side.

Pataudi found DDCA management "stingy" and thoughtless. Players were denied proper refreshment. There were days when the management had declined to provide sufficient quota of soft drinks. One or two office-bearers were vocal in saying as to why should a "Muslim" captain Delhi. This was a height of absurdity. It was sheer foolishness to give an unneccessary communal touch.

As the 1965 season was about to begin, Pataudi let Mehras know that he would not be able to play for Delhi any more. He did not give reason nor was he asked "why". He switched to Hyderabad.

Akash Lal, a fine opening batsman, was made captain. He too had his share of controversies with the Mehras. But the caravan went on.

# 94

# A Strange Procedure Followed

In wilderness for more than a decade, Vizzy resurfaced when it was finalised that the West Indies would be touring India in 1948. Vizzy now president of the U.P. Cricket Association (UPCA) requested de Mello for the allotment of a three-day match against the tourists. de Mello readily agreed. The match, East Zone versus West Indians, was scheduled for Lucknow.

As the match was allotted to Lucknow, Dr. A.C. Chatterjee was leaving for London Olympics as manager of the Indian hockey team. He asked the university skipper P.R. Chauhan to help in laying the pitch at Gomati (university) ground. Before leaving Lucknow, Dr. Chatterjee had ordered the treasurer to give Rs. 400 to Chauhan as initial expenses for laying the pitch.

As Dr. Chatterjee left for London, N.N. Mukerjee (Habul) retuned to Lucknow after coaching Indian hockey team at Mumbai. He immediately declined to give advance to Chauhan saying that Lucknow would not be able to raise the requisite amount of Rs. 7,500 as guarantee money for the match. Habul was then officiating as general secretary of the Lucknow Sports Association.

As LSA withdrew at last moment, the search was made for another venue in UP. The Board in general and de Mello in particular were upset at Lucknow's last minute withdrawal. Allahabad, one of the good cricketing centres, came forward to stage the match.

The Palia-Banerjee-Wahidulah combination brought about West Indians downfall at Allahabad. This was the only match tourists lost. Skipper Palia arranged the field meticulously. Shute Banerjee bounced the ball. The West Indians main batsmen went for hook. Wahidullah, diminutive, leapt now this way and now that way to bring about spectacular catches at mid-wicket.

The guarantee money was advanced by Sir Hargovind Misra (Kanpur). Upset at Vizzy's repeated interference into day-to-day functioning of the Allahabad Cricket Association (ACA), D.S. Pande also acted tough refusing to share profits with the UPCA. The controversy had already existed between UPCA and Allahabad. The cause for controversy was Mohammad Mustafa who was opposed to ACA secretary Pande.

Vizzy was the boss of U.P. cricket. It was a ritual with him to resign before the annual general meeting when elections of office-bearers of the U.P. Cricket Association were held. The meeting was invariably held after sumptuous lunch, hosted by Vizzy. As he placed meeting in order after roll-call of members, about half-a-dozen members, known and unkown, would say in chorus "No Vizzy, no UPCA. Now. the entire house would appeal to Vizzy : "Sir we need you to guide us". Following persistent requests (all pre-planned and pre-arranged) Vizzy would withdraw his resignation with "tears rolling down his cheeks". This was a drama enacted every year with Allahabad's Mohammed Mustafa, secretary UPCA, as master of ceremonies.

It was in mid 1950s when Vizzy tried to befriend with Amarnath, who had grown in stature in Indian cricket politics. Vizzy had invited Amarnath to lead UP in Ranji Trophy. To Amarnath's credit, he had not made a commitment but he had not declined the invitation either. No contact could be established with Amarnath for some days despite frantic telephone calls. Vizzy, in the meantime, appointed Balendu Shah captain of UP team for Ranji Trophy. A good wicket-keeper, he was one of the candidates for the Indian team to tour Australia in 1947. A cultured politician from Tehri Garhwal (he was an MLC and was even offered by the Chief Minister C.B. Gupta a ministerial post if he joined Congress). Belendu even occupied the special room in the Vizzy Palace (Varanasi). The following morning Amarnath arrived. Balendu had was not only thrown out from the captaincy but he was even asked to vacate the room. Balendu was extremely bitter on Vizzy's crude handling.

Vizzy, also president of the Andhra Pradesh Cricket Association (APCA), was now all ready to seek elections for the office of the president of the Board. The year was 1954-55. J.C. Mukherjea, Board president for three years, was seeking re-election. Two other heavy weights were in the fray. They were Surjit Singh Majithia (deputy union minister) and Anthony de Mello.

There was no love lost between de Mello and Amarnath, who carried a few votes with him. Mukherjea was also uncertain of his re-election. After considering the situation, de mello and Mukherjea withdrew from the contest.

Senior politicians, bureaucrats and diplomats were canvassing for the remaining two candidates, Vizzy and Majithia. A keen contest was expected at Bangalore on October 10, 1954. But the battle royal did not come off as Majithia's (he was not present in the meeting) candidature was withdrawn by Amarnath after his name was proposed and seconded. Vizzy thus became Board president unopposed.

A bitter controversy surfaced. Could Majithia's name have been withdrawn after it was proposed and seconded? A debate followed. But the contest did not take place. Majithia perhaps did not have enough support. But why did Amarnath propose his name when he was not certain of his strength?

# 95

# An Amusing Explanation

Iftikhar Ali Pataudi did not enthrall in England in 1946 both as a player and as a captain. India lost the three Test series 0-1 but the team returned in one "piece" without any acrimony or controversy. This was more than satisfactory in view of previous two acrimonious tours in 1932 and 1936.

Pataudi was not in dazzling form. He was not at the best of his health. Still he nurtured a hope of leading India on a tour to Australia in 1947. His assessment showed that de Mello, now President of the Board, was in favour of Merchant to appease him for the allegedly wrong done to him a year earlier.

Merchant was duly elected captain in December 1946. Eight months later some time in August 1947, he withdrew from the assignment on account of deteriorating health. Groin ailment was the cause for his withdrawal. Some Board members were heard as saying that Merchant withdrew because he was not happy that Amarnath should have been appointed as vice-captain. If this could be correct, why did he take so long to withdraw? This, however, remained a mystery.

As Merchant pulled out of the team, two other established batsmen, Syed Mushtaq Ali and Rusi Modi withdrew. Mushtaq Ali walked out of the tour on account of sudden demise of his brother while Modi assigned no reasons for his withdrawal.

When announcement of elevation of Amarnath was made, he was in Patiala. Mohsin Ali Naqvi, in his article in National Herald (Lucknow) said: Amarnath made a cowboy dash from Patiala to Delhi. The journey was made partly by car, partly by train and partly on foot, specially from Kurukshetra to Delhi". When asked what was the need for Amarnath to undergo all this trouble when Patiala was so well-connected with Delhi, Naqvi said : "This was what Amarnath himself told him".

With Fazal Mehmood also withdrawing as Lahore had fallen in Pakistan, the Indian selectors had to select four substitutes. The time was short. It was not an easy task. The selectors were divided. Amidst this confusion, de Mello assumed all responsibility of nominating Rangachari, Rai Singh and Ranvirsingh. These three were chosen in place of Merchant, Mushtaq and Modi while Chandu Serwate came in place of Fazal. There was resentment but de Mello did not bother. The substitutes joined the team in Perth before the tour commenced.

As the period of mourning was over, Mushtaq was persuaded by the Maharaja of Holkar for his joining the team. He sent a telegram to de Mello for joining the team. But the Board did not entertain his request saying that he had earlier also ditched the country when Hassett's Australian Eleven was playing in India. Mushtaq Ali was naturally upset at Board's handling. The team had not yet taken off from Kolkata for Australia. But de Mello sent him a telegram saying that replacements had already been finalised and it would be improper to bring about further change. Mushtaq knew it was a plot engineered by some interested persons.

India was no match to Australia. Initially there appeared some reservations among players. But Amarnath and manager Pankaj Gupta saw to it that there was no division among players.

Pankaj Gupta, short and round, was as shrewd as de Mello and Amarnath. He was at his brilliant best when he was "spirited". He did not submit accounts when he returned from the Australia tour. He gave a novel reason : "All vouchers had been blown by a gush of strong wind as I was sorting them on the ship", he offered this explanation. He went on to say that even paper weight on vouchers had blown away. This was amusing. What was more amusing was that the Board accepted it. He was then Board secretary.

In 1984 the Board charged five Test players for billing two parties for single air Journey. Sunil Gavaskar rose in defence of the players. The intention was not to cheat. If it was not cheating, what was it? The Board did not take action against erring players. But it threatened to bar any player guilty of similar offence in future for official cricket.

# 96

# Another Sin At Kolkata

The largest cricket stadium (Eden Gardens) and the ICC president (Jagmohan Dalmiya) enjoy many firsts. But it is also the worst centre for crowd-management. Had there been any other centre, it would have been "black-balled from staging any international match for a few years, if not more. But who can touch Kolkata as long as Dalmiya is at the helm of affairs?

Apart from earlier rounds of trouble against the West Indies team and the Australian team, there was unprecedented problem in the 1996 World Cup semi-final. As if these incidents were not enough, another serious trouble erupted in the 1999 inaugural Asian Test Cricket Championship.

"Disgraceful", "Sin in Eden" and "Kolkata image sullied" were among many adjectives used as a section of the hooligans translated "Chennai good behaviour" into "Kolkata hell".

The India-Pakistan match in the first ACC was staged with all the pomp and show. It was being staged after 1-1 draw of the two-Test series at Chennai and Delhi. There was hope that India would repeat the performance given at Delhi where Anil Kumble became the second bowler in history to claim all 10 wickets in an innings. The first was Jim Laker (England) against Australia.

India were sitting pretty initially, but then they threw away the Test. It was a case of snatching defeat from the jaws of victory. That was nothing unusual for Indians. They had done it before and they would continue to do so. As if this ignoble performance was not bad enough, the hoodlums upstaged Sainik jawans misdeeds by committing a "murder of cricket". It was day-light murder, witnessed by thousands of people of all walks of life. Kolkata should have been "black-listed" so that similar ugly instances do not recur.

The seeds of unpardonable behaviour of crowd violence were sown a day earlier when Sachin Tendulkar was run out in most tragic circumstances. He accidentally collided with Shoaib Akhtar. The TV slow-motion replays showed that both were watching the ball and this led to their running into each other. None was to blame. Nadeen Khan's throw dislodged the bails while Tendulkar was not yet home. The third umpire was referred to by the field umpire. K.T. Francis scrutinised the incident repeatedly before ruling Tendulkar run out. It was a fair decision and it should have been accepted by all present.

Supposing Nadeen's throw had hit Tendulkar or any other fielder and the ball had sailed for a boundary. What would have umpire done? He would have been duty bound to award a boundary plus run or runs already made. If this is in order, as per rules, then why can't batsman be given out run out if he is not home.

There was nothing unsporting if Wasim Akram did not call Tendulkar back. There was no infringement of laws. Also, he was not given out wrongly. Why then expect "mercy" from the rival captain?

When this "unfortunate" incident took place, the organisers should have announced on PA (Public Address) system that what had happened was in accordance to laws. It would have removed all misgivings that existed in stands. This is the minimum that Dalmiya and his men should have done.

How can spectators be pacified when authorities are themselves guilty of several violations? There are instances when a few office bearers have actually incited the spectators to indulge in violence. Many ills that exist in Indian cricket are because of ill informed officials.

# 97

# An Obnoxious Behaviour

The Board of control for Cricket in India (BCCI) officials showed that they lacked in planning and foresight when they allotted the opening one-day international between India and West Indies in 1983 to Srinagar. The result : Indians were hooted, booed and jeered. India Lost the match as also there were slogans of "Pakistan zindabad".

The unpardonable behaviour of a section of the spectators was a slap in the face of Indian patriotism. The day's events that unfolded showed that the throng of spectators was tuitored to shout anti-India slogans even when there were occasions to applaud them. It was shocking; it was not cricket.

In a sporting contest, spectators are expected to cheer players for their excellent doings regardless of the side to which they belong! The Caribbeans got a good gallery even when appreciation was due to Indians. This was shameful.

The spectators' behaviour was so obnoxious that the game had repeatedly been disturbed by trouble-makers. Stones were hurled at some Indian players and the Indian captain was for a moment contemplating whether it was advisable to continue with the game at the centre where atmosphere was vicious. The West Indies officials were heard saying that the crowd support was so vocal that "we thought we were playing in our own country".

It was learnt that the Jamait-Tuleba, the student wing

of the Jamat-Islami was the main culprit in shouting anti-India slogans. Known for its unsavoury past, Tuleba remained unashamed of its anti-national role. It held the view that Kashmir was not an integral part of the country. Religious fanaticism was the cause for this unhealthy trend obtaining in Srinagar.

Dr. Farooq Abdullah was at the helm of affairs when the match was in progress. He could have brought the situation under control, had he taken adequate measures. But, for some strange reasons, he was mute observer at the ground.

The fault was clearly of the Fixtures and Programme Committee of the Board for starting the tour at the centre, which was hostile to the country. The West Indies got a head-on start. Clive Lloyd and Wes Hall were grateful to the Board for fixing the itinerary to their advantage!

The spectators had come prepared to humiliate Indians. They often waved a huge poster of Imran Khan. They once flashed it at Gavaskar who, in a grand gamesmanship, held his right thumb and forefingers together. They visibly felt satisfied and did not cause more problems to him.

Dr. Abdullah expressed his apologies for crowd misbehaviour at the subsequent get-together. His apologies were indeed genunine. But there were some local politicians who were heard saying that he could have prevented spectators from misbehaving, had he made sincere attempt because he continued to be extremely popular in Kashmir, particularly in Srinagar.

Some senior players stayed back in Srinagar to enjoy the scenic beauty. They were all treated royally and they were provided the security personnel. Says Gavaskar, in his book Runs'n Ruins : "I believe sportsmen may be booed and jeered at but nobody in his right mind would want to injure a player". Gavaskar goes on to say : "I have been asked whether I would play in Srinagar again and my answer is yes, because one does not hold any grudge in cricket and in any case one swallow does not make a summer".

These are indeed philosophical words. But how one wishes that he had displayed similar kind of attitude towards spectators of Kolkata where he declined to play against Pakistan!

# 98

# Silver Jubilee—An Eyewash

In a bid to celebrate silver jubilee in 1953, the Board made frantic efforts to get an official Australian team to undertake tour of the country. The Australian Cricket Board expressed its inability to tour the country because of its previous commitment else here.

Unable to get a favourable response from the ACB, the Board officials tried to secure an unofficial Australian side. They entered into protracted correspondence with Australian umpire Barlow. But this move also failed.

Determined to have an overseas team, come what may, the Board through Pankaj Gupta prevailed upon George Duckworth to raise a Commonwelth side. Lucrative terms were provided to Duckworth. The team came. But the itinerary underwent several changes to accommodate voting members. The situation became so annoying that Duckworth and his players did not know what the itinerary was. Not only this but some of the fixtures made different reading from the itinerary announced.

In addition to five unofficial Tests, there were two Indian XI matches of four days' duration. There were several other matches in which virtually the Test team was fielded. The result : visitors were upset and bitter as Duckworth went on record saying that he had brought his team to play five Tests and not a dozen Tests.

Hyderabad Cricket Association (HCA) was assured of

a Test match provided it laid a turf wicket. The HCA laid the turf wicket and also raised facilities on the ground for the two teams. The Board secretary visited the centre and accorded his approval. Yet the Test was not allotted to Hyderabad and it was given to the UP Cricket Association which held the Test at Lucknow's jute matting. The HCA was offered the Indian XI match but it snubbed the Board declining to accept the offer.

The selection panel of C.K. Nayudu (chairman), C. Ramaswami, Amarnath and Dutta Ray chose, among others, Jasu Patel and Mushtaq Ali for the first Test at Lucknow. The match could not by played on schedule dates because of rioting by Lucknow University students.

For the next Test at Delhi, Patel and Mushtaq Ali were sidelined. While Patel's exclusion could be understood as the Test was on turf, why was Mushtaq Ali dropped? He was a player, who was as proficient on matting as he was on turf.

It was subsequently learnt that Mushtaq Ali was chosen for the Lucknow Test at the insistence of Vizzy, vice-president of the Board. Vizzy's plea was that Mushtaq Ali's presence would help secure full house at Lucknow. It was further learnt that Vizzy, also president of the UP cricket Association, had sent telegram to each selector for the inclusion of Mustaq Ali. Should vice-president of the Board have sent such telegram and should selectors have paid heed to it? Obviously, selectors did give weightage to Vizzy's telegram as Mushtaq Ali should have been an automatic choice for the Delhi Test also if he had been chosen on form.

Arjun Nayudu, who was brought in the team in place of Patel for the Delhi Test, bowled eight overs in two innings without securing a solitary wicket. On the inclusion of Nayudu, Vijay Merchant went on record saying that : "Sometime I feel that Mankad's faster ball is quicker than Nayudu's fastest". another question that arose was aslo why medium pacer was brought into the team in place of a spinner?

The selection of the team for the Kolkata Test was made on the fourth day of the Mumbai Test, which was second as the first Lucknow Test could not be held because of riots. The selection of the side was advanced because one selector wanted to leave for his "home" earlier. C.V. Gadkari was made 12th man but he scored a century on the fifth day after the Kolkata Test team was finalised. When the Kolkata Test began, Gadkari walked into the team while Gaekwad was demoted to the position of the 12th man. This arbitrary action was taken without taking captain Hemu Adhikari into confidence. The decision was shocking as the team had only one opening batsman Pankaj Roy. In the Mumbai Test also there was only one recognised opening batsman—Vinoo Mankad and Niran Tamhane had to open the innings. The result was that Tamhane failed since he was not accustomed to playing a moving ball. Dissatisfied at Tamhane's style of batsmanship, Polly Umrigar was asked to open. He also failed.

For the Chennai Test, Ghulam Ahmed was made captain. Why was Adhikari removed after he had captained in only one Test? Was one Test enough to assess captain's calibre? Adhikari was appointed vice-captain of the Indian team that toured England in 1952 under Vijay Hazare and he should have been an automatic choice for captaincy in 1953. What was deplorable was that Adhikari was subsequently eased out of the team. A sheet-anchor on many occasions, he was treated shabbily by the selectors.

The Commonwealth team's tour, ended with a match against the Prime Minister's XI at Kolkata. Like chopping in the Indian team, the Commonwealth side also underwent many changes. A failure financially, Worrell and Ramadhin left the side midway through the tour and Simpson left a few days later. Jack Iverson (Australia) and Watkins (England) were the replacements.

After the conclusion of the tour at Kolkata, the Board officials woke up from their slumber and held an eye wash of a function at Delhi. The function was styled as Board's silver jubilee celebrations! The function lacked in glamour, decency and decourm. There were no players from two teams-Indian and Commonwealth. Only Barnett and Duckworth attended as a matter of courtesy.

# 99

# Board's Faulty Scheme

In August 1953 it was announced that Vinoo Mankad and Joe Hardstaff would train promising youngsters from Octorer 1 under the scheme of Rajkumari Amrit Kaur. Both Mankad and Hardstaff were renowned player-coaches and some centres affiliated to the Board of Control for Cricket in India (BCCI) had made elaborate preparations to raise promising youngsters from their respective areas.

Suddenly, something went totally wrong with the much-talked about scheme and it fell through before it was taken off the ground. Both Mankad and Hardstaff regretted their inability to function as coaches.

Mankad was not informed of his appointment until October 1 although he had made repeated inquiries about the scheme. Unsure of the scheme, he entered into contract with Purshotam Rungta, Founder president of Mumbai's Rajasthan Cricket Club. The contract covered a period of three years from October 1 to March 31 every year from 1953 to 1956. "One in hand is better than two in bushes", was Mankad's philosophy. Eventually, the Board's scheme was scrapped.

Similary, Amarnath wanted to conduct coaching at Kanpur in mid 1950. The plan did not materialse.

Alan Moss, the Middlesex and England fast bowler, came to India in January 1958. He was scheduled to visit Metropolitan cities to unearth prospective fast bowlers.

But he stayed at Mumbai's CCI. He refused to leave Mumbai as he was not happy with the scheme.

Moss went on record saying that the youngsters that were provided to him were not cut in for physical work out. Most of them did not have talent for fast bowling nor did they have physique for it. Only Ramakant Desai had in him some capacity to become a decent fast bowler. But even his bouncer was a "suspect". Polly Umrigar did often attend nets. He smacked these yougsters all over the place. He enjoyed batting against these innocuous looking fast bowlers.

The scheme, according to Moss, was a total flop and no tangible result could be achieved. There was no planning and the boys, who came for training, lacked in basic material. He stayed in Mumbai for four months and all the money spent on him by the Board was a total waste.

In an unplanned bid to develop fast bowlers as also provide leading batsmen to play fast bowling, four West Indian speedsters were drafted into playing domestic competitions. The visitors, placed in different zones, did figure in matches but the experiment was a failure, as expected.

Roy Gilchrist, short and stocky, was one of them. He was sent back by his skipper Gerry Alexander for bowling too many bouncers to his university mate Swaranjit Singh at Amritsar. Gilchrist, an extremely quick bowler, had couple of balls standing up as tall, hefty, left-handed Amritsar born Swarnjit came to bat. The more his skipper asked him to quieten down, the less he was obeying his skipper's instructions.

Following skipper's stiff direction Gilchrist bowled a good length ball. Swaranjit drove it. While running, Swaranjit asked Gilchrist "How did you like the stroke". This had a maddening effect on the quickie. He hurled one of the quickest deliveries. It whizzed Past Swaranjit's ear. Then there was no helmet.

If West Indian fast bowlers' participation in domestic competitions did not help the Board's move the scheme to send fast bowlers to Alf Gover's School (England) also failed. Both Dattu Phadkar and Salgaokar returned totally disillusioned. While Phadkar lost his pace that he possessed Salgaokar returned much heavier than what he was. Gilchrist had a problem at Kanpur. He had gone to the post office to buy stamps. When he asked the clerk as to how many stamps (meaning price of stamps) would he needed to send a letter to his home country, the clerk was unable to answer him. He repeated but the clerk could not understand his 'lingo'.

Infuriated at his indifference, Gilchrist rushed inside the cabin, pulled him out and man-handled him. Commotion arose. Police was summoned. He was hauled up for manhandling a Government clerk on duty. The Kanpur and Board officials, luckily, reached on the spot and a very ugly situation was averted.

Poor Gilchrist, essentially a well meaning fellow and outstanding fast bowler, has currently been passing through a pitiable plight back in his country. A loner, he often visits a pub where he drinks his glass of beer in solitude. Once "Pocket dynamo" Gilchrist was rated as fast, if not faster, as Harold Larwood. Initially an off-spinner for Parish (St Thoms) he was asked to open as fast bowlers played truant. He grabbed the opportunity.

When Holt was ill, Gilchrist prayed for his speedy recovery. It was a great gesture because it was Holt who was responsible for his being sent back from Amritsar.

La affaire coaching, the Board discontinued with training programme for Juniors. After procrastination for decades, the board eventually established an academy. There is now a controversy whether it should continue to function from Bangalore, or it should be shifted.

# 100

# Merchant Admits His Mistake

The difference in age between Prof D.B. Deodhar and Vijay Merchant was enormous. They belonged to different eras. Both were self-made and were strict vegetarians. If Deodhar was considered as "father" of Indian cricket, Merchant was an epitome of grace at the crease. Both were more friends than mere colleagues. Both had developed healthy respect for each others ability and skill. Both wore a label of "principled players". Deodhar died on October 27, 1987.

Deodhar was an established player when Merchant was showing his prowess. Deodhar was the captain when Merchant was chosen in the team. First time, Merchant played under Deodhar was in 1929 then in 1934 and again in 1936 for the Hindus in the Mumbai Quadrangular. Deodhar was the captian in 1940 when Merchant was a member of the team in the unofficial Test between India and Ceylon (now Sri Lanka). There were several other festival and charity matches in which Deodhar was the skipper and Merchant a player.

An unseeming controversy between two great Hindu players surfaced in 1934. Deodhar had successfully captained Hindus against Europeans. He should have contined to lead the side. But he was dropped from the final.

Merchant was one of the selectors. He reportedly agreed with other selectors who held the view that Deodhar was too old at 42 to continue to captain and also play for the Hindus.

It was not a happy decision. Merit and not the age should have been the guiding factor for the selection.

Deodhar was reportedly unhappy that Merchant, of all persons, should have agreed with other selectors. This was bad. What was worse was that Yuvraj of Patiala was brought in to captain the side. The Hindus lost the final. He was then in his 20s. It was an atrocious decision which was perhaps taken for considerations other than skill. It was then said that he was being groomed to lead India on the tour to England in 1936. But it did not happen

Deodhar was upset at his exclusion but he was determined to prove that Merchant and his co-selectors had erred. He proved his ability as he went on to score century in the trial match in which Merchant also figured. Deodhar regained captaincy in 1936 and the Hindus defeated a strong muslim side. He scored a useful half-century.

For a while, there was a misunderstanding between Deodhar and Merchant. But Merchant made ample amends a few years later when, while delivering a speech on the occasion of the golden jubilee function of the P.J. Hindu Gymkhana (Mumbai), he expressed his sincere regret for being party to Deodhar's exclusion from the team in 1934. Merchant went on to say that it was a mistake to have chosen Yuvraj to captain when seniors, like, C.K. Nayudu, Jai and Godambe were available.

This speech saw two great friends bury the hatchet.

# 101

# Patil Arrives In Solitary Splendour

The wise men of Indian cricket Board officials and five selectors felt in 1979 that there was no need to have more than 12 players for a match against the visiting side. Two reasons were advanced. One was that the "reserve" players for the Test or one-dayer would not waste their time in pavilion and would be free to play local and other matches. The other was that sufficient money would be saved if the side comprised 12 instead of 14 players. After protracted discussion, the Board decided to have the team of 12 players. It also decided that two "local" players would be kept in readiness, should an occasion arise for them to field.

The decision of 12 players for the match was not strictly adhered to subsequently. There were occasions when 14 or more players had been chosen. That was, however, Indian Board which could violate its own decision without assigning any reason.

Came the second Test againt Pakistan at Nagpur which was an awful centre for players, mediapersons and officials. Good hotels were scarce. Players were unable to snatch proper rest after a day's rigorous play. Observations, suggestions and even protests were unheeded by high and mighty of the Vidarbha Cricket Association (VCA).

On the eve of the Test, Mohinder looked doubtful as he

was indisposed. He also had "tiff" with his colleagues over distribution of prize money. He was on a heavy dose of medicine but he rose unfit on the morning of the match. This was bad enough. What was worse was that the selectors had made up their mind not to include Roger Binny although he had batted exceedingly well and also bowled quite well in previous match. Why was he not being included when there was a clear-cut vacancy was difficult to understand. It seemed that the powers that-be had certain different designs and ideas up their sleeves.

There was a considerable uncertainty in the Indian camp as to who 11 players would take the field. Out of blue came the startling news. Sandeep Patil had been recalled. There could have been no complaint whatsoever in his induction in the team. But there was no plane nor could he have reached by a train on time for the Test. There was a flurry of activity at the VCA stadium. In arrived Nagpur's most influential politician. He revealed that after a lot of effort, he had been able to convince the Maharashtra Government that Sandeep Patil might be provided state plane to arrive in Nagpur for the match.

The Maharashtra Government agreed. The plane was got lined-up to take off from the Santa Cruz Airport. The commander was waken up from his sleep for the flight. But Patil was untraceable. Vigorous search was undertaken. He was eventually located. His "coffin" (kit bag) was sent from home to the airport. He himself dashed to aiport from wherever he was. The plane took off late. But VCA authorities were informed that Patil was on his way to Nagpur. He arrived in solitary splendour. Skipper was asked to include his name among 11. Luckily, India batted first. Had India fielded first, it would have been the discretion of the Pakistan skipper whether to allow a substitute or not.

The entire drama of including Patil in 11 lacked wisdom. It was a brain-child of a politician Salve who, when he had made up his mind on any issue, he would have it implemented regardless of how wrong or foolish a decision or an idea was. What was most deplorable was that skipper Kapil Dev was not consulted. He was merely told that Patil was playing and he was rushing from Mumbai to be on time for the match.

Patil, who had arrived at fag end of the first day's play, had night's rest before he went in to play. He did not seem fully focussed. After a well-time drive, he did not move in sufficiently for his hook shot and was caught off Azeem.

# 102

# An Intelligent Strategy Denounced

Rajesh Chauhan running backward while Srinath was on his run-in to catch Aravinda de Silva raised a controversy in the drawn India-Sri Lanka Test at Mumbai in 1997.

There was nothing unethical or objectionable in what Srinath did. It was, in fact, a well planned strategy to trap a batsman. Srinath bowled a short-pitched bouncer inducing de Silva to hook. Chauhan moved from mid-way position to backward area. de Silva duly hooked only to be easily caught by Chauhan.

What was unethical in this strategy? It was an intelligent ploy as it had so often happened before in Test cricket. Both Srinath and Chauhan should have been congratulated for evolving of a strategy to bring about a downfall of a seasoned batsman instead of denouncing them.

One of the finest TV commentators Geoff Boycott, for exmaple, reacted sharply at the practice adopted by Srinath and Chauhan. One felt that he was more emotional in his observation than practical. He observed: "When the batsman was concentrating on the ball in the bowler's hand, the fielder ran backward to a deeper position. de Silva could not see that happen, hooked the ball to what he felt was a vacant area, only to see Chauhan make a simple catch".

de Silva was furious at Indians. He was also unhappy with his partner Mahanama who, according to him, should have drawn his attention or prevented Srinath from bowling.

Many well known umpires and retired Test stars did not subscribe to the observation of Boycott. They said that neither laws nor the spirit of the laws had been violated by Srinath and Chauhan. In support of their argument, they said: "If a fielder, stationed in the country in front or behind a batsman, is allowed to move forward many steps as a bowler starts his run in to deliver the ball, why can't a fielder move backward"?

de Silva's suggestion and Boycott's observation that Mahanama should have stopped Srinath if run-in is not a tangible solution. If this can be allowed, then every time a bowler over-steps, the non-striker can shout no-ball reducing the game to a mockery.

The game is already heavily loaded in favour of a batssman. There are innumerable restrictions placed on bowlers; there are restrictions on placement of fielders. A batman is now "armed" with as much protective gear as a soldier going on war. Any more restrictions will render the game more lop-sided than has been at present. Says a veteran player : "if movement of a fielder without disturbing a striker is unethical, then, perhaps, bowling a googly is more unethical".

There is an instance of a fine strategy adopted by Learrie Constantine to outmanoeuvre Don Bradman at his dazzling best. Constantine bowled two balls on middle-off stumps and Bradman duly cut them. Constantine then bowled one ball one foot or about behind the bowling crease. It was a similar outwinger. But the ball took a friction of a second longer to reach. Bradman went for the same stroke. He missed the ball and was dismissed. Would this strategy be considered as unethical?

The Test had another controversy. Sri Lanka were facing defeat. The umpires S. Bucknor and debutant V.

Jayaprakash closed the match on account of insufficient light. The Indians thought that the light had improved considereably when the match was closed. Maybe, the umpires will henceforth be "armed" with a gadget to determine the light!

# 103

# Tradition Not Respected

More often than not in Indian cricket, traditions have been flouted and rules have been bent to help a section of players and officials. A sad chapter indeed, but it is shocking that violations of traditions and breaking of rules should have taken place during the regime of Ranjsingh Dungarpur, who is "married" to cricket and who played first class cricket in 1950s and 1960s for Rajasthan and Central Zone.

Sri Lanka team's tour in 1997-98 started with a delayed match against Board President's XI at Cuttuck (Nov 14-16) as the visitors were busy with Anshuman Gaekwad benefit match at Baroda a day earlier, that is, Nov 13.

Following the conclusion of the Baroda match, prize distribution and other functions, the visitors could board the plane late and arrived at Cuttuck around 2.30 a.m. They were naturally tired and could reach the Barabati Stadium late and the match began about 90 minutes behind schedule.

It was just a mere chance that local spectators, known for their rowdysim, did not create rumpus for the delayed start. They could have easily resorted to any crude method and that would have caused a needless problem and anxiety to the local organisers.

Should Board have allowed a benefit match to be played a day earlier and disturb the opener? Why did

Board allow this? Was it because Gaekwad was an important wheel in the scheme of things of Indian cricket? Was benefit match for Gaekwad more important than the tour opener? There were several other questions that arose projecting Rajsingh in a vey poor light.

This was not the first time Rajsingh was guilty of violation of traditions. It was in 1976-77 when England were touring the country and Rajsingh was one of the selectors. He was unable to watch the boys in action at Guwahati. He asked Ken Barrington to "look for a promising youngster in the team. It was understandable that Rajsingh could not reach Guwahati, but why depend upon English manager?

In an after dinner speech, Barrington said that he was functioning in two capacities as a manager of the touring team as well as Indian selector!

There were four other selectors on the panel. Why could not Rajsingh depend upon them or one of them instead of asking Barrington to do his job?

# 104

# Slavery Attitude Continues

To Australian batsmen off-spin is as much a "death" as quick bowling to Indians. It was England's Jim Laker, who took 19 wickets in the 1956 Manchester Test against Australia. It was again Jasu Patel, who took 14 wickets for 124 runs to help India outplay Richie Benaud's Australia in the second Test at Kanpur in 1959-60. (Benaud, however, was candid enough to say that his team was beaten fairly and squarely instead of doubting the legitimacy of Patel's action.)

It was an Australian umpire and Australians who called Sri Lanka's Muttiah Muralitharan a "chucker". The Sri Lankan Cricket Board did not accept Australians' viewpoint. They accused Australians of needless prejudices. The Sri Lankan off-spinner returned to play Test cricket.

It was again these kinds of authorities and players who doubted Rajesh Chauhan's action. In the India-New Zealand series in 1995, some suspected his action which, according to many experts and analysts, was peculiar. A round-arm action, an angular run-in, a leap and his arm brushed his ear as he delievered the ball. His elbow seemed to wear a kind of "bend", but he did not secure any benefit of either obtaining a huge turn or quickening through the pitch. His action was certainly not graceful; it did not povide any aesthetic beauty to watchers. But it was a "passable" action.

When some over-rated players and officials raised a

question mark against Chauhan's action, he was sidelined. It could not be ascertained as to who was that "authority" which asked Indian selectors not to consider him for selection. His "grounding" was uncalled for. He was disappointed and upset. He was sent to England for "scrutiny". Why England? Was there any one more knowledgeable on the art of off-spin bowling than India's E.A.S. Prasanna and Venkataraghavan? Venkat was, in fact, the best person to provide his opinion. A fine off-spin bowler in his time, he is an outstanding umpire holding world ranking. But it is a case of "ghar-ki-murgi-dal-mafic".

In England, on a virtual trial, Chauhan was "advised" by Fred Titmus to undergo minor changes and adjustments in "action". He was essentially opposed to any change in his action. He thought—and so did many—that there was nothing wrong or objectionable about his action. Ashok Mankad, one of the shrewdest observers, had advised him that he should not undergo any change in action. This was before he had made a mark in the arena of international cricket.

It is a downright mockery to spot a bowler with suspect or objectionable action at international level of Test or one-dayer. A bowler with a "suspect" action, if at all, should be spotted at a tender age of 12-14 or about. It is total tomfoolery to refer a bowler (international grade) with "suspect" action, to the ICC. Supposing ICC with the aid of best of authorities "clear" a bowler. But the umpie, as dispassionate as any in the world, reaches the conclusion that he throws or chucks the ball. Should he call him? If he does not, it means he is failing in his duties just because ICC had cleared a bowler.

Chauhan lost precious two years of his cricketing life as no firm opinion could be formulated. He was then granted a temporary reprieve. He was declared eligible for selection on the tour to Sri Lanka, where he was a success.

The two-member panel of Sunil Gavaskar and Kapil Dev watched Chauhan bowl at the National Stadium for more than an hour. But they did not pronounce their judgment. They returned to ICC asking for more footage of action replay of Chauhan before they could arrive at a conclusive decision.

Indecision on Chauhan's action continued. This was because Indian Board did not handle the situation with the required firmness. The officials, always suffering from needless inferiority complex, played into the hands of people who were not exactly unbiased. Amidst this vex scenario, Australia's Bob Simpson raised a question mark against Chauhan's action. This was enough. Poor bowler was again shown the door. He was sidelined from the competition in Dhaka.

Let there be no nonsense. Test stars or one-day exponents are not necessarily the best in all aspects of cricket. They are human beings and they can also err in their judgment. There are quite a few who may not have figured in the arena of international cricket but their knowledge is second to none. John Kupputh, for example, did not know swimming. But he added in his exceptional knowledge scientific coaching methods. He produced more world beaters than many well known swimming coaches and swimmers. Similarly, in cricket there are quite a few observant people who thought that Chauhan was more sinned against than actually sinning (throwing or chucking). The Indian authorities should have taken Simpson's opinion with a bagful of salt because Australians hate off-spinners!

There are some, who feel that young spinner's life was unnecessarily destroyed by authorities who have pronounced prejudices against Indians. The Indians continue to be "slave" even after 55 years of independence.

The laws say the umpire is the sole judge. He has to adjudicate on each individual delivery, not just a basic action, which may be altered.

The Indian authorities should have ignored Simpson's observations leaving Chauhan in the hands of the umpires.

Law 24(2) Says : Fair Delivery-for delivery to be fair,

the ball must be bowled, not thrown. If either umpire is not entirely satisfied with the absolute fairness of a delivery in this respect he shall call and signal "no ball" instantly upon delivery.

A "throw" : "A ball shall be deemed to have been thrown if, in the opinion of either umpire, the process of straightening bowling arm, whether it be partial or complete takes place during that part of the delivery swing which directly precedes the ball leaving the hand. This definition shall not debar bowler from the use of the wrist in the delivery swing".

# 105

# A Well Organised Racket

Taking a team of youngsters abroad for a fortnight or a month or more is a well organised racket in this country. Parents beg, borrow or steal funds of Rs. 50,000 or more to help their wards to join the team. The "lucky" youngsters have to rough it out in the middle as also occasionally undergo insults and humiliations from over-bearing and pompous officials. The boys are not allowed to ask questions nor are they given any answers. Such tours are nothing but "dadagiri" or "personal kingdom" of handful of officials, who have translated such tours into lucrative business. The officials, coaches and managers make hay while sun shines. This is at the expense of youngsters' money. These officials carry gifts for the hosts and collect presents from them for themselves and their own families. When these officials shop in excess, they hand over suitcases to youngsters resulting in that these boys are deprived of buying their own essential articles.

The cricket team should normally comprise 15-16 players. But it is not so for these kinds of trips. The team consists of 20-25 persons, including some who are not remotely connected with cricket. Visas are secured for them in the name of cricket. Some of them break away after reaching there. They, in fact, do not return with the team. For such acts, the so-called persons contribute a far bigger amount than other youngsters. This enriches so-called officials, who are at the helm of affair. There have been instances when shrewd officials organise matches with embassy bigwigs with a view to befriending visa officers. Such get-togethers help them obtain visas without any hazzle.

An official of a well known club in Hyderabad was once apprehended for FERA violations. The same official was a member of the official Indian team for the 1983 World Cup in England and was questioned for carrying excessive quantity of tea leaves. He was imposed a heavy fine. The same official along with Delhi based official, bought tickets from a travel agent on credit. Subsequently cheques were issued. They all bounced. The agent filed a suit in the Delhi court. While Hyderabad based official secured a "bail", the Delhi-based official absconded to Bangladesh.

Another official representing a well-known Congress unit, took the team abroad. He charged a sizable amount from boys for air passage. But he brought about pressure on Air India and managed "complimentary passages" from the airline which also provided T-shirts and other equipment. No one knew what happened to the huge amount of money collected from boys?

According to rules, the group travelling under GIT (Group Inclusive Tours) scheme, the team is entitled to heavy discount in addition to free passage for two or more persons. While the boys have to pay for their travel the officials accompanying the team travel free in royal style.

The clubs assure youngsters that lodging and board would be provided by hosts. But when the team reaches UK, for example, the boys are lodged in mandir or Gurdwara where lodging and board are free. But the boys are made to pay. There have been instances when teams have taken with them cooks who don't even return with the teams. What is the cause for concern is that expenses incurred on such cooks are debited in the account of boys.

The departure of such teams is invariably associated with a lot of pomp and show. But the boys return from such tours disappointed and dejected. The matches held there are mere "farce". Only favourites play and others are made to cool their heels in the pavilion. When favourites succeed, the news is released to press.

It is nothing but fraud in the name of cricket tours. Such trips should be banned straight away. This will be a great service rendered by the Board of Control for Cricket in India.

# 106

# Compton Feels Cheated

It was a tall-scoring memorable Ranji final between Holkar and Mumbai at Mumbai in 1945. It was a match of matches in which no quarters were asked for and none given. As several leading players were playing, spectator-response was also encouraging. Every run was cheered for regardless who made it and spectators made a lot of noise on the fall of each wicket.

Denis Compton, friendly and debonair, was stationed in Mhow for awhile during his service in the British army. He was a batsman, akin to Mushtaq Ali, also of Indore, in unorthodoxy. Australia's renowned writer, Ray Robinson, wrote something like this: "If Compton and Mushtaq were batting together—this did happen sometime—the spectators would not visualise who is the striker and who is the non striker". Those were the days when cricket was a game which was delightful and delighted the spectators.

During short span of his stay in Mhow (near Indore), Compton had made many friends because of his easy-going style and friendly attitude to all, junior and senior. He enjoyed every minute on the ground and, when off it, he was seen among people enjoying jokes. He was one of the few Englishmen, who was prepared to laugh at himself and it rendered him all the more popular with locals. The players also respectd him because he was a good influence on them. To youngsters he was all the more important because he was ever ready to give them useful tips.

Despite the presence of C.K.Nayudu, who was a strict disciplinarian, the atmosphere in the dressing room was that of carefree and gaiety when he was around. On the field, he along with CK saw to it that the atmosphere was electrifying. CK took the match so seriously that he did not let his players have drinks during interval. He felt that "drinks" even in humid and sultry weather reduced fielders' concentration. Wrong or right he was the boss on the field.

When Compton arrived for the match in Mumbai, he was warmly greeted by all members of the team, including skipper Nayudu. Compton used to like playing at Mumbai as much as playing at Yashwant Club (Indore).

Just before the rival captains went out for the toss, an Indian merchant (not Vijay) and a staunch supporter of Holkar told Compton that he would provide him an incentive for Holkar's win over Mumbai. Says businessman: "Mr. Compton, we are very honoured to have such a worthy player in our team. I will give you a Rs. 100 (£7.10 then) for every run you score over a hundred". "I will try my best for Holkar to win the final", said Compton, adding "I do hope you are serious about giving me the promised incentive".

Compton duly completed his century and raised visions of Holkar's win over mighty Mumbai. He raised his "topee" to acknowledge crowd's vociferous applause. His thought then switched over to businessman's offer. He pondered then that every four meant 30 pounds to him. It was a big money in those days. It was more so because his salary, allowances and perks were not very high.

Holkar could not shock Mumbai. Compton went on to score an unbeaten 247. His knock played a vital role in Holkar making a fight of the final.

As Compton was returning, he began to calculate that he would soon be richer by about 1100 pounds. As he removed his leg-guards, batting gloves and box, he went in the pavilion in search of the businessman. His search proved in vain. Then he asked CK as to where that club official was. "Oh Denis, I have an urgent message from him for you", said Nayudu, adding: "He has been recalled to Kolkata on the most urgent business".

Compton lost 1100 pounds but he reportedly felt bitter at the cheating. Who would not ? Compton (78) died in May 1997.

This may be a cheating by a businessman, but there is a very amusing story concerning another Holkar player, left-hand spinner Hiralal Gaekwad (Ghissoo). Like Compton, he had helped Holkar win the Ranji Trophy. Maharajah of Holkar, who employed most of the players, was watching the exploits of Hiralal. Match over, he summoned Hiralal: "Bole Ghissoo, kiya chahiye?" Hiralal could have asked for anything, including a house, and Maharajah would have gladly presented it to him, so happy was he over Holker's win.

Do you know, what Hiralal asked: "Sir, a cycle as I stay very far away from the ground!"

# 107

# Englishmen Were Not Sporting

Englishmen came as traders in this country. They soon realised ready-made availability of untapped gold-mine. They spread their wings; they widened their umbrella. From their first innings of traders, they translated it into a Raj with their policy of "divide and rule". Their assessment was that there was no love lost between the Hindus and the Muslims and Parsees hated both.

Strong, stronger and strongest Englishmen grew with the passage of time. They needed recreation. They spread the concept of sports. Cricket was one of them. If they played a pioneering role in installing cricket, which is now a national discipline in the country, Parsees were the first to take to cricket. Soon there were exchange of matches between Europeans and Parsees. The contests were razor-sharp: win or defeat meant a lot to both teams.

Parsees were quicker in picking up technique than Elglish-traders settled in India. The Parsees also developed their own skill and temperament to match or even outclass Englishmen. Naturally, it promoted intense rivalry. As no team wanted to lose, unseemly problems surfaced.

It was 1890 when the match between Parsees and Mumbai Gymkkhana (all European), was billed. But it was cancelled. The Gymkhana secretary A.P. Gould went on record as saying that the match had given rise to "display of feelings" even before the start of the game. Some others, particularly Framji Patel, thought that the real reason for calling off the match was not "emotional feelings" but as to who would supervise the match.

The system prevailing then was that each side would provide a knowledgeable person who could umpire with fair degree of impartiality. While Parsees saw nothing wrong in this system, the Englishmen insisted that both umpires should be Europeans. Parsees were confident to take on Europeans with their umpires but some seniors among them felt that it was a reflection on their character. Terming this demand as "extra-ordinary", they rejected it.

The umpiring problem persisted. Even when Presidency matches began, many eye-brows were raised by the local Englishmen. Some mischievous Englishmen gave a twist to the issue of umpiring. Their viewpoint was how could they accept decision (judgment) from one belonging to a subject race. Once Parsees were told that they could nominate one of the two umpires but he should be an Englishman. This was nothing but an instance of adding insult to injury.

Parsees did not agree to European demand. Parsees suggested several names of ex-players, who could supervise the match competently. Among them were the names of Framji Patel, M.D. Kanga and D.J. Tata. Parsees were then asked to nominate a panel of three umpires. This was understandable. But there was a foot-note to it : If all three unpires were found unsuitable, the English umpire would have to officiate the match.

John Greig was Europeans' mainstay in Presidency matches which evoked much enthusiasm. Once he was stumped off Nayudu. He stayed put saying that the bails had not been adequately "dislodged", as stipulated. The decision was contested because it was given by a Hindu umpire M.F. Pai. Organisers subsequently decided that henceforth the umpires would be from a community other than playing a match.

The King does no wrong. This was the philosophy of the English team, official or otherwise, that visited India when they were the masters. Indeed they were the rulers but it did not mean that they should insist on having their own umpires. They arbitrarily finalised the playing conditions. Their judgment could not be challenged. They played matches at their terms. No questions could be asked and no answers were expected.

Cricket in pre-independence days was sponsored by Maharajahs who, for their own benefits, would do anything to please white "Sa'abs". Vizzy, for example, excelled in sychophancy and got away with murders because of active support from "Raj".

When Gilligan's MCC was playing in India in 1926, there were several incidents. One that needs narration is: In a combined Hindu-Muslim versus MCC match at Mumbai, C.K. Nayudu was beaten. The ball rebounded off wicket-keeper's pads and dislodged the bails. The ball had gone so close to the stumps that even a batsman like Nayudu thought he was genuinely bowled. Nayudu was about to start his journey towards pavilion when his partner Vithal asked him to check from the umpire Warden, a parsee, who ruled him not out. Warden was himself a player of proven ability and skill and his decision should have been accepted gracefully. But Englishmen expressed their resentment, which showed that they were after all not as sporting as they ought to have been.

According to Prof D.B. Deodhar, who was a staunch Hindu and who had many brushes with authorities, the Englishmen were so upset with that decision that they created a lot of fuss even in dressing room. That needless row in dressing room was bad. But what was worse was that they refused to mix or mingle with Indians on the lunch table. They chose to sit separately among themselves. This action showed that they were not playing cricket, as it should be played, but they were tyring to project themselves as masters.

Apart from this incident, Gilligan was generally held in a very high esteem for his attitude to cricket players belonging to India. He was impressed by Indians technique, style and ability and he played a key role in Indians forming a proper organisation to promote the game. A true ambassador, he played a pioneering role in stabilising

Indian cricket which was without a parent body to control cricketing activities in the country.

The Nayudu incident however proved one thing that Englishmen were pleasant and friendly when the going was good for them. But they were not exactly sporting when the going was not good for them.

When Bengali Schools lost to British rivals, Kartik Bose, a diminutive, orthodox batsman, wrote to the Englishman on February 13, 1926, assigning reasons for home boys indifferent display. He also offered an explanation as to why players belonging to Sporting Union were refusing to turn up for the match.

Bose, one of the most respected players in Kolkata, says: "For some considerable time back we have been picked out for abusing and slanging by certain section of the public. In an Anglo-schools match whenever any of us came within shouting distance, he was showered with filthy abuses".

There was no understanding between local organisers and Kolkata Cricket Club (CCC), all European club. The CCC did not have any faith in the Indian as a player. The All-India team for the second unofficial Test at Eden Gardens from December 31, 1926 against touring MCC team had as many as seven Europeans. Only four Indians were among eleven. This was shocking because a team comprising all Indians had shocked MCC at Mumbai.

The match saw an amusing incident taking place. Heavily-build and tall Maharaja of Patiala was playing for MCC. How and why was he playing for MCC, there was no plausible reason. But the day's play was interrupted for seven minutes as Maharaja's precious ear-ring was lost when he was at the crease. While he was searching for it, so did his partner Maurice Tate. For some strange reason, Maharaja glared accusingly at C.P. Johnstone, who was fielding at hand-shake distance. Suddenly, Maharaja found earring stuck in his hair-net. The controversy, however, died down soon.

# 108

# Groups Within Groups

A representative side from England, under the captaincy of A.E.R. Gilligan visited India in 1926 and played as many as 34 matches, 26 of which were considered first class. The visitors had impressed every one in the matches played in Northern part of the country. In Mumbai they were to take on a very strong Hindu team.

Ramaswami, a Cambridge blue in tennis, was one of the players chosen to play for the Hindu. He was not much known for his cricketing ability. But he was selected as he had played one marvellous innings against R.J.O. Meyer who had destroyed many a reputations while playing for the Europeans in the Quadrangular. Ramaswami batted freely and hit a sledgehammer century. Many known Hindu authorities and critics had watched him make a mincemeat of the Mayer's bowling. This innings became his passport for selection.

Despite his hurricane innings, Ramaswami was not a very accepted choice for selection in the Hindus team. Vithal was the Hindu captain and he kept asking from many as to who this Ramaswami was.

Even in those days, the Hindus were a divided unit. There were more than two groups. C.K. Nayudu and L.P. Jai were opposed to Vithal. They met Ramaswami in the dressing room about an hour before the match was to start. They started talking freely although they had not met each other before. While discussing various aspects of cricket, both Nayudu and Jai impressed upon him that he was duly chosen by the selection committee and that he should not stand down, should skipper Vithal ask him to do so.

Lo and behold ! As Nayudu and Jai left the pavilion, in came Vithal. Taking the plea of two days of arduous train journey from Chennai to Mumbai, he advised Ramaswami that it would be great if he chose to rest in the interest of the team.

Ramaswami, already fore-warned, said he was quite willing to oblige provided it was the decision of the selection committee which had duly chosen him for the match.

Vithal was keen on including his favourite by the name of Mahale of Mumbai. Looking at the firmness of Ramaswami, the skipper did not pursue the matter as he did not think it proper to suggest selection committee for the change at that late hour.

Ramaswami duly played the match. He could merely make one. The highlight of the match was hurricane hitting by Guy Earle who, in rattling up 130, hit as many as eight sixes and 11 fours. In other words 92 of his 130 came through sixes and fours. One of the sixes broke glass pane of the pavilion in Mumbai Gymkhana.

When Ramaswami failed, there were protests. But the high point that there were intrigues in plenty in those days became obvious.

The scenario in Indian camp even now remains unchanged. During "Raj" regime, there were problems between "Princes" and "Commoners". Then there were "communal problem". Following division of the country, there are now "language problems". The "dressing room" is a "partitioned area". If two are talking in punjabi, five others are conversing in Telugu or Tamil, two are making fun of others in Marathi and some may be discussing in Bengali. In such complex situation, can a team of 14-15 be one unit? This is a peculiar problem existing in this country. Languge disparity is one of the major causes that hurts Indian cricket.

# 109

# A Genuine Mistake

A dashing opening batsman Farokh Engineer was 14 in the fourth Test against the West Indies at Chennai in 1974-75 when he was given out caught by Greenidge off Julien. The ball looked like having gone off the bat. It travelled low and fast and Greenidge grabbed it instinctively. As the ball stayed lodged between Greenidge's fingers, every fielder rushed to congratulate him. Engineer stayed put. He seemed to think that it was not a clean catch. The umpire upheld the appeal, which was loud.

In the following morning papers, the photo, prominently displayed, made it clear that the catch was not taken cleanly. What Greenidge, other fielders and umpire thought was a fair catch, appeared unfair through the eye of the camera.

Gordon Greenidge says: "If I had thought it otherwise, I swear I would have admitted it and Engineer could have batted on. The photo shows that the ball hit the deck the very same moment it lodged between my fingers. No wonder Farokh waited for the signal and even now all I can do is to apologise because at the time I had absolutely no idea it had been grounded. For all the gamesmanship in the game, I genuinely thought it to be a fair catch."

When Greenidge went out to open West Indies innings on the following morning, there were boos and jeers and cat-calls from a section of spectators. Like Engineer, the

West Indies opener also could make 14 before he was caught by Solkar off Ghavri.

Unlike most other players, Greenidge at least was man enough to apologise. He was a player who had risen to the Test status through sheer hard work and many hazards. During his apprenticeship, he had encountered many rough and tough situations as a professional. He was one of a very few gentleman-players.

For the groundstaff boys it was virtual hell in England in those days. Among other boys, he had to pick waste paper as also discarded food which often got soaked by the overnight rain. He had to pick up before the next day's play began. He was also called upon to sweep it. In his words, he says :" As in the army anything that did not move had to be painted".

Greenidge's book, written in 1980, shows how tough was the life of a professional, even as late as 1960s.

# 110

# Spirit Of Game Violated

Dasmond Haynes, a fine opening batsman, was playing superbly. He had completed his half-century and moved on to 55. Kapil Dev's incoming delivery grazed Haynes's bat and hit his pads. The ball was crawling precariously towards the stumps. Haynes instinctively picked the ball up.

Indians, trailing 0-2 in the series against West Indies in 1983-84, nurtured the hope that they might win the fourth Test and reduce the lead. Governed by this instinct, they appealed loudly and appealed vehemently. The umpire M.V. Gothoskar took his time. He considered and reconsidered the appeal. There indeed was a violation of the law 33 but the appeal was against the spirit.

When Indians persisted, he had no option except to declare the batsman out "Handled the ball".

Haynes walked back disappointed. He thought that the Indians had resorted to tactics that were not exactly good for the game. His skipper Wesley Hall was angry. He felt that good sense should have prevailed upon Kapil Dev and his men and the appeal should have been withdrawn.

The Law is quite straight-forward. It states that "either batsman on appeal shall be out Handled the Ball if he wilfully touches the ball while in play with the hand not holding the bat unless he does so with the consent of the opposing side".

Whatever the Law, the appeal did not enhance India's

image in the world of international cricket. The consensus was that there indeed was a violation of Law by Haynes, but India violated the spirit of the game. This violation was worse than Haynes's infringement.

Although there are nine instances of the batsmen being given out "Handled the Ball", it was first instance of the batsman being given out in Test cricket.

The most amusing instance is that of W.H. Scotton, 18, playing for Smokers against Non-Smokers, East Melbourne, 1886-87. As the last ball of a high-scoring match was delivered, Scotton was anxious to secure the ball as a souvenir. He played it softly and then ran to pick it up. This was done before "Over" had been called. There was an appeal (some fielders were equally keen to have the ball as a souvenir), and he was given out.

Good or bad, the law is expected to stay in the book. In order to avoid an unpleasantness, it is paramount that a batsman should keep his hands off the ball at all times.

# 111

# Funny Board Rules

"A wife is a distraction to a player and his performance". This was the view of the Board officials for many years. In a special general meeting in Mumbai on April 1, 1982, it stipulated five rules to "discourage" players from being accompanied or joined by their wives on the tour to England.

The five-point contract, as signed by the players before taking off for London on April 30 was:

1.  Wives will not be allowed to accompany the players from the beginning of the tour,
2.  Wives will be permitted to do so as far as possible after the first half of the tour. Even then, such a request must be routed through the manager with his recomnendation. Wives will then be allowed to accompany their husbands, provided the permission is granted by the president.
3.  Wives will not stay in the same hotel.
4.  Minimum penalty for a player infringing these stipulations will be that 50 per cent of the amount, which is retained by the Board, will not be paid to him.
5.  The manager will be empowered to give two warnings to a player. In case, the player persists in not abiding by the instructions of the manager, the manager may impose any additional penalty.

The rules were lax, vague and weak. They betrayed knowledge of the officials. Take rule 2, for instance, it specified that wives would be permitted to joint their husbands "as far as possible" after the first half of the tour. The duration of the tour was 76 days. The team arrived in London on April 30. The first half was devoted to County matches. In accordance to the rules, she joined her husband before the first Test began on June 10. In other words the Board officials thought she would not be distraction to her husband for Tests!

There were many infringements on this tour alone. The wives did stay separately either in other hotels or with friends and relations. But they were with their husbands most of the time during evenings and also during nights. In subsequent tours, like the one in Australia, when Wg Cdr Salim Durrani was the manager, he surrendered his suite for players to stay with their wives. Then there were instances when juniors (three or four) were clubbed together so that husbands could stay with their wives. All in all, there were more violations than adherence to the rules which were merely on paper.

The consensus in those days was that wives were definitely a "hindrance" to their husbands. Some die-hard officials were heard saying that, unlike wives of Englishmen, Australians and New Zealanders, who egged on their husbands to perform on the field, the Indian wives were merely interested in shopping.

The Board made several attempts to "discipline" players on this count. But the players were too smart for the Board.

# 112

## Gavaskar Cries "Wolf, Wolf"

A genius in batsmanship and stolid compiler of runs, Sunil Gavaskar has had a knack or highlighting or creating or even fabricating a news story to suit his interest. He has been one who has had maximum brushes with people connected with cricket. He has had maximum controversies with his colleagues, seniors and juniors, and with his rivals from different countries, like, England, Australia, West Indies, New Zealand and Pakistan. He had problems with umpires, with officials and with mediapersons. The study shows that five stars, including Bishan Singh Bedi and Kapil Dev, put thogether have not had caused as much rumpus as he has since entering into arena of first class cricket. Yet, he thinks that he has done no wrong and all the blame lies with others.

Gavaskar says that one Delhi journalist made "advances" at him while driving a car back from "Beating of Retreat" to the hostel where he was staying in January 1969. Now what "advances" could a journalist have made while being on the wheel? If the journalist chose to make "advances" to Gavaskar, surely he would have made attempts to make similar "advances" to various others, sweeter than the former India captain. In the absence of any such history of evidence or complaints against the journalist, one is inclined to believe that Gavaskar's assertions or claims are no more than mere figament of imagination to secure cheap publicity and give a bad name to the unnamed journalist. It is a fact that Delhi Journalists are less partial and parochial than Mumbai journalists.

Sample what Gavaskar says in his book entitled "One-Day Wonders" (pages 21-22): "When I was playing in the Vizzy Trophy in Delhi in 1968-69, this person offered to take me to the rehearsal for the Republic Day parade. I went straight from the ground in a car and saw the very impressive "Beating of the Retreat", as the parade is called. It had become quite dark as we were returning to the hostel we were staying at and on the way to the hostel this person made an indecent advance which I promptly repulsed, even telling him that he was like an uncle to me." He said: "Please do not tell anybody or else I will ruin your career". Since nothing really had happened, I did not bother, but confided the story that evening over dinner to Naik who asked me to forget it and just concentrate on my game. It is obvious that while I did not even think much about it, this person has not forgotten the rebuff and has been critical of everything that I have done, ever since. Ajit Naik jokingly remarked the other day, "what he could not do to you physically, he is doing in print. All I can say is good luck to him. I actually feel sorry for him now".

The incident, purported to be imaginary of course, took place in Jaunary 1969. He mentioned it in his book published in 1985. Why did he take so long to write about it? Was he afraid that this journalist might "ruin his cricket career"? Since he emphasises that he believes in honesty, fair-play and truth, he should be man enough, if he is man enough of courage, conviction and responsibility, to name the journalist and say what did he really do to him? will he?

# 113

# Menace of Age Manipulation

Eversince age-group competitions have been born, there have been allegations and controversies against some players, considered much over-age the competitions in which they have taken part. There have been innumerable instances of players of 16 years or about taking part in competitions meant for 14 and under; the players of 18-19 years are seen rubbing shoulders with boys of 16 and under, while players of 23-24 figure in matches meant for under 19. The noble concept of age-group competition has been flouted with monotonous regularity at every stage.

Parents and dispassionate officials have lodged protests and made vehement complaints against this havoc. But the authorities, including Indian Board, have done precious little to introduce curbs to minimise this evil, which has "killed" the concept of the age-group tournaments.

A grossly over-age player has pushed out a genuine youngster causing widespread disappointment, dejection and demoralisation. Like a system of "dowry" in this blessed country, the evil has been spreading. Since the authorities have been turning deaf ear to this virtual heinous crime, more and more people have been indulging in this unholy practice which has destroyed the very fabric of junior cricket.

Coaches, physical directors, principals, parents and players are all guilty of violation-directly or indirectly. The major fraud is committed by the coach who, in order to enhance his reputaion and prestige, induces a promising youngster to manipulate his age by leaving one school to another. The coach, already in league with the physical director, records youngster's age two or three years less than what it was recorded in the first school. There are several other uncanny methods of altering the age.

There are several interesting instances of age mainpulation or non-bona-fide students taking part in official championships. The one that is worth narrating is that a manager of the university team had carried with him a university letter-head and a rubber stamp. He submitted the list of players or swimmers with changed names and ages after reaching Jaipur. How can any one challenge it? If a die-hard does protest, the reply from the concerned school, college and university will take days and by that time, the competition will have ended and teams would have dispersed.

India won the Lombard World Championship for under 16. The final was between India and Pakistan at Lord's. Both India and Pakistan were guilty of carrying over-age players. One player of India team had to change his passport. He had influence and he could do it. The organisers, Lombard (England) were disturbed at downright cheating. The result: The World Cup for under 16 could never be held again. When Indian team returned one player had to face litigation (age).

There are seveal methods to minimise this unholy practice. One is medical examination of all participants a day before the meet begins. It may mean an extra expenditure. But it is worth it to make the play-field equal for all players. Another is that a defaulting player and institution should be debarred for three to five years. The coach concerned should be black-balled and his bosses, Government or non-Government, duly informed for his breach of age-old norms, rules and ethics.

There are coaches who receive money from parents for the manipulation of ages. Parents, gullible as they are, agree for manipulation of ages of their kids because they are keen for their wards to succeed in life. Coaches in this country have played havoc with youngsters. This is a country where dunkeys ride our boys of merit and skill. This is all because of coaches who draw salaries from their employers and also a hefty honorarium from schools, colleges or universities. They also retain their say for the selection of the teams!

Dilip Vengsarkar, one of the renowned Test stars, says : "The boys looked over-age not only for under 16 tournament, but who would surely raise eyebrows if they were included in an under 19 line-up for that matter".

Vengsarkar adds: "When an over-aged boy is pitted against those under-16 physically he is definitely at an advantage. In fact, I was amazed to see some of the north zone lads sporting well grown beard. Now that is some physical growth indeed for a boy supposedly less than 16 summers old!".

In Patiala in the Vijay Merchant (under 16), a UP player unabashedly showed three age certificates. One issued by the head of the school and other two issued by two municipal corporations. All three certificates had different dates of birth.

# 114

# A Providential Recovery

Sunil Manohar Gavaskar's entry into the world on July 10, 1949 began with a controversy. No wonder he has been wrapped up in controversies more than any other Test star.

Gavaskar's arrival was normal in a crowded Mumbai hospital. There was nothing unusual about his birth. There were, however, stream of visitors as Gavaskars were a very popular family. Among visitors was one Narayan Masurekar, a family relation. He noticed a tiny hole at the top of child's left ear-lope. No one else had observed it although quite afew visitors had come on the day of arrival.

Masurekar, called 'Nan-Kaka, visited the hospital next day. He picked up the baby from Mrs. Gavaskar's bed. But he was visibly taken aback as he found that the baby he had picked up did not have the small hole that he had noticed a day earlier.

Nan-Kaka protested. He raised an alarm. A search of all the cribs was undertaken. Eventually, the baby with a hole on left ear-lope was located. He was serenely sleeping on the cot of the fisherwoman. He was brought back to the rightful owner and the baby lying on Mrs. Gavaskar's bed was duly returned to the woman, who had borne him.

Investigations were undertaken as to how this vital mistake took place. It was found out that all newly born babies were given bath, as was customary, and in doing so, the nurse had made a mistake in changing the babies. It was an unintentional lapse. But recovery of Sunil to his rightful mother was providential because had Nan-Kaka not noticed that vital hole on the left ear-lope, Sunil might have borne different name and lived in different surroundings. But he might have still risen as world's leading batsman because talent and concentration were in-built in his system. The cause for the happiness was that Sunil retained his true identity of Gavaskars. Indeed Gavaskars nursed and nurtured him to become a batsman-and-commentator of great quality.

When Sunil started walking about, he swung his bat while his mother was the bowler. The ball was then a rubber ball (tennis). Once Sunil hit the ball hard. It was flying in the direction of his mother, who was as quick in withdrawing from the ball as Gavaskar subsequently became in withdrawing from the line of rising deliveries. Once Sunil's shot landed on his mother's nose and she started bleeding. She washed her face and continued to bowl at her son with the same enthusiasm as before.

Not many in those days could have imagined that this tiny youngster would surpass all the doings of his uncle, Madhav Mantri, who played for India as a wicket-keeper batsman in 1950s. Mantri did not train the youngster but provided him lesson on philosophy of cricket. He also emphasised upon him the need of team-spirit and value of hard-work.

When Sunil wanted to get into his uncle Mantri's pullover, the veteran player explained to him that he should "earn" it through his dint of hard-work instead of wearing his uncle's sweater. Sunil got the message and decided to work on his game to earn it.

# 115

# Rough Treatment To Madan Lal

It was a match between knowledge and "yes Sir". The public relations official won the match hands down causing hurt, humiliation and betrayal to the knowledgeable man wanting to uplift fielding ability and skill of the Indian team.

The actors in this unholy drama were Madan Lal, a cricket manager (coach) and Ali Irani, a physiotherapist, when India were on tour to Sri Lanka in 1997.

On the basis of complaint made by Ali Irani, the Board secretary Jaywant Lele wrote a curt and humiliating letter to Madan lal saying that the physical training of the team was the responsibility of Ali Irani and not his. The letter was handed over to Madan Lal by the administrative manager Ratnakar Shetty. Madan Lal thought it was a kind of a routine letter and did not even open it. The following morning, when he began training the players, Ali Irani quietly asked him whether he had read the letter delivered to him by the manager. When Madan Lal said that he had not read it, Ali Irani added an insult to injury by telling him that he had been stripped off the responsibility and physical training of the team was his job.

Madan Lal returned to his hotel room. He read Lele's letter and was fuming in anger. He should have straightaway sent a fax message or made a lighting call resigning from the office of the cricket manager. But he did not act thinking that it would bring a negative round of publicity to the country.

What was the cause of fall out between Madan Lal and Ali Irani? Madan Lal, in his own wisdom, had invited Tej Kaul, of Sports Authority of India (SAI), to attend to boys problems at the Bangalore camp prior to team's departure. Madan Lal had reportedly taken permission for Kaul's induction in the camp. But Ali Irani felt that it was a subtle move by Madan Lal to get him replaced by a man of his own choice and zone. This gave rise to suspicion and Madan and Ali Irani drifted away as the team landed in Sri Lanka.

Like his predecessor Bishan Singh Bedi, Madan Lal also started adhering to "regimentation" in the sanguine hope that team's fitness level would improve. His methods of training were not as drastic and rigorous as Bedi's, but they were not likened by many seniors, including Azharuddin, who was no longer captain.

Already disturbed at selectors move of removing him from captaincy, Azharuddin was not on the same wave length with Madan Lal as before the team reached Sri Lanka. This became clear when Azhar showed the handle of his bat to Madan Lal on reaching his century against South Africa at Kolkata. It was "Up yours" sign. This shocking incident was an outcome of misunderstanding that existed between the two over the extent of injury that Azhar had sustained.

On the tour to Sri Lanka, Madan Lal did not approve of the findings of Ali Irani on injuries sustained by some players, including Sidhu. Ali Irani felt that his competence and sincerity were being questioned by Madan Lal after his continuous service to the Indian team for about a decade. The cracks between the two widened.

After protracted deliberations, Madan lal dashed off a letter from Sri Lanka to the Board president Rajsingh Dungarpur. The letter was straight-forward. Madan Lal wanted to know what his terms of reference as a cricket manager were?. Rajsingh should have acted. But he chose otherwise until the team returned when he had a detailed discussion with Madan Lal.

Azharuddin had a suspicion that Madan Lal had played a pivotal role in his exclusion from the team for the Independence Cup. Just as Ajit Wadekar on the tour to England in 1974 had considered Bedi and a few others "Pataudi's men", Azharuddin thought Madan Lal was Bedi's man. It was far from true. Madan Lal always had his own mind and he was one person who did not carry any prejudices or malice against any player, irrespective of which zone he came from.

Madan Lal's one-year contract included rigorous programme and tough assignments. He had, by and large, performed superbly. He should have been continued as a cricket manager. But he was summarily sacked without even informing him about the change. There was no "thank you" to him. He rightly felt hurt. His question was: Why was cricket manager dropped when the same team, same captain and same selectors were retained?

# 116

# Gavaskar Loses Cool

It was, in essentiality, a clash of personalities between Sarfaraz Nawaz and Sunil Gavaskar on television during the Pakistan-Sri Lanka Test match in the 1998-99 season. When Tony Greig, in a meaningful and provocative interview, asked Sarfaraz background of betting and match-fixing, the Pakistan "superbat" categorically stated that it should start with Asif Iqbal and Gavaskar who, according to him, were the "original fixers".

A livid Gavaskar lost his cool and lambasted Sarfaraz in unspeakable language. "Such scum of earth should not be on television. He should provide evidence for his charges. These are harsh words to say on television but they must be said", Gavaskar remarked live on television.

Seeing Gavaskar's mood, Geoff Boycott had to take over the commentary to distract attention from the outbursts of Gavaskar.

According to Sarfaraz, "sometime, there is betting on a particular delivery being bowled. The bookies signal to the bowler from the stands and the ball is bowled accordingly", said Sarfaraz. Imran Khan had also pointed the finger at Asif Iqbal when he was captaining Pakistan on tour to India in 1979-80. He (Asif) had told his rival captain. G.R. Vishwanath, that he had lost the toss even before picking up the coin. The reference was to the drawn Eden Test.

When Sarfaraz made these allegations on television, he was summoned by the PCB chairman Khalid Mahmood asking him to refrain from making these kinds of allegations. Sarfaraz was further told that Gavaskar was supportive of Pakistan that they did not deliberately allow Sri Lanka to make it to the final of Asian Test Championship final ousting India in the bargain.

Sarfaraz, however, stayed adamant. He said : "I will produce the bookie, who paid them". "I believe such people need to be brought to justice," said Sarfaraz, adding : "Match-fixers have to be hanged publicly. It is a treason case and penalty for treason is death, nothing else". "Sharjah is a den of gamblers", emphasised former Pakistan fast bowler.,

On the allegation that Pakistan had allowed Sri Lanka to reach the final through bonus points, the tournament director, Dulip Mendis said that the rules were not flawed by Pakistan. "I saw nothing wrong in the match and Sri Lanka played with a positive frame and earned points", Mendis said. His views were endorsed by Gavaskar, one of the three members of the championship's technical committee. According to Gavaskar, there were no flaws in the rules but this is the first championship and there can be many changes in future. "I cannot read minds to say there was anything wrong in Pakistan's way of playing", he added.

"Sarfaraz charges are all bunkum" was the reaction of Rajsingh Dungarpur, then president of the BCCI. Standing solidly behind Gavaskar, he said : "Sarfaraz's accusations of match-fixing are garbage".

Despite a legal threat from Gavaskar, the Pakistan's former pace bowler was emphatic in his charges. He reiterated that India and Australia should hold inquiries into match-fixing and bribery instances and the process must start from the 1980 season.

# 117

## Both Are Spoil Sports

The newly formed National Cricket Academy's (NCA) team playing a tour opener against Zimbabewian XI at Indore in the 2000-01 season turned violently controversial. The Countil's respected and knowledgeable member Sunil Gavaskar was critical of the move in his syndicated coulmn. To this, the Council chairman and former BCCI president Rajsingh Dungarpur took an exception. He reacted sharply. Words hard to forget and forgive were exchanged by two bigwigs. They also traded charges against each other. Some die-hards felt that they were both guilty of bringing disrepute to the game.

To Gavaskar's criticism, Rajsingh said : "One gentleman (read Gavaskar) being a member of the NCA said that the academy should not have been given a game against Zimbabweians. Such people should either resign from the academy or take it on, or fall in line. You can't run with the hares and hunt with the hounds. These are your big names".

Rajsingh also said that 'Gavaskar had got away with things in his playing days". He made several other allegations against Gavaskar, including his 36 (in 60 overs play) in the 1975 World Cup and his Melbourne walk out.

Gavaskar's view was that he had not criticised the board but he had made an observation that there were other players (other than from NCA) who deserved to play. After resigning from the Council, Gavaskar said : "Dungarpur was a self-confessed failure". He added : "People who live in glass houses should not throw stones at others". Gavaskar also accused Dungarpur of adhering to "double standards". Gavaskar went on to say : "I played the game for my country with pride and my pride does not allow me to be in the same committee chaired by a man for whom I don't have respect". After saying all this, Gavaskar stormed out of the meeting.

Holding that the row between Dungarpur and Gavaskar was 'unfortunate', the BCCI president A.C. Muthiah said : "It was their personal opinion and the stand-off between them would be sorted out soon". Muthiah however said that the issue was avoidable and suggested that the officials should desist from going public with their opinions. "I think this is unnecessary and impulsive behaviour. And this will keep happening with every one giving personal opinion".

The impact of the 'big fight between two big fellows' was such that no business could be transacted in the board meeting pertaining to fixturers, finance and marketing committees.

As tempers cooled down, Dungarpur extended Sunny an alive branch. He said on Christmas day that 'if Sunny withdrew his resignation, it would be considered". He added: "After all, he is yougman who tends to get carried away at times", adding : "We are not in a hurry to find a replacement".

On the NCA issue, Dungarpur was not much to blame. But the media tore him apart. One newspaper, in its editorial, called him "spoilsport" and also said : "he had graduated from being called joker to being termed senile by his critics. He was taken to task for his harsh observations about Sourav Ganguly during net practice at Colombo". The editorial concludes by saying : "...the tragedy of Indian sports is that the game suffers while the spoilsports thrive".

La affaire NCA, both Gavaskar and Dungarpur were

faulted by dispassionate cricket followers. "While being Council member, Gavaskar should have avoided criticisiing his own family", said two senior observers. Dungarpur should have exercised restraint instead of going to town against "little master" whose contribution in international cricket cannot be doubted.

As Jagmohan Dalmiya brought about a coup in beating the sitting president A.C. Muthiah at Chennai on September 29, 2001, Rajsingh Dungarpur resigned from the NCA and Sunil Gavaskar, as expected, became the new chairman.

According to Rajsingh, he resigned from the NCA because he did not accept Dalmiya's desire to become president when Muthiah had yet to complete this term. "When I was challenged by Dyaneshwar Agashe during my presidency, Dalmiya stood like a rock behind me. He said that I must complete my term. By the same yardstick, why didn't he let Muthiah complete his three-year term, that too when he had done such a fine job? That is why I chose to stand by Muthiah", said Rajsingh.

Much as one may appreciate Rajsingh's principle, he had flouted it while unseating S.K. Wankhede for N.K.P. Salve to take over. He had then gone along with Dalmiya and I.J.S. Bindra. Wankhede's term was reduced from three years to two at the behest of Rajsingh who had the support of Fatehsingh Rao Gaekwad. Says Salve : "...Maharaja of Baroda, however, very graciously said that at any rate we will end this controversy and elect me as the president unanimously and that thereafter the president shall hold the office zone-wise and not on the basis of seniority as vice-president, and hold office only for two years". Since this fateful day, all rules concerning seniority and zone-wise have been flouted with impunity. Rajsingh has been party to all these violations.

On Gavaskar, Rajsingh, in an interview on October 3, 2001, says : "... "without a doubt he is a right man for the job. I have no problem with Gavaskar. I have worked under him. I would not have had a problem. I have nothing but admiration and affection for him".

A few months ago, Rajsingh was highly critical of Gavaskar la affaires NCA. Either Rajsingh's criticism then was wrong or his recent "words of wisdom" are meaningless. If only "Raj Bhai" and his friend Gavaskar go through their clippings and opinions from time to time, they will realise that they are better somersaulters than world's best divers.

Gavaskar, for example, writes more words in a month than any other sports editor in a newspaper. He earns in a month more than the sports editor gets his salary in a year : Should a person of his eminance also hold offices in different bodies, national and international?

"There is no controversy over fifth coach (Gursharan Singh) in North Zone Academy", said Rajsingh. Rajsingh adds: "It was just a misunderstanding due to lack of communication. There is no controversy and all five coaches will now be concentrating on providing the best training to the boys".

Rajsingh had to eat these "words of wisdom" again. Says Rajsingh : "...The NCA committee met here (Mumbai) and it was unanimously decided that Gursharan Singh would not be part of the NCA North Zone Academy". Why did he say that there was no controversy? Why can't he withhold his personal opinion? Why should he insult or humiliate a former Test player? Does he have a right to contradict himself just because he is a Rajsingh Dungarpur?

(In lighter vein)

# From Personnel Department

As a result of Board's new "Effective programme" as well as declining standards, management considers it necessary to take measures to remove "dead wood" from the Indian team. A reduction in force plan has been developed which appears to be the most equitable in view of our team's declining standards. The plan is simple and has the concurrence of the entire Board without any dissent.

Under the plan, senior players will be placed on early retirement, thus permitting the retention of players, who represent the future of the team. Therefore, a decision to phase older players through early retirement will be placed into operation immediately.

The programme has been befittingly named as 'RAPE'. (Retire Aged Players Early). Players who have been raped will be provided an option to stage a come-back in the team, provided that while they are being RAPED they request a review of the players record before actual retirement comes into effect. This phase of the operation will be called "SCREW" (Survey of Capabilities of Retired Early Worriors). All players, including captains, who have been RAPED and SCREWED are free to put in an application for "SHAFT". (Study by Higher Authority following Termination).

Following detailed and dispassionate discussion by

Board's office-bearers, it has been decided that players/
captains may be RAPED once and SCREWED twice, but
they may get SHAFT as many times as the Board deems
appropriate.